Colin Greenland was born in Dover in 1954 and wrote his first book, about a fire-engine that laid an egg, five years later. His doctorate study of 'New Wave' science fiction was published in 1983 as *The Entropy Exhibition*. From 1980–82 he was Arts Council writer in Residence at the Science Fiction Foundation. His books have been translated into seven languages including Russian, and have won awards in Britain and America. Active in many roles – reviewing, lecturing, running workshops – he has become one of the most distinctive and best loved of British sf writers.

Critical acclaim for the Tabitha Jute series:

'Tabitha's amazing adventures have repercussions not only for herself and her beloved ship, but for the entire universe, known and unknown.' LISA TUTTLE, *Time Out*

'Tabitha Jute . . . A cussed, cantankerous, self-centred Han Solo – who saves the world regularly, pulls all the sexy guys, and still ends up all alone in the launderette of life, watching her socks go round.'

  GWYNETH JONES, *New York Review of Science Fiction*

'A heroine so real she even keeps tampons in her handbag.'

  The Face

'One of the m   n years.'

  The Times

'Everything   novel.'

  MOORCOCK

Voyager

COLIN GREENLAND

The Plenty Principle

HarperCollins*Publishers*

Voyager
An Imprint of HarperCollins*Publishers*
77–85 Fulham Palace Road,
Hammersmith, London W6 8JB

The *Voyager* World Wide Web site address is
http://www.harpercollins.co.uk/voyager

A Paperback Original 1997
1 3 5 7 9 8 6 4 2

A catalogue record for this book
is available from the British Library

ISBN 0 00 649906 6

Set in Postscript Ehrhardt and Univers Light by
Rowland Phototypesetting Ltd,
Bury St Edmunds, Suffolk

Printed and bound in Great Britain by
Caledonian International
Book Manufacturing Ltd, Glasgow

Many of the stories in this book first appeared elsewhere:

'The Traveller' in *Zenith: The Best in New British Science Fiction*, edited by David S. Garnett (Sphere, 1989)

'Grandma' in *13 Again*, edited by Anne Finnis (Scholastic, 1995)

'The Station With No Name' in *13 More Tales of Horror*, edited by Anne Finnis (Scholastic, 1994)

'A Passion for Lord Pierrot' in *Zenith 2: The Best in New British Science Fiction*, edited by David S. Garnett (Sphere, 1990)

'Miss Otis Regrets' in *The Fiction Magazine*, edited by Judy Cooke (Winter 1982)

'The Wish' in *Other Edens II*, edited by Christopher Evans and Robert Holdstock (Unwin Hyman, 1988)

'Station of the Cross' in *Tombs*, edited by Edward E. Kramer and Peter Crowther (White Wolf, 1995)

'Candy Comes Back' in *In Dreams*, edited by Paul J. McAuley and Kim Newman (Gollancz, 1992)

'Masquerade and High Water' in *The Book of Dreams*, edited by Neil Gaiman and Edward E. Kramer (HarperCollins, 1996)

'The Travelling Companion' in *Strange Plasma*, edited by Steve Pasechnick (Edgewood Press, 1995)

'Temptations of Iron' in *Michael Moorcock's Elric: Tales of the White Wolf*, edited by Edward E. Kramer and Richard Gilliam (White Wolf, 1994)

'Going to the Black Bear' in *The Weerde: Book 1*, edited by Mary Gentle and Roz Kaveney (Penguin, 1992)

'Nothing Special' in *Temps: Volume 1*, edited by Alex Stewart and Neil Gaiman (Penguin, 1991)

'In the Garden' as a chapbook (Birmingham Science Fiction Group, 1991)

'The Suffer the Children Man' as a broadcast reading (BBC Radio 4, 3 November 1995)

ACKNOWLEDGEMENTS

This book comes with many thanks to Brian Aldiss, Mike Moorcock, Dave Garnett, Chris Evans, Rob Holdstock, Julia Moffatt, Anne Finnis, Judy Cooke, Paul McAuley, Kim Newman, Ed Kramer, Pete Crowther, Steve Pasechnick, Neil Gaiman, Alex Stewart, Mary Gentle, Roz Kaveney, Ellen Datlow, Pam Fraser Solomon, Mike Harrison, John Clute, Stella Hargreaves, Maggie Noach, Jill Hughes, Jane Johnson, Patsy Antoine, Jim Rickards, Sally Lincoln, Bryan Talbot, Mary Branscombe, Susanna Clarke, Milfordians and Blotters old and new, and all other providers and supporters whatsoever and wheresoever, witting or unwitting, now and hereafter.

CONTENTS

I

MONSTERS

The destruction and devastation of whole native populations in Tasmania and the Americas taught us at last, far too late, about the discontents and diseases that unwary explorers may carry with them when they venture into the unknown. It's interesting to speculate too what unrecognized gifts they may bring home with them when they come, and for whom.

This story was written for Dave Garnett, one of the most perceptive and scrupulous editors a writer could wish for. For whom a writer could wish. No writer could wish for a more perceptive and scrupulous editor than.

Well anyway.

The Traveller

THAT WINTER THE WIND from the mountains was fierce, prowling and shaking all around the house like a great wolf. It scattered the icicles from the trees in the park and licked the thick snow that crested the walls into strange peaks and curlicues. From the window seat in the drawing room I watched it at play: desolate entertainment indeed, but I could not always be reading. When I was alone, and not reading, I preferred to stare from the window than face into the centre of the room like any civilized and sociable person, for the drawing room reminded me of my father.

Father had departed some months previously on another of his journeys. Indeed, he was rarely at home any more; and when he was, preferred the solitude of the study and the laboratory to the company of mother and myself. Yet even in his absence the drawing room seemed imbued with an aura of him. His pipes lay on their rack above the fireplace. Albums of his travels, bound in dark leather, filled two shelves either side, and two glass-fronted cabinets of queer mementos flanked the window where I sat. Neither mother nor I ever sat in his chair.

When the sun shone I would go riding in the park, sometimes as far as the lake, but never off the estate. I would see people, very often, running away or trying to hide among the trees; or little children in rough clothes, staring at me as I rode by. They had stolen in from the village or the farms, in search of shelter, or expecting to find something,

I know not what, on my father's land that they could not find at home. Perhaps they had no homes. Georgei would have driven them off, had I told him. I would never tell him. When my father was absent Georgei was never so assiduous about the estate, especially in winter. Georgei was not so young as he had been.

In the long nights I could hear mother coughing in her bed-chamber. I believe now that her cough relented somewhat while father was not there to trouble her, but she was never altogether at peace with it. As the time drew near for his return, however, she grew morose and restless. I would see her from the window riding off through the snow with Sasha panting at her heels, as if she were hunting something; but she came back each day empty-handed. By some common, unspoken consent we did not mention father, nor go down into the cellar.

The day father was due home she could settle to nothing. She strode in and out of the room needlessly rearranging things and continually glancing at the clock.

'Put on your black velvet, Isa,' she said, exactly as if I were still a little girl. 'And for goodness sake tidy your hair.' Then, when I returned downstairs in the dress she had recommended, she found fault with it at once. 'One would think you were attending his funeral,' she said. 'Well, it must suffice. It is the hour.'

From the bureau in father's study she took a ring of keys. The ring was small, the keys only two: a large one of black iron and one of brass no bigger than my little finger. She shook them briskly, without looking at them, and went before me down the cellar stairs.

With the longer key she unlocked the door of the labora-tory. Within, all was stillness and gloom. The air was stale from long enclosure. I went to climb on the workbench and open the little window high in the wall, but mother stopped me. 'There's no time for that.'

Georgei had covered the cabinet and all the equipment in dustsheets as soon as father had departed in September. Together mother and I pulled them off. Roughly I folded them as mother began to cough. 'Quickly, Isa, quickly,' she said, and tugged the great switch that governed the electrical machinery.

Revealed, the cabinet resembled more than anything else a single wardrobe, quite plain but for the small window of black glass set in its door. Already a faint crackling could be heard from inside. When I looked, I saw a tiny tongue of lightning flicker behind the glass.

Mother pulled a chair from the workbench, gave it a perfunctory dusting with her hand, and set it to face the cabinet. The inside of the glass was radiant. I do not know how it should be expressed. It was as if it were frosted with light.

From the shelf above the bench mother brought down the tray that held the decanter and placed it beside her as she took her seat. She righted the little tumbler, poured brandy into it, and drank it at a draught, not looking at me. All her attention was concentrated upon the window of the cabinet, where the glow now sparkled and prickled.

I stood behind her chair. Inside the cabinet I could see something thickening, a form taking shape where there had been none before. I tucked my hair behind my ears and stood up straight, resting my hand lightly on my mother's shoulder, the very picture of the dutiful daughter. Except at times like this, I was not accustomed to touch my mother.

My father was now complete. The fuzz of light went out abruptly and the glass misted over before his face. He was breathing.

My mother rose, took up the little brass key, and unlocked the cabinet. A strange smell flitted through the room, like soap and salt and violets, all at once. Inside the cabinet my father stood in a trance. His eyes were tightly closed, his hands folded on the scuffed and ancient satchel slung about his neck.

His garb was strange. He had on the rubber cap with wires attached that was necessary for travelling, but otherwise above the waist he was clad only in a rudimentary under garment of some kind, a brief black bodice that left his arms quite bare. There was a lurid design worked on the front of it, altogether barbarous, of a human skull set about with flames and chains. Also he had on a pair of coarse trousers of indigo blue, but greatly faded. Strangest of all, however, was his face. His face was bare. He had lost his great beard and moustaches.

Mother took his hand. He shivered; he trembled. He opened his eyes. He looked straight at me. He opened his mouth, but said nothing. He dribbled.

'Isa,' said mother, indicating the tray, though she looked neither at it nor at me, but only at father. I took the upturned tumbler, filled it swiftly with brandy, and gave it to her. She held it to his lips and tilted it.

His eyes rolled as he swallowed. He snorted in a great breath through his nostrils, and sighed gustily. 'Magdalena,' he said. His voice sounded stifled, as if by some constriction or obstruction of the throat. He stepped stiffly out of the cabinet into mother's arms, where he lolled, smacking his lips as the brandy took effect. 'Isa,' he said then, gazing into vacancy over my head. He spoke a phrase in a language I did not know, and stumbling out of my mother's embrace, came lurching towards me. 'Isa!' he cried again, and hugged me, crushing me to him, bruising me with his satchel. The chemical odour I had smelled when mother opened the cabinet seemed to emanate from his body, like an embrocation.

I found the intensity of his greeting embarrassing, and then alarming; but I bore it. To my shocked imagination, my father was like a wild animal, intending to devour me. I told myself it was pleasure at seeing me once more.

He was raving. 'There are women everywhere!' he announced. 'More than you could possibly imagine!' He released me to gesture wildly, waving both arms above his head. I cannot now remember what else he said. While attempting both to calm him and to avoid accidental injury, mother and I paid no attention to his words. He was often thus incoherent on his return.

Soon enough he had put on his brown silk dressing gown and was striding up and down with the glass of brandy in his hand.

'One surprise after another,' he said. He paused in his striding to open his satchel, and began to dig around in it. 'I beg you, dearest, do not tire yourself,' pleaded my mother. Father dismissed her anxieties with a brisk shake of the head. He did not look at her, but only disturbed the contents of the satchel.

I wondered where he had been, and for how long. The question is not as eccentric as it sounds. Sometimes when he came home he would seem older than I expected, as if he had been away longer than we were aware. By his own account, he often had; though the more he told us, the wilder and more elaborate his tales grew.

He would speak at first of a realm where horses were unknown, and every man travelled by means of a balloon of gas which he wore in a canister at his back and inflated at need by tugging a cord. By the end of the week, the tale would be exaggerated beyond all proportion. 'Great cruciform ships of steel roam through the skies, swept back and forth across the face of the globe by artificial winds!'

Though mother would never admit such a thing to me, I knew that she deliberately made herself forget everything he told her of his travels, so as not to catch him out inadvertently in an inconsistency, for nothing angered him more than to be contradicted when he was in the wrong. I had adopted the same policy of incurious acceptance; though I would wonder, in bed that night, what he had meant by his exclamation about women.

My father was not a large man. Nevertheless, observing him that cold and uncomfortable afternoon, I thought that if he seemed no older on this occasion of his return, he was yet diminished somehow; and I thought by his shaving. We were clearly not to mention it. It was as if a portion of his power had resided in his beard, like the wizard's in the fairy-tale.

Perhaps it was I who had grown older.

'I'm ready for a bath,' he said. 'Accompany me. Both of you.'

His very eyes commanded us.

Georgei, like a good servant, had anticipated his master's wish. Smoke had been rising from the bath-house chimney for an hour. While mother and I assisted one another to unlace our stays, father stripped off his dressing gown and his peculiar costume. I saw that his depilation extended no further than his chin.

In the bath-house he would not rest, but strode about in the steam, slapping his shoulders. His eyes never left us. Mother and I sat mutely on the bench until I could stand this scrutiny no longer. I begged leave and went in to break the ice in the cold bath. Father scorned it. He ran from the door, calling mother to follow. I glimpsed them from the window. He was tumbling her naked in the snow. I heard her laughing and coughing pitifully, while father shouted my name. I ignored him and plunged at once into the icy water.

Having washed and dried myself quickly, I was dressed before my parents came back indoors. I took the opportunity of examining the strange clothes my father had been wearing, which lay discarded in the corner of the dressing room.

The blue trousers were made of stout cotton stuff, such as a labouring man might wear. That they were so faded seemed to bespeak years of rough use and laundering; but the cloth was as new, and stiff with starch. The bodice was a brief, primitive kind of garment that might, but for its size, have been made for the merest child, for it was nothing but two rectangular pieces of smooth black cloth sewn together, all of a piece with two short flat tubes protruding at its upper corners by way of sleeves, and a hole worked for the neck. For all its crude form and hideous embellishment, I thought it would be a light and comfortable garment to wear in warmer climes; yet dare not take it up and try how it might fit me.

After bathing we sat together on the couch in front of the drawing room fire, drinking tea and eating currant bread. The wind had got up again, and was flinging snow at the windows. It only emphasized our comfort, and made us cherish the warmth. My father spoke further, more coherently if no more lucidly, of his discoveries. 'It is not as I had expected. They do not think of the machine as a saviour. They look upon it as a mistress, to be wooed, to be accommodated. And there are those who disregard her, who enjoy her largesse while insisting that the duty of mankind, the purpose of society, lies elsewhere . . .'

He opened his trophy satchel and spread the contents in his lap. Mother made a show of polite attention which masked, I knew, sincere disapproval. For years she had been witness to the arrival of such things in her house: curios, fetishes, inscrutable to her and so neither pleasant nor useful, but rather disquieting. My interest, however, was genuine; for now I was relaxed, comfortable in clean, dry clothes and properly warmed inside and out. At such times the fancy is apt to extend itself most pleasantly. Father's stories might be fact or fiction, but his souvenirs were real enough, I felt: not comprehensible, perhaps, but separate in their existence from whatever interpretation he might put upon them. They spoke to me with silent tongues of worlds where everything was not shrouded in snow and disdain.

Father was nodding, with mother's arm about him. His eyes were all but closed. I leaned over to examine this latest trove. He permitted me to touch some of it, which I did with gingerly curiosity.

There was a kind of wallet, square and flat, made of a remarkable substance he had shown us before, like glass but quite unbreakable. It was cunningly hinged, and contained in one side a little book of coloured paper, and in the other a silver mirror in the shape of a circle, with a circular hole at the centre. The mirror was small enough to encompass with the fingers of one hand. Father encouraged me to detach it from the case. It was as light as a seashell, and had writing printed on it. Some of the letters were unfamiliar.

There was another silvery item, a wafer of soft metallic foil as thin and pliable as paper, but studded with a double row of discs. To my fingers it seemed that things like tiny buttons were enclosed within the metal. Father's explanations became exiguous and vague. 'They have banished all disease,' he said, distantly, and yawned.

Also there were pictures, more of the highly detailed miniatures on glossy card he had brought back on other occasions. These, reluctantly, mother joined me in examining, while father lapsed into slumber with his head on her shoulder. Foolishly I wondered whether everything in this strange new world was polished and shiny. The pictures seemed to suggest it was so. Everything they showed – the sleek carriages, the glass palaces and aerial pagodas, the subterranean orchards and the men who tended them, clad in their electrical armour – all these marvels were depicted with astonishing precision and fidelity. Yet fidelity to what? For such things never were on sea or land; nor under it, I felt sure. Other pictures, showing scenes of violent death and smouldering ruin, mother slipped under the pile with a wince, and I made no further attempt to inspect.

When the pictures were done, mother rang for Georgei to help her put father to bed. I went to my room and attempted to read; but the poet's words resisted me, and swam like senseless motes before my eyes. My mind was too full of father's tales to absorb any other matter. I seemed to see men and women with silver hair, their clothes embroidered with scenes from atrocities, beckoning me into glass chambers to the wild music of invisible orchestras.

I hoped my father would sleep out the rest of the day; but in vain. At six o'clock I was dressing for dinner when, without so much as a preliminary knock, the door flew open and father came striding in. He was still in his gown. I was sitting at the dressing table in my chemise and petticoats, combing my hair. He halted behind my stool, looking at me in the glass. His eyes were full of a fierce humour; his right hand was behind his back. The eternal fear I had so easily forgotten in the warm, peaceful afternoon rose up again and seized me by the throat.

'What is it, father?' I asked, as calmly as I was able.

'They think they know it all,' he said, intently, but indirectly, as if continuing a conversation we had that minute broken off. 'They think they see everything. They *think* the men underestimate them. Well, so they do. So they do, Isa.'

He smiled. There was no humour in it.

'Indeed?' I asked. I was capable of no more.

'It takes another kind of man,' said father, 'a very special kind, to understand them.'

He laid his left hand on my shoulder.

'I understand them, Isa,' he assured me. 'I do.'

He squeezed my shoulder.

'I see them, and I understand them, and I see that they are no different, Isa! No different from you.'

He took the comb from my hand and tossed it onto the dressing table. Then he took a fistful of my hair. 'Without all this,' he said, tugging it. 'But otherwise – no different.'

I cried out, calling for my mother, but she did not come. I suppose she was not in hearing, or was in some way incapacitated. In the glass I saw father bring out from behind his back a great pair of scissors; and despite my pitiful complaints, he chopped away at my hair until it was nothing but ragged ends all over.

Perhaps I should have turned on him then, but instead I retreated into silent tears. In truth I could have clawed his face for my curls dropping like shorn fleece into my lap and onto the floor; but I knew better than to provoke him further. His wild mood was upon him, as so often when he returned from a visit to those other worlds that were the subject and whole source of his passion.

'Now you look like one of them!' He stood behind me smiling and staring at me in the looking-glass. Through my tears I thought I resembled no one indeed, unless it were some poor mad lunatic of the village; and I wondered who they were, burning in his memory, that he must perforce disfigure and abuse me so. Were they the ones who had shaved off his beard?

My mother stifled an exclamation when I appeared at table; but she asked no question, nor voiced any protest on my behalf, despite my wretchedness. With her own hair he had not tampered; perhaps she feared to cause him to think of it.

Throughout dinner father drank heavily and spoke in awesome hints of the conduct of war. He spoke not of the glories

14

of the cavalry, nor yet of the courage of the foot-soldier. 'Two men,' he said, again and again, 'two men shut up in a small room underground, watching over the sleep of great engines of destruction. Who are they? Nobody! And on the other side, what? Two more! The same men, it might be. The very same.' His mood had become sombre again, as if he were appalled at the spectral visions he conjured up for himself. He looked unwell.

His meal unfinished, he pushed away his plate and rose awkwardly from the table. I stared at my food. I had eaten nothing. Father leaned towards me an instant as if to berate me; then veered aside and seized my mother by the wrist. By main force he drew her thus pinioned to her feet and pulled her after him upstairs. In bed that night I buried my head beneath my pillow, but in my mind I could still hear my mother's cries and entreaties.

Next day, as usual after a day of such exertions, father remained in bed, resting. Mother did not wish to see him. I took up his morning draught on a tray. He lay in his nightshirt against a mound of pillows, breathing noisily through his mouth. His eyes were sunken in sockets black with fatigue. As I set the tray carefully upon his knees and directed his hands to the beaker, I saw that his beard was growing through anew, like a dark shadow smeared across his pale jaw.

His skin seemed clammy, his muscles tense. An unpleasing smell rose from him. It occurred to me that, far from being an idyll in a paradise free of all disease, his adventure had exposed him to some pestilence unknown to us, some more cunning and indifferent plague. He seemed hardly to know me. He drank his medicine with tremor in his lip.

He gave a profound shudder then and at once relaxed. In the grip of his beloved morphia he began to tic and twitch, as if his body were a-crawl with energy.

He was making a tiny noise. I put my ear closer to his lips. He was singing. 'No loss, no problem,' he sang, over and over again. 'No worries, no error, no sweat.'

He looked suspiciously at me. In shame for the ugliness he had inflicted upon me, I was wearing a headscarf, like a peasant woman. Perhaps it confused him. Before I could move away he had taken hold of my arm again.

'If you knew where I came from – and where I have been –' he said, hoarsely; 'if you knew to what sights I have been privy in certain rooms, shall we say certain upper rooms, in the city . . . ?' He nodded, stiffly. 'Then, madam, you would not use me so lightly. You would accord me more respect.'

I laid my hand on his. 'Hush, father,' I bade him. 'It is I, Isa.'

'Isa?' He furrowed his brow. 'There is not enough light in here. I thought you were your mother.'

I knew it had not been to mother that he had been speaking, not even in his distraction.

'Shall I open the curtains, father?' I offered, as much to get away from the bed as to secure him such comfort as cold grey daylight might afford.

'Do.'

But while I stood at the window, attending to his wish, he heaved himself out of bed and approached me from behind with a springing step that quite belied his appearance of exhaustion. It seems to me now that he was always coming upon me from behind. He caught me under the arms and kissed my neck. I drew my head sharply from him.

'Isa,' he said. 'My daughter. How fortunate you are not to take after your mother. I can see in you the form of the woman you will be.'

He pressed himself against me, loathsomely. I resisted

him. He seemed to have no strength. He released me and fell back against the bed.

'You will be as good as any son, won't you, Isa?' he said mockingly, but with something of his former debility. 'As good as any son.'

For a moment I thought I was free. I thought his relapse was complete. I was wrong. 'Except one thing!' he cried, and once again he came lurching at me.

My nerve broke. I twisted violently from him and fled the room, sweeping the door to behind me. But father had already grasped the edge of the door and was forcing himself through even as I dragged at the handle. He grasped at me. I flinched, let go the handle and ran along the passage with him at my back.

I reached the door of my own room and there turned to defy him on the threshold.

'How dare you?' I cried. I tore off the scarf from my head and threw it at his feet. 'How *dare* you?'

'I dare,' he said, with a grimace. His eyes seemed to start from their dark hollows. He reached for me.

I whirled into the room and snatched up the first thing I seized upon, the stool from the dressing table. I backed away from him, swinging my stool as he came at me, holding it by two legs and trying to hit him with the seat. I should have clutched the seat to me instead, and thrust at him with the legs. I knew nothing of fighting.

Father seized the stool and wrested it from me. He flung it away and came on, his arms spread wide. Now the dressing table was at my back. I could retreat no further.

I put back my arm and felt steel beneath my hand. It was the scissors, the scissors with which he had cut my hair. I caught them up and brandished them at him, jabbing the air.

He seized my wrist, wrenching at me. I dropped the

scissors. They fell to the floor between us, open. Father bent for them, and I heaved clumsily at him with my shoulder and caught him on the nose. His head jerked back; he staggered and lost his footing, collapsing and scrabbling for the scissors as he fell. I crouched to snatch them up. He grabbed at me and pulled me down after him; but I had the scissors in my left hand. In desperation I thrust them at him. One blade pierced his nightshirt and struck home in his stomach. It was a horrid, yielding sensation, like stabbing meat with a skewer.

At once, there was blood, spreading across the cloth of his shirt and welling through onto my hand. He clasped his hand to the place, knocking my own hand and tearing the wound. He cried out.

I rose in a strange state of fright. I recall crouching over him: it can have been an instant only, but it seemed longer, far longer. I was thinking I should help him, but I could not bear to touch him.

I ran to fetch my mother; but as soon as I was out of the room, leaving him behind there struggling on the floor, I suffered a change – I know not what to call it, a change of heart, a change of mind. In that pause I seemed to see my mother hurrying to my room and, at first sight of him, drawing away, shouting for Georgei. And Georgei would come, stumping up the stairs, and see to father as best he could, somehow staunching that horrid flow, bandaging it, and returning father to bed. And what then? Would the madness not redouble then? Would the tyrant defied not be twice the tyrant?

And what if he did not recover? What if he died? Would my mother then protect me? Or would she deliver me up to the law? Would she even hesitate?

All these questions occurred to me that instant, in the passage outside my room; and I did not know the answer to any of them. They have occurred to me again, since, frequently, severally and together; and still I do not know.

What I did know, there and then, was that it was in my power to escape them all. I ran downstairs, tearing at the buttons of my dress. From the closet by the garden door I dragged the old boots I wore for skating; and from the dressing room father's outlandish clothes that lay where he had discarded them. In the laboratory it was the work of a moment to throw the heavy switch and release the electrical power. While it spread humming and buzzing into the machinery, I pulled on the clothes and the rubber cap of wires, and laced my boots; and then, as the strange cold light began to glow behind the little black window, turned the key in the lock and stepped into the cabinet.

Upstairs, my mother began to scream.

I have always been a great lover of graffiti. In the Oxford English Faculty library the gnomic, witty inscriptions on the toilet walls (FREE THE TVC 15; HAMLET AND LEAR ARE GAY) were quite as enthralling to me as the hallowed texts on the shelves. Later, years of travelling on London Underground taught me to admire the intricate fantastic baroque tribal iconography with which young volunteer artists so generously decorate not only the drab grey rolling stock but also the dreary outer reaches of the Metropolitan Line.

I just wanted to make that clear in case any of them should happen to read the story that follows.

The Station with No Name

THE STATION IS THERE. You don't always pass it; only sometimes, going underneath the river. The trains that do go that way don't stop there. Nothing stops there any more. It is the station with no name.

Probably it's only an ordinary station, one they closed down for some reason, a long time ago. Perhaps the roof fell in, and hurt somebody. Perhaps people were buried here, under the rubble, for some time, and afterwards no one could bear to use it, so they locked it up and left it.

There is hardly enough light to see by; only a sort of mucky, grudging, dark brown light that filters down from somewhere up above. It looks like the bottom of the sea. You can just about make out the platforms, the exits like low square mouths full of darkness.

As your train passes through, though, the same thing happens almost every time. There is some kind of fault or bump you go over in the track, and the train wheels spark, and at that instant the whole place lights up, stark and lifeless in the cold white glare. You see the bare walls, the locked gates, the shrouds of dust over everything like an abandoned tomb. It's only for an instant. If you happen to be looking down at that moment you'd never know it was there, the station with no name.

Mark and Kix hadn't even meant to go that way that night. They had been mucking about up the District Line when this bloke came after them and they had to run. They'd had to jump two trains to lose him, and that had taken them right out of ZEE-5's territory.

Mark was not happy about that. For one thing, he hadn't finished his throw, and that always got him annoyed. For another, he didn't know whose territory this was, exactly.

Kix was laughing his face off, though, as always. Kix always had a good time, whatever. He looked around the car, picking out names they knew. 'STAC, look! POET! FA-Z!'

Mark didn't care whose name there was. There was only one name he cared about.

Kix was mad, a crazy man, he didn't care about anything. It didn't bother him that they'd had to fall through the doors of a train that was going the wrong way. Mark took things like that personally. He didn't want to be heading south of the river. He had no business down that way. Anyway, it was nowhere, who ever went down there anyway? No one.

Kix was complaining happily. 'I was really going good there,' he was saying. 'I was just getting the highlights, fsss . . .' He imitated himself spraying the ceiling of the train, next to POET and someone's orange blur that had dripped and run.

Mark was not listening. He had been staring out of the window and seen a flare of electricity light up the station with no name.

He had seen the walls of brown tiles with little veins in them like marble, and the big blank medallions where the station name should be, and the platforms with black spiky railings blocking all the exits. It was dark again now, the shadows pulled in tight, but the light had flashed and shown him the station.

The train hadn't stopped. There wasn't supposed to be a station there. There was no station on the map.

None of that bothered Mark. What made him light up,

what made tonight a good night suddenly, a really spectacular night, in fact, was that there was a station, and nobody had hit it yet! It was incredible. When the train light had splashed the walls, there was no answering dazzle of paint. No BAF, no DIET, not even 230, and 230 was everywhere.

Kix, naturally, had missed it. 'You're such a nerd, Kix,' said Mark at random.

Kix pulled out his can. He aimed it at Mark and pretended to spray him. He grinned. Mark didn't grin back. Miles too late, Kix looked out of the window, as if sensing something had happened. He saw nothing. There was nothing to see.

They got off at the next stop, jumped the barrier and ran along the road and round a corner into a smelly bit of waste-land behind a supermarket. On the back wall of the shop they bombed a couple of locals, ESKIMO and DODGE, total unknowns, then Kix said he had to go home.

'My dad's coming,' he said.

'Your dad?' Mark said. 'He won't come.'

Kix gave this massive grin. 'No,' he said.

Mark, who had two parents, which was two too many, couldn't let it go at that. He felt like leaning on Kix, pushing him with it. 'Your dad never comes,' Mark said.

Kix laughed, but it was weak, not a real Kix cackle. His dad was the only thing Kix didn't think was just one huge joke. 'No, but,' he said. 'I just got to go, right?'

'Yer!' jeered Mark. 'Go on, then.'

As if he had been waiting for permission, Kix put his can in his pocket, pulled his cap straight, pulled his jacket straight. He laughed a sneering, happy laugh and departed.

Mark sprayed a hard burst of blue at the wet black rubbish lying around. He was glad Kix had gone. Now he could really move. He gave Kix five minutes, then went back to the station, keeping out of sight of the man at the barrier. There was a local map on the wall by the entrance. Mark studied it, memorizing street names. Then he ran out, and off in another direction.

He ran along a street of factories with shuttered doors. VACANCIES said the boards, in white letters, but all the card slots underneath were empty. Perhaps those were the vacancies they meant.

Mark's footsteps on the pavement were quiet, as though the street wanted to hide his presence. No one else was about, and hardly any traffic. Mark went left and cut across a yard. He was following the train line.

He ran across a road and behind a line of hoardings with posters for rum and Rothman's and car tyres. The street-lights showed that kids had been at the posters, but Mark didn't pay any attention to that. Only dweebs bombed posters.

Behind the hoardings, out of the light, he scrambled, and found a dusty brick building. It was two small shops, gutted and boarded up, with a dark gap in between.

That was it. It had to be.

In the gap was a door. It wasn't the proper door, it was a door from somewhere else that they'd brought and nailed into place. There had been glass in the door once. Now there was plywood blocking the hole where the glass had been. Some of the plywood was just hanging there, loose. It had been ripped away in one go, as though someone big had come this way in a temper.

Mark squeezed through the hole in the door.

Inside it was utterly black. One foot at a time, Mark crept across the floor away from the door. The floor felt like tile, big tiles and grit and rubbish lying around.

Mark got out his lighter, shook it, turned the flame up full and flicked it on.

He was in a circular hall with empty ticket windows, ancient yellow tube maps, so strange you could hardly tell that's what they were. There were triangular sooty marks at the top of the walls as though they'd used to light the place with candles. Turning to look behind him Mark glimpsed a pair of sentry boxes for ticket collectors and a big hole going down into the ground. Then the lighter got hot and he had to let it go out.

Mark stood there in the dark, breathing the musty, shut-up air. This place was just incredible! He felt like an explorer breaking into a pyramid in Egypt. There was no gold, unless you counted the dull brass trim around the glass of the ticket windows; no priceless old pots, only empty bottles of cider and battered beer cans. What there was was something better. Bare space. Yards and yards and yards of it. And not a fleck of paint anywhere.

Mark flicked his lighter again and laughed. He was pleased with himself. He was glad he hadn't told Kix about this. He imagined Kix's face when he brought him down this way next. He would wait until it was just coming up, then he'd hold his hand up mysteriously and point out of the train window. And Kix would look, obviously – and at that second the lightning would flash out from under the wheels, and there it would be, the whole place one gigantic throw, both sides of the track, all his!

First he had to get down on the platform. And he had to do it now, this minute, while his head was full of it and his blood was up. The Name would not hang about.

Putting his lighter away to save it, Mark moved carefully forwards. He could make out the shape of the two boxes, and behind them a big black hole in the soft grey clinging dark.

He stood on the brink of the hole, blinking in the tiny breeze that blew cold air and grit from far below. His eyes grew used to the gloom. He could see what was beneath him now: two deep pits, shockingly huge, where the escalators had been torn out; and over to one side, a half-open door.

Mark went to the door and pushed through it. There was a black iron spiral staircase, leading straight down into the ground.

Going down in total blackness, he flicked his lighter once. Nothing showed through the gratings beneath his feet. His trainers, so quiet on the street, sounded loud and clumsy on the metal stairs. In the shaft there was no breeze. The air was dead. Thick cobwebs trailed in his face.

Mark emerged at the bottom. He could see weak light leaking through from the platform. It showed him high railings barring his way. He fumbled about and found a gate without a handle. He shook it. It was locked. The railings were rigid, the cross-bars too far apart to climb. Mark jammed his foot against one of the uprights and tried to bend it, but it wouldn't give.

He kicked the railings. There was a dull metal thud; and after it a small dry, pattering sound that whispered away through the dark like shuffling feet. Mark held his breath, listening. The noise did not come again. Probably it was just the rattle of a train, far away in the tunnels.

He stumbled around the lower hall until he found the bottom of the escalator bank. Underneath he could just make out a lot of metal, brackets and supports. He climbed in a little way into the dark hole, planted his feet and got hold of a strut, a long strip of steel with round holes in it. He put his weight on it and bent it away from where it was bolted. Then he jiggled it until he could swing it around on its bolt and hauled it back, bending it the other way.

Several minutes Mark worked on the strut, working it loose. He worked on it so hard he didn't notice the eyes gathering around him in the darkness until there were quite a lot of them.

Mark felt the hair on his arms bristle. He whipped out his lighter and flicked it on.

Rats. Black rats, big ones black as coal, creeping up out of the depths of the escalator pit to watch him. They didn't seem to mind his flame and didn't even move until he stamped his foot. Then they turned tail and vanished, instantly.

Mark breathed hard. He put away his lighter. He heaved on his strut.

The eyes were back.

With a shout, he snapped the strut off. It was good and heavy. He swung it round his head like a rat-killing club. He felt good. 'I am the Name!' he told the rats.

He bashed the side of the pit with his strut and then climbed out and went back to the iron railings where the gate was. He hit the gate, three times, aiming right at the lock. On the third try the lock gave with a sweet smart crack and the gate swung open as though he was only too welcome to come through to the platform; as though it had been waiting all this time for him and him alone.

The station with no name lay like a sunken wreck at the bottom of the dark brown sea. Beyond the crevasse of the rails, the other platform leaned away in the murk, curving like the hull of a big ship. There were the blank signs, the blocked exits, the empty spaces where posters were supposed to go; the long window of the waiting room like an unmarked slab of slate. All ready and waiting for him.

Mark threw his strut clanging resoundingly into a corner. Later for the other platform. He stood square to the wall. He listened to the big hollow silence of the underground, the tunnels running off for miles to every corner of the city. He made an announcement, in the imitation black voice he liked to talk in sometimes when he was alone. 'I mek my Mark,' he said. He shook his can. The ball bearing rattled

29

crisply inside, the sound of eagerness. Mark started to write.

He put his initials on each of the doorposts. Just warming up. Winding up to it, like a footballer before the match. Mark v. the Rest of the World. No contest, really. He sprinted down the platform, ready to open up some of this space.

Okay. O. K. The Name. A large specimen. Something to make the Monday morning cattle blink in disapproval as the lightning flared and it leapt out at them. Here, right in the big station sign. In all the station signs, each end of the platform and in the middle. Starting here.

Mark made an M. The M he made did not look like an M. If it looked like anything, it looked like a fat blue balloon with invisible rubber bands wrapped round it. It gleamed down at him from the tiles. It was very blue, like a streak of sky glimpsed through the roof of a cave.

Mark whooped. His voice rang in the lifeless halls of the station with no name.

He shifted his stance, stood with his feet wide apart; shook up again; did the A. The A was like a razor unfolding, hooked in the fat side of the M. The wide curves of the M and the wicked thin curves of the A looked good together like that. Mark did the R, propped against them. The flick up at the end of the R was neat and sweet.

'Sweet as de banana on de tree,' said Mark, aloud.

As soon as he stopped speaking, he heard the small whispering sound again. This time it sounded like someone in one of the passages crumpling up some paper. It was such a tiny sound, you would think you could hardly hear it, but in the deep silence of the station with no name Mark could hear it very clearly.

He knew now it was just the rats, or else dirt sifting down from old brickwork, disturbed by his own movements, most probably. Nothing had moved down here for years by the looks of it. But the tiny noise gave Mark a sudden over-whelming sense of being completely alone, in the dark, far underground, in a place no one even knew was there. No one would come here to look for him. Not even the rest of ZEE-5.

Mark worked a lot on his own, of course. But most of the time there were the others not far off. Even if there was no one else, Kix would usually be hanging around. For a minute Mark almost wished someone else was here, not Kix, Poet or Norman or someone, to admire his handwriting and keep guard. ZEE–5, it was a really slick logo, should he do that somewhere?

No chance, he thought. Let them find their own deserted station. Later, when they see what I've done, the others will be all over it. A major ZEE–5 raid! He smiled. He did the first bit of the K, with the fins that always made him think of combs, and then a slashing upstroke.

'What do you think you're doing?'

The hoarse voice was close. The shock of it was like needles in his ear. His spine contracted painfully.

He spun, and saw an old man standing there. An old man with long white hair and a white beard, white you would have to say, but also yellow and brown and matted with filth. He was wearing a ragged coat and trousers that unravelled halfway down his calves, and boots tied up with string.

A wino! A wino had nearly made him muck up his throw!

Mark scowled. 'Interior decorating,' he said.

'Young vandal. Should be horse-whipped.'

The voice was like an old door creaking in the wind. The man shuffled closer, trailing shreds of newspaper after him, carrying something awkwardly under his arm. He was as thin as a rail and his eyes were sunk so deep in his skull you couldn't see them at all. He was in a world of his own, though, obviously.

31

Mark turned away from the stink. 'Where did you come from?' he asked.

'Up the street,' said the old man impatiently. A sheet of newspaper under his foot lifted in the breeze from the tunnel, tearing slowly as it fluttered.

'I haven't got any change,' Mark lied. He lifted his can again.

'I don't want your money,' said the old man contemptuously.

Mark sighed. He lowered his can again. This old bloke had put him right off now. He could barely see where he had been going to go with the rest of the K.

He turned to the man. 'Look, just get out of here, all right? Just go away.' He tried to push him away without touching him. People like that shouldn't be walking around on their own. He barely looked human. And he smelled something terrible. 'Go on. Right away.'

'Young thug! I shall report you . . .' As the antiquated figure lurched back along the platform, it clutched its luggage to its withered chest. It was the remains of a briefcase, tied up badly with a lot of cord and string. The two halves of it were slipping apart, scattering more ragged paper in the dust. Wrestling with it, the old man looked to Mark like an ancient commuter, lost on his way home. He hadn't had the brains to take a train he didn't know, and so he'd been stuck here, forever.

'How *did* you get in, anyway?' asked Mark. 'You didn't jump off a train.'

'No trains until they clear the line!' nagged the man. He plucked at one of the tattered papers protruding from his case, as if it was a document to prove the point. 'The bombers got the line.' He said it as if Mark was supposed to know what he was talking about.

He was getting on Mark's nerves. 'The bombers got your

brain, more like,' he said. 'The line's not blocked. I came that way, right?' he said, pointing with his thumb. 'And the train went that way. So.' He felt better now, more in command. 'You're not supposed to be here any more than I am, so just belt up, all right?'

The old man came skating towards him, faster than any wreck like him had any business moving. There was black mould on his clothes, and big dark blotches on his skin. He opened his horrible mouth wide, in Mark's face, practically. He had a grin bigger than Kix's.

Mark shook up hard and started spraying again.

'Pack you off up the front and let Hitler sort you out!' wheezed the old man.

'Get lost, granddad, I'm warning you.'

Where now? Mark strode away from his persecutor, along the platform. There, the timetable! Shrivelled paper pasted on the wall, no one wanted to read that any more. MARK MARK MARK. He was in his stride now, whipping each one off in three moves, five seconds, less.

Then someone else turned up. Another one of them! A woman, this one was, a young woman thin and white as a fish in a headscarf and carpet slippers that were rotting on her feet. She came tottering out of nowhere with her hands stretched out. 'Mister,' she whispered. 'Please mister, have you seen my Betty?'

She put her hand on Mark's arm. Her hand was cold and damp as a lump of putty. A wet, bad smell came off her. Not alcohol. Not even meths or glue. Her voice was soft and weak as a moth scrambling inside a lampshade. 'Please mister, have you seen my Betty?'

At that moment there was a noise in the southbound tunnel. A light. A train coming.

Without thinking, Mark seized hold of her cold hand and pulled her back in the shadow of a pillar. The train, a track maintenance rig, clanked slowly past, long and blind and low and yellow. The woman stood behind Mark until the train had gone. She was so close her smell enveloped him, making him feel sick. She was worse than the old man.

Here came the old man now, shambling towards them. He was getting so animated bits were falling off him. 'Is this young layabout interfering with you madam?' he creaked. 'Fetch the station master!'

Mark pushed him away, hard. It was like pushing a greasy sack full of chicken bones and jelly. 'You stupid old dosser! You just stay out of my way, right?'

'But my Betty,' whined the woman, helplessly. 'She's not even four . . .'

'She's not down here,' said Mark. 'Go and look somewhere else.'

The woman was not as young as she looked. Her mouth was a mass of wrinkles. She seemed very ill. Her eyes were no more visible than the old man's, black holes in her chalky face. Below, shiny wet lines trailed down either cheek, as though a snail had crawled up into each socket.

'There were so many people . . . and she's so little . . .'

Mark wrenched away from her. What did they have to bother him for? What difference did it make to a couple of derelicts if he hit the station? It wasn't their station anyway, it was his.

'Mister . . .'

Mark set his teeth and worked on.

In a while number three turned up. This one had a London Underground uniform on, or the rags of one, decaying and caked with filth. His grey hair sprouted up through the crown of his cap like a frostbitten bush. 'Oh my god,' said Mark wearily. He felt his stomach heave as the man approached. Grimly he concentrated on the angle of an A.

'You're not supposed to be on my station,' said the man,

in a voice like a frog shut in a filing cabinet.

'You want to look after it better, if it's yours,' said Mark loudly.

'You shouldn't be down here,' the man persisted. 'You ought to be in the main shelter.'

'You ought to be locked up,' said Mark.

'What's your name?' the man demanded.

'Donald Duck,' said Mark. MARK, he squirted.

'I haven't got you on my list,' said the man, and then he gave a low chuckle.

Mark had had enough. He was obviously completely loopy, like his mates. 'Go and play with your trains!' said Mark. He started to move towards the stairs.

'You won't get any trains here, sonny,' called the 'station master' with pride. 'The trains don't stop here any more.'

Something in that gloating croak made Mark pause. He looked back uncertainly at the decrepit silhouette. 'You've been down here too long,' he said.

'Since the warning . . .' the figure cried, and the echoes rang and ebbed away to nothing along the tunnel.

Mark was running up the stairs. At the top he looked back. The old fraud was stumbling after him, lurching slowly towards the staircase. Mark laughed. He couldn't catch him in a million years. He probably couldn't even get upstairs.

Mark ran across the bridge, lazily, arms and legs flying free. He felt as if he could leap down to the platform in one enormous jump. He did it in three.

He looked back across the rails. They were all there, both men and the old woman too, lined up at the edge of the platform, watching him. The first old man was still holding his disintegrating briefcase, clutching it to him as though he thought someone was going to take it away from him. The woman was clasping his arm, stroking distractedly at wisps of ancient hair escaping from her scarf like stuffing from a ruined armchair. The man who thought he was the station master was standing in a strange posture, leaning forward, running his hands slowly up and down his front. There was a kind of eagerness about them, like an audience assembled for a pop concert. Mark saw a glimmer of drool fall from the station master's mouth and drop down onto the tracks. They couldn't take their eyes off him.

It was just like being on stage. Mark was the star. He would give them a performance, all right.

Mark capered for them, swivelling his hips. He strutted up the platform, taunting them. 'You can't fool me. The war was fifty years ago. You couldn't have been here all that time. You wouldn't still be alive!'

He shouted louder. His voice rang across the lightless gulf. 'You're nuts, all of you. You don't even know what year it is. Why don't you go and bother the Salvation Army? Go and set fire to yourself under the bridge with the rest of your mates, yer, go on!'

Tiring of them, he went to see if he could get in the waiting room. He could do a little redecorating in there. He put his hand on the doorknob and, stiffly, it turned. Mark went inside.

Went into the waiting room, where the others were. All of them, gathered. Quite a lot of them, altogether, waiting in the waiting room at the station with no name, huddled over their belongings, their grimy shopping bags filled with slats off broken crates and butchers' knives. In every corner they sat and stood and perched, among heaps of slimy bones and hanks of hair and empty shoes. Their faces were veiled with the cobwebs the spiders had spun across them and the rats had eaten their feet, but still they stood up when Mark entered the room, stood up to welcome him.

It was only right and proper. Mark was the Name.

*

Kix thought it was all right, riding in the back of the police car. He leaned across the copper to look out the window, to see if he could see anyone he knew on the street. The copper pushed him back in his seat.

The driver was on the radio, talking in codes and numbers. It was just like on the telly. 'Why can't we have the siren going?' said Kix, goofily.

'Leave it out,' the copper grunted.

'Round here you last saw him, was it?' called the driver.

Kix pointed through the windscreen. 'Down behind the TruSave,' he said. They spent a long while poking around the back of the supermarket, rattling doors and stirring the rubbish in the bins with a long bit of wood. Finally they told Kix to go home. 'Buy a ticket,' the copper advised him, looking him straight in the eye. Kix sniggered.

On the platform he saw a POET and a lot of fresh JAWJ's. He wished he'd brought his can, but the cops would only have taken it off him. Then the train came in and he got on it, and sat looking at his reflection in the black window.

That was how he came to see Mark's great throw. There was a big white electric flash suddenly, and there it was. Kix yelped aloud and knelt on the seats, pressing his face to the window. It was brilliant. It was everywhere, all over the place! MARK, MARK, MARK everywhere in huge great sprays. It was great. It was the greatest! As the train rocked on and the after-images faded Kix laughed and laughed, while the other people in the carriage frowned and tried to look as if he wasn't there.

He wondered why Mark had changed his colour. Mark had been using blue. There was no sign of any blue back there. It was all red: bright red and sticky-looking, as if it was still wet.

'The Station with No Name' was the first story I wrote for the Point Horror anthologies published by Scholastic Children's Books. This was the second. What interested me (and the editors, when I suggested it) was the idea of stepping back, away from the assumptions and encumbrances of the horror genre, to the primary emotion itself. I chased the story all over the place before I got it right, but the principle was always clear: that this should be a horror story with no supernatural component. And the most horrifying thing, I decided, to the innocent intolerance and vigour of the young mind must surely be the devious and wrinkled decrepitude of old age.

Grandma

'NOW THEN, ROBERT,' said his mother for the twentieth time, 'are you *sure* you'll be all right?'

Rob, who was watching the cartoons out of sheer boredom, gave a loud sigh. He slumped down further in the armchair, scraping his heels through the deep-pile carpet.

His mother was trotting up and down the hall, accumulating shopping bags. 'I don't like leaving you with her all day,' she said, as if they hadn't been talking it over and over for weeks.

'Mum, I'll be all right!' All he had to do was give her her dinner and help her to the bathroom, and give her one of her tablets if she got 'worked up', as Dad called it. It wouldn't be the first time he'd done those things for his grandma, even if he couldn't exactly say he liked doing them.

'But are you sure you can manage, poppet?' his mother went on. Rob hated it when she called him that.

'Dinners in the fridge,' he recited, in a singsong voice, 'Grandma's tablets in the bathroom, Grandma's fags in your room –'

'Cigarettes, Robert,' said his mother, automatically. 'Three minutes in the microwave on full power,' she said. Rob supposed she was talking about their dinners now, rather than the cigarettes. 'Three minutes each, remember, and make sure it's really hot before you eat it. I've put Grandma's tray out ready.' She was looking in the hall mirror, checking her lipstick. 'You will put the ironing board away for me,

41

won't you, darling?' she said. 'I wish you could come with us.'

'Mum, it's the Ideal Home Exhibition,' said Rob, reaching into the magazine rack beside his chair for the remote control.

'You used to like it,' she said.

'I used to like being taken out in my pram to see the ducks,' growled Rob, turning the sound up so she wouldn't hear him.

His mother came into the lounge in a great wave of perfume. 'Don't watch that thing all day,' she told him, 'and whatever you do, Robert – Robert, are you listening? Whatever you do, don't –'

He chorused the line with her. 'Don't let Grandma downstairs!'

Outside his dad started sounding the horn. Still flapping bags about and dispensing random advice and reminders, Rob's mother kissed the air at him and ran out of the house.

Rob stood by the window with his hands in his pockets as they drove away. Then he went and made a mug of coffee, and a mug of tea for his grandma. He leaned on the ironing board while the kettle was boiling. When the tea was made, he carried the mug upstairs and stood it on the floor while he turned the key in Grandma's door.

Rob's grandma was sitting on her bed, in all her clothes. Her eiderdown was on the floor and she had managed to knock the radio off the bedside cabinet again. It was still playing, lying on its back somewhere among the ancient junk that Grandma kept piled up like a fort around her bed, her boxes of clothes and stacks of old papers. A choir of children was singing happily about little flowers that open and little birds that sing. The room smelled bad, the way it always did, of old clothes and old slippers and old woman.

'Hello, Grandma,' he said loudly. 'I've made you a cup of tea.'

Grandma moved her mouth about resentfully. She looked at Rob like a sentry with orders to shoot intruders on sight.

Rob locked the door and brought her the mug. 'Here you are,' he said. 'Take it, then.'

Rob's grandma's glasses were half an inch thick. She stared suspiciously into the mug. 'What's this?' she demanded.

'Rat poison,' said Rob.

'What?' said the old woman, screwing up her eyes and opening her mouth at him. The last hair on her head straggled over the wrinkled pink skin like strands of white cotton. 'What? I can't hear you all the way you mumble.'

'Tea, Grandma,' said Rob, louder. 'I've brought you a cup of tea.'

Grandma took the mug, grudgingly. 'I suppose we haven't got any cups and saucers,' she said, sarcastically.

'It's got three sugars in, Grandma,' Rob said, 'the way you like it.'

She ignored that completely. She was looking past Rob as though she expected to see someone standing behind him.

'Where's your mother?'

Rob pulled a face. Between Mum saying everything fifty times and Grandma making you say everything fifty times, conversation was a bit limited in this house.

'Mum and Dad have gone out,' he reminded her. He picked up her eiderdown and put it back over her thick old legs. Grandma's legs always made him think of the pale white fatty joints of meat piled in the freezer at the super-market. 'They'll be back soon,' he lied. He knew better than to try to explain about the Ideal Home Exhibition. He wondered if the Ideal Home Exhibition would have some-thing that could turn your grandma into an Ideal Home grandma, a smiley one with rosy cheeks who would sit in a rocking chair and suck humbugs and knit woolly hats for everybody instead of wandering around the house at all hours of the day and night, knocking over the ornaments. 'Drink your tea,' he told her.

'People today have got no respect,' said the old woman.

Rob found the radio behind one of the boxes of old clothes Grandma would never wear again but would never allow anyone to throw out. He picked it up and stood it back in its place on the bedside cabinet, next to her magnifying glass and her indigestion tablets and her photo of Grandpa. The children had stopped singing; now there was somebody playing the organ.

Grandma glared at the radio with hatred. 'I don't know what you want to put that on for,' she said, as if it had been his idea. 'I can't understand a word they say.'

Rob switched the radio off. Grandma had started drinking her tea, making horrible slurping noises like an old dog.

The last time they had left her with the door unlocked she had come down in the middle of the night and started messing about in the kitchen, thinking she was cooking breakfast. If she hadn't dropped the teapot on the floor and smashed it they might never have woken up and caught her. She had turned the cooker on, all four burners and the oven, and the kitchen was full of gas.

Her room got stuffy with the door locked all the time. They couldn't even open the window, Rob's father had screwed it shut, just making sure. Rob looked out into the garden. Next door's cat was sitting on the roof of the shed, gazing down at the sparrows on the ground as if it wanted to put a bet on one of them and was judging their performance.

'I'm going down to have my coffee,' Rob told his grandma. 'Are you going to have a little sleep before your dinner?' Yes, he wished at her. Yes. When Dad talked to Grandma he would keep nodding his head, trying to get her to imitate him, to make her agree to whatever it was. It never did any good.

'I want my cigarettes,' said Grandma.

'You have your cigarette after your dinner,' Rob said.

Grandma stuck out her teeth at him. 'I want my cigarettes,' she said.

'Later,' Rob said. 'You have your cigarette later.'

Grandma put her head down. She looked as if she was going to spring off the bed and headbutt him. 'Where's your mother?' she said. 'Tell her I want my cigarettes.'

Rob could hear the frantic cartoon music playing downstairs. 'The doctor said you could have one cigarette after your dinner,' he told her.

'I want to have them here,' said Grandma implacably, 'so you don't forget.' She turned to her bedside cabinet and started to pull things out of it, as if she thought the cigarettes might be somewhere in there. She knocked her photo of Grandpa over. Rob made a dive and rescued the tea before that went everywhere too.

Grandma was pulling paper hankies out of the box and dropping them on the floor. 'I can't find them!' she said, her voice rising. 'What have you done with them?'

'All right, all right,' said Rob. He went out of the room, locking the door behind him. 'Smoke yourself to death,' he said aloud, as he fetched the packet from the shelf inside the door of his parents' room. 'Government health warning, old people can cause fatal diseases.'

He unlocked Grandma's door and went back in to her. She was sitting on the bed still, crushing the tissue box in her yellow hands. Her eiderdown was on the floor again. Rob leaned over to give her the fags. 'Here you are, Grandma.'

She looked at the little white packet as suspiciously as she had looked at her mug of tea, as if it really might be rat poison this time. 'People have got no consideration,' she said, snatching the packet from Rob and clutching it tight.

'Don't squash your cigarettes, Grandma,' said Rob. He

picked up the eiderdown and put it over her legs again.

With a look of triumph on her face, Grandma buried the packet of cigarettes away in her lap somewhere. As she did so she caught sight of her tea where Rob had put it, on a pile of faded old magazines, out of danger. She groped determinedly towards it, threatening to fall off the bed. 'Give me my tea!' she shouted. 'Give it to me!'

'Calm down!' Rob shouted back. He picked up the tea and held it away from her. 'Calm down! Grandma! Now then!'

'You don't know what I put up with,' said the old woman, full of injury and indignation, clutching at the air in the direction of the mug.

'Sit back and you can have it!' It was more like looking after a baby than a grandmother.

'Not good enough for you, I suppose,' she grumbled. 'People these days.' She seemed to come to rest, to be still for an instant, so Rob gave her the mug.

'Don't spill it, Grandma,' he warned.

The old woman sat back, breathing through her mouth, slopping tea on her cardigan. She drank, her hands quivering with the effort. 'I don't know why we can't even have the radio on,' she said resentfully. 'I suppose that's too much to ask now, is it.'

Rob wiped her cardigan with a tissue, trying not to notice the sour smell of her. He put the radio back on, tuning it to a rock station and turning it up extremely loud. Pealing guitars blasted out, over a cannonade of drums.

'Oh!' cried the old woman. 'Oh! Oh! You –! You –! '

'All right, all right,' said Rob. He twisted the dial at random, found some soft strings playing, turned the volume right down. His grandma glowered at him. 'That's to put you to sleep,' he told her. Funnily enough, it seemed to work. Very soon he could see her head begin to sway, her eyelids starting to close. He took the mug out of her hand. She mumbled, barely protesting.

Rob hurried downstairs, quietly. He went and got his cooling coffee and took it into the lounge. The cartoons had finished. Now there was an old western on, a musical. People riding around on horseback, singing. It looked really stupid. He tried the other channels. There was skiing, a gardening programme and a thing that reckoned it was a teen magazine, with teen pop videos and lots of people showing off on roller-skates. Rob went back and watched the musical. It was stupid, but there was nothing else to do till dinnertime except his boring homework, and that could wait.

Rob's heart nearly stopped when his grandma said: 'I can't find my cigarette lighter.'

He jerked his head round. She was standing in the doorway like a bulldog looking for somebody to bite. He must have forgotten to lock her bedroom door.

'It's upstairs, Grandma,' he said immediately. They had taken Grandma's lighter away before they had even started locking her in. Thank goodness she hadn't actually gone and found it.

Rob got up and went towards the old woman, trying to herd her back towards the stairs. 'Let's get you back to bed, then, and I'll fetch it for you.'

Ignoring him, Grandma came lumbering into the lounge. She went to the little table beside his dad's armchair and picked up the big glass ashtray. 'I don't know what you think you're playing at,' she said. 'People today haven't got the sense to tie their own shoelaces.'

Fortunately, there was nothing in the ashtray. Rob reached out and grabbed hold of it before she could drop it or smash something with it. Grandma hung on.

'That's right, Grandma,' Rob said, thinking quickly. 'Let's take the ashtray up. What a nice ashtray. That's what we need, isn't it? Come on, then. Shall I carry it for you?'

She stared at him belligerently over the ashtray, as though he was a thief trying to steal this trophy from her. Her eyes looked weird through her thick glasses, like something forgotten at the bottom of a bottle. 'Let me carry the ashtray, Grandma,' Rob said.

'I need my lighter,' she said very definitely, as if he was the one who was deaf and stupid.

'When you're back in bed I'll fetch it for you,' he promised. He pulled on the ashtray, trying to tow her out of the room. 'Come on, Grandma, back upstairs. It'll be dinnertime soon,' he said.

She grunted and swayed her head about. It was like trying to lead a cow into a slaughterhouse. She would neither come nor let go of the ashtray. Rob let it go. 'Carry it yourself, then,' he said.

Grandma lurched backwards, the heavy ashtray sliding from her grip. It fell with a thump, denting the thick carpet.

Grandma went red. 'Now look what you made me do!' she scolded.

Rob stepped forward and kicked the ashtray under the sofa, out of reach.

'You pick that up, young man!' Grandma raged.

'Pick what up, Grandma?' asked Rob.

'That, that –' She was losing it already, forgetting the word, then forgetting what it was she was trying to find a word for. Bending forward, towards the vanished ashtray, she caught sight of the magazine rack. Purposefully she reached inside.

'Do you want something to read, Grandma?' said Rob. 'You've got your papers upstairs,' he reminded her.

She'd got hold of some catalogue of Mum's. She was pulling it clumsily out of the rack, holding it by the cover with the pages hanging down. The cover was starting to tear from the weight of them. He would have to hide that before Mum came home.

'You don't need that, Grandma.'

'You've got no right,' she said, standing up.

'Put it back,' said Rob. 'Come on, Grandma.'

'Put what back?' she asked, aggrieved. 'I don't know, ordering me about, I don't know what –'

'Put Mum's catalogue back where it goes,' he said, patiently.

The old woman looked at the heavy publication hanging from her hand. She twisted her head at an angle, as if trying to read what it said on the cover without lifting the book up to her face.

'They have nice things in here,' she said conversationally.

Rob gathered his forces. He put his hand on her arm. 'Well, let's take it with us, then, Grandma, shall we, eh? You can look at it in bed.' But she turned away from him, pulling her arm free. She was moving towards the book-shelves now, catalogue in hand.

Rob dived to intervene, almost toppling the standard lamp that stood in the way. 'I'll help you, Grandma!'

'Bookshelves are the place for books, young man,' wheezed Grandma righteously. 'Not on the floor for people to tread all over.' She reached up shakily with the catalogue, trying to push it in between the books on the shelf. The books at the end of the row started to tilt.

'Careful, Grandma,' said Rob. 'Let me do it!'

He made a grab for the books. Some were already sliding off the end of the shelf. He threw up his hands, half to catch them, half to shield his face. He saw she was looking at him with a fixed, intent little smile like a malicious toddler. She started to push the row of books along the shelf onto his head.

'Grandma! No!'

She got hold of the shelf, lifting the end of it up off its bracket, and shoved it at him. As Rob threw himself to one side, the rest of the books, road atlases and DIY manuals and books of pictures by Constable and Canaletto, big hard books with sharp corners, slid down the shelf in a colourful avalanche and hit him on the shoulder, in the chest, on the side of the head.

His face stinging, his ear ringing, Rob skipped back, tripped over the flex of the standard lamp and fell back into Dad's chair. The lamp came crashing down, just missing his arm. The cream satin shade hit the wall and buckled and he heard the bulb break.

Wide-eyed, he stared at his grandma. 'Grandma, be careful! You could hurt somebody!' He heard himself shouting. He sounded just like his dad.

The old woman stood in the middle of the room like a wrestler gloating over an overthrown opponent. 'Look what you did,' she told him. 'You didn't ought to have done that.'

Rob, breathing hard, was trying not to be angry. She was just a loony old woman. She didn't know what she was doing, half the time. He knew that. But that look he had seen in her eyes, that was an evil look. Like someone that really meant to do you harm. The glasses. It must have been her thick glasses, making her eyes look all twisted up like that.

Then five shots rang out. A horse whinnied shrilly in terror. Women started to scream.

Blinking, Grandma swung around on her heel, looking for the source of the noise.

'No, Grandma, that's just the TV.' Rob ducked in front of her, shielding the set from her, groping around behind his back for the button and switching it off.

'I'll show them,' Grandma said. 'Frightening people like that.' She seemed to be looking around for another weapon.

Rob scampered for the door, pulling at her sleeve. 'Here, Grandma!' he called. 'Here! Grandma, here!'

She swayed towards him, then back towards the silenced set. He had to get her out of the lounge and back upstairs before she really damaged something. A broken lightbulb was one thing, a broken TV would certainly be another.

'I'm going to get your lighter,' announced Rob. He walked out of the room importantly, stamping his feet down. He started off upstairs. If he could get her upstairs, perhaps he could get one of her tablets into her. Two, three, a whole bottle of tablets. That would calm her down. 'I'm going to get your cigarette lighter, Grandma,' he called.

He heard her following him. Then halfway up the stairs, he looked round and saw Grandma go stumping down the hall, into the kitchen.

He just made it in there as she collided with the ironing board. 'This way, Grandma,' he said, catching hold of it before it could fall.

She turned and looked at him as if she'd never seen him before. Casually, with one hand, she tipped the ironing board up on its hinge. The iron slid off and crashed to the floor, narrowly missing Rob's foot.

His heart was thumping. It was all getting out of control. Every instinct told him to lash out at her. But this was like a fight in a nightmare. She was an old lady; she was his grandma. You couldn't fight your own grandma.

'Upstairs!' he said.

She cursed him.

'All right. All right, Grandma.' Rob made himself act and speak calmly. 'Look – let's put this all away, Grandma, shall we? Mum would like that, wouldn't she? She'll be pleased.' More and more he sounded as if he was talking to a baby. Busily he wrapped the flex of the iron around its cleats, then folded up the board, swinging it into an upright position.

'Grandma, could you pass me the ironing board cover, please?'

The cover for the ironing board was where Mum had put it, on top of the washing machine, folded up. Grandma located it, foggily, and picked it up in one fist. She held it up, squinting at it. It started to come unfolded, tapes flapping.

'Doesn't look very clean to me,' she observed.

'Let me have it, Grandma,' said Rob.

'It needs a good wash, this does.' She went to the sink and turned the tap on, hard. Water splashed everywhere.

Rob pushed past her and turned it off. He took the ironing board cover out of her hand. 'We'll put it in the machine,' he said. 'In the washing machine, look. That's what we'll do.'

'We never had no washing machines,' said Grandma, contemptuously. But she let him take the cover.

Rob crouched down and opened the door of the machine. 'Here,' said Grandma. 'Here.'

He sensed her above him, moving something across the draining board. He looked up just in time to pull away as she started pouring hot water over him.

'That's what we'll do!' cried Grandma. Now she was imitating him.

Spitting, Rob wiped his face with his sleeve. 'Grandma! You could have scalded me!'

He couldn't take this any more. In a minute she would be turning on all the switches and pouring water into the sockets. Abandoning the struggle, he dashed for the stairs.

'Well, where are you going now?' Grandma shouted after him.

Just you come and see, he thought.

Grandma's bedroom door was open. Rob pushed it open wider. The key was still in the lock. He snatched it out, and ran into his parents' room. Then he looked around frantically. Where was the lighter? It wasn't on the shelf where they kept it, near the fags. Rob groaned. They must have put it away in a drawer or a cupboard somewhere, 'just to be on the safe side' – it was one of his dad's favourite phrases these days. What had they done with it?

From downstairs came the complicated sound of two or three things going over together.

Rob grabbed his mother's lipstick from the dressing table and ran back to the top of the stairs. He leaned out over the banister. Explosions and cries rose from the TV, a burst of fiddle music. Something exciting was happening on the wild frontier.

He could see Grandma in the kitchen, wrenching the lead out of the kettle. He held the lipstick out where she could see it.

'Grandma! Grandma!' he called. 'I've found it! Here's your lighter, Grandma, here it is!'

It started to work. Grandma dropped the kettle with a clatter and came along the hall. She stood there at the foot of the stairs, peering sideways at them as if they were some new kind of puzzle she hadn't encountered before. 'Well, what good is it up there?' she demanded, sarcastically.

Rob shook the lipstick at her. 'Come and get it, Grandma . . .'

She put one heavy slippered foot on the bottom stair. 'I don't know what you think you're doing,' said Grandma wearily, 'playing about like that.'

'Come on, Grandma . . .'

Grandma came labouring upstairs, breathing hoarsely, working her whole body. She had shoulders like a road-digger's.

Rob danced backwards to the door of her room, holding the lipstick up in the air. 'The first woman of a hundred and ninety-nine to attempt the south face of the Eiger without oxygen!' he cried, as Grandma mastered the final stairs.

She came trundling towards him, the kettle lead dangling from her fist. She was still complaining. 'If your mother knew –'

Rob backed into Grandma's room. It was working. He was winning the battle. He felt exhilarated now.

Grandma came in after him, like a rhinoceros entering its house. Rob threw the lipstick on the bed, where he could see the cigarettes still lying; then he turned, took hold of the old woman and steered her in the same direction. She kept moving, dazedly, while he stepped neatly behind her back and locked the door, pulling out the key and sticking it in his pocket.

'You think I don't know what goes on down there,' said Grandma in a loud voice; but on the contrary, she sounded baffled and confused.

The eiderdown was on the floor. Rob picked it up and dangled it in front of Grandma like a bullfighter's cape.

Under the cover of the eiderdown he chucked the cigarettes and his mother's lipstick in the bedside cabinet: out of sight, out of mind. Then he whisked the eiderdown away. 'Olé!'

He started straightening her bed, tucking the blankets in, making a performance of pulling them tight. 'Come on, now, Grandma, dinnertime,' he told her. 'Back on your bed now, and let's get you some nice dinner, shall we, eh?'

'Not right,' Grandma pronounced. 'People these days.' She set off to walk around the bed, banging awkwardly into the side of the chest of drawers.

'This way, Grandma!' shouted Rob. 'Grandma!' He smacked the bed with his hand.

She wasn't taking any notice. She was coming round the

foot of the bed. Her trunks and boxes were getting in her way.

'What do you think's for dinner, Grandma?' asked Rob wildly. 'It might be shepherd's pie, Grandma! Your favourite! Mmm!'

She bore down on him, knocking a pile of papers over. He grabbed her arm, hauled her towards the bed.

She resisted him. 'Trying to pull the wool over my eyes,' she accused him.

'Pull a plastic bag over your head, in a minute!' said Rob, losing his temper.

She came at him with the kettle lead. The plug hit him on the head. She had the lead around his throat. She was throttling him.

Rob's hands went to the lead, pulling at it. He felt Grandma trying to put her hand in his pocket. She was after the key. He barged her with his shoulder, but she was like a rock. She was all on top of him suddenly. He got a purchase on the lead around his throat and inhaled, blindly, choking. His face was full of smelly cardigan. She trod on his toe, hit him in the chest.

He twisted away from her, jerking the lead from his throat. All her weight was on his back. He tried to push her over, on to the bed, but he couldn't shift her. They staggered together like an eight-limbed monster. Rob felt the key go from his pocket.

Gasping, he saw a gap and put his head up into clear air. He could see the key, in Grandma's hand. He made a desperate lunge for it.

'Oh no you don't!' she cried.

There was a smash and tinkle of breaking glass. Grandma had thrown the key straight through the window.

Rob pulled free. The old woman just stood there, swaying, nodding her head proudly. 'What do you think of that?' she said.

Rob opened his mouth to tell her what he thought of that. Then he heard himself start to laugh.

'What do I think?' he echoed. 'What do I think?' He went and tried the door. Of course it wouldn't open. He shook it. 'You've done it now! We're both locked in now!' It was hilarious.

Grandma subsided, sitting down heavily on the bed. It squeaked hideously under her. 'Throwing things out of the window,' she said disgustedly, as if he'd been the one who had done it. 'You just wait till your father comes home.'

'Yes, well, we're both going to have to do that now,' said Rob. He was exhausted. Green and pink lights were coming and going inside his head. His ear was still hurting where the books had hit it. 'We'll both just have to wait for them to come home,' he said. What they would say, Rob didn't know. At least he wouldn't ever have to look after her on his own again, though, that was for sure.

'I don't know what you're laughing at,' said Grandma, some moments after he had stopped. She was trying to pull the eiderdown over her again. She wasn't getting very far. 'Throw everything out of the window, why don't you.'

Rob looked outside. Birds were flitting from tree to tree. A cool breeze was flapping the washing in the gardens, the same breeze that was now streaming in through the broken pane. Rob wondered where the key had landed. He didn't suppose he could see it anywhere. He stood on a chair and pressed his face to the glass.

Beneath Grandma's window was a narrow slope of slates that ended in a grey plastic gutter. Rob could see sodden dead leaves in the gutter, and unidentifiable bits of rotting furry black slime. Maybe the key had fallen in there.

He turned. There was a big straight-edged shape falling towards him. It hit him, hard.

Then he was on the floor, with part of the chair digging into him. There was something on top of it, on top of him. It was incredibly heavy. It was crushing him.

It was the wardrobe. He was pinned under Grandma's wardrobe. He heard a voice yelling out in shock and pain. It was him.

Grandma's face came round the wardrobe. It came very close up. It had skin like old wallpaper and cracks like ancient mud. There was a pair of thick glasses on it, from behind which big eyes were staring at him, like something in a case at the zoo.

A crepy yellow hand held a lipstick in Rob's face.

'This isn't mine,' said Grandma.

Rob jerked away from her. Pain grabbed at his hip, savagely. Everything went dark blue, with red round the edge.

Grandma was walking away from him. He was trapped under the wardrobe, and she was walking away.

Rob shoved at the wardrobe. Pain bit him in two. The wardrobe didn't budge.

'You think you're so clever, all you youngsters today,' said Grandma. He couldn't see her any more. He heard the bedsprings clash and jangle. Grandma was climbing onto her bed. 'You think you can do anything you please,' she told him. The noise of the springs continued while she settled herself, puffing and blowing as she laboriously rearranged her pillows. 'You've got no consideration.'

Rob felt cold and clammy. He was sweating. He thought he might have wet himself. He was going to be stuck under the wardrobe for hours, until Mum and Dad came home, until they could get the door open. He could feel his foot, turned the wrong way. It felt like somebody else's.

Grandma's voice continued, righteous and unstoppable. 'When I was your age I had to do what I was told. If you didn't like it, you had to go without! Some people have got no right, just barging about willy-nilly without so much as a by-your-leave. Now look at you.'

She seemed to think it was his fault, that the wardrobe was on top of him. It hurt. It hurt, it hurt, nothing had ever hurt so much, nothing could.

Rob heard the radio go on. It was the middle of the racing results. A man's voice was saying rapidly: '– *On the Nod, 5–2; second: Bright Day, 8–1; third: Hungarian Rhapsody, 5–1; eight ran.*'

'Now this is more like it,' said Grandma.

Rob passed out.

He dreamed he was a racecourse. Hundreds of horses were galloping over him, pounding him with their hooves. Rob could see people walking about. He saw police in uniform; he saw some sailors, and a boy selling newspapers, and his mum and dad. He tried to shout out to them, to tell them he was under the ground, but when he opened his mouth, nothing came out.

Suddenly he was awake again. The radio was still playing, the same voice reading out the same meaningless names and numbers. Rob's head was at an angle, hard against the wall. He could see part of the ceiling, and the top of the wall opposite. He was dizzy. He thought he was going to be sick. He could smell something. A sharp, pricking smell.

He tried to rock the wardrobe from side to side. It hurt, it hurt, it hurt –!

Something was floating across the ceiling, something thin and shapeless. Smoke.

'Grandma?'

His voice sounded like a little boy, somewhere else, in a different room, a different world.

Now he could hear a soft crackling noise. Smoke began spilling over the top edge of the wardrobe, white and grey, dribbling into his face.

Startled, he sucked in a lungful. He started coughing. The cough hurt. His leg hurt worse. He squirmed in pain and felt the broken chair shift. He tried to push his back up the wall, clutching at the side of the wardrobe, straining to see over it. He gained perhaps six inches. The pain made him scream.

When he stopped screaming, he looked at the scene before him. Then he screamed again.

The room was hazy. The smoke was everywhere now, everywhere Rob could see. At the centre of the smoke was Grandma's bed. The crumpled bedclothes were burning nicely, curling up in flame, throwing a cheerful, dancing, red and orange glow onto the possessions of the old woman's life that she kept piled round about. Her boxes and carrier bags full of musty, many-times-mended clothes, her hoarded heaps of magazines and newspapers, all were blazing merrily as rubbish on a bonfire. Heavy black fumes were pouring out from under the eiderdown that trailed across the rug. A wave of heat came drifting across to Rob, and a reek of burning feathers.

'Grandma!' croaked Rob, choking. 'Grandma, no!'

But there she was, sitting up in the midst of the flames, puffing happily on six cigarettes at once and smirking like a mad Guy Fawkes. She held her lighter up to show him. It glinted gold in the firelight.

'It was in my pocket all the time!' said Grandma, contentedly.

Like 'The Traveller', *this story was written for the Zenith anthologies of Dave Garnett. Once again he showed me how to take the faint pencil sketch of which I was so proud and turn it into full-blooded impasto.*

The Commedia dell'Arte characters and attitudes are a tiny homage to Michael Moorcock, the most generous of writers and of men, as is the narrative tone, which, when we were writing Death is No Obstacle, *Mike told me was something he had taken from George Meredith. One of the most encouraging things about the lonely and largely pointless business of writing fiction is the way these little borrowings and repayments go on and on from hand to hand eternally, often invisibly, but surfacing here and there like coloured threads in a tapestry. One sentence in this story, about 'the gala concert on Artemisia to celebrate the opening of the new Trans-Galactic Passage', was the germ from which the whole of* Harm's Way *later sprang.*

A Passion for Lord Pierrot

IN THE LAND OF ANISE, on the planet of Triax, it is the hour after dinner. Lord Pierrot sits alone in his apartment, playing the accordion. He reclines on a couch and plays a slow, sad tango. A melancholy fit is upon him, for he remembers the past, the years before he came into his inheritance.

He is thinking of other nights, nights of gaiety when he sauntered with his comrades through yellow gardens on the moon, the same moon that now shines on the lake, turning it the colour of fine honey. On those nights he had not a care to his name, and the songs he sang were merry. He was young then, Lord Pierrot, and now he is old, as they reckon such things on the planet of Triax.

Lord Pierrot's whole apartment is most sumptuously appointed. The furnishings are made of velvet, the floor of glossy yellow hardwood imported all the way from Peru, on Earth. Splendid specimens of the local wildlife decorate the walls, represented by their severed heads. But tonight Lord Pierrot is not comforted by luxuries, nor by the trophies of his skill in the slaughter. Tonight there will be no comfort for him but in the arms of his paramour, Daphne Dolores.

He will go to her now, this minute. He rises and tucks the accordion under his arm, to entertain her, later, with some music. With this thought he steps from his chamber into the shaft and goes down, out of the front door into the stifling night.

Lord Pierrot crosses the lake by means of his little rowing

boat. The moon is bright. Tomorrow night, he thinks, it will be full. Across the water he sees a light in the window of the lodge that stands upon the other shore. Moon or no moon, that is his beacon, his guiding star.

He moors below the lodge, in the lee of a black rock that shelves out like a parapet over the water. The rock was brought back from the Horsehead Nebula by Lord Pierrot's father, at a time when society admired such actions. Lord Pierrot climbs upon it now and stands gazing at the moonlit lodge. A languid breeze toys with his pale hair.

In the silence he hears the door of the lodge open, and then he sees her, sees Daphne Dolores, running to greet him.

'Daphne Dolores!' cries Lord Pierrot, and he springs from the rock. At once she is in his arms. He holds her very tightly, though not inconsiderately. He feels the beating of her heart, that splendid organ. Its rhythm betrays only a slight sign of exertion – or is that passion, passion for Lord Pierrot?

'Daphne Dolores,' murmurs Lord Pierrot ardently. 'My love.'

'My darling,' Daphne Dolores replies, in rapture.

Daphne Dolores is slight and becomingly small of stature. She looks up at Lord Pierrot and presses the palm of her hand to his breast in a way that he finds irresistible. Her blue eyes sparkle in the moonlight. At this moment he would do anything for her, anything she asked. At this moment he would give up his wife, his house, his lands, his laboratories, and take her away on a journey to another star, a journey to last a lifetime.

Fortunately, Daphne Dolores does not ask him to do so. She does not ask him for anything. It is not in her nature to ask for things.

The most she will ever ask him is: 'Are you pleased to see me?'

Lord Pierrot is inflamed with love for her. He kisses her fiercely, bearing down on her in his hunger for her lips.

She returns his kiss as avidly as he gives it her, Daphne Dolores. Thus they remain, a minute or more, as they reckon these things on Triax.

Then they enter the lodge, and close the door upon the night.

Lord Pierrot bids his darling extinguish the lamp that guided him across the lake. He prefers darkness for these meetings. He does not like to let Daphne Dolores see his face too clearly, for it will remind her that he is old, and remind him too of what she is.

She is a young woman, Daphne Dolores.

She obeys him in this request, as in all things, and returns to him at once.

Lord Pierrot is solicitous. He pays full attention to the woman in his arms. He must not waste an instant of her company. He kisses her again, hungrily, as if he could somehow suck new youth from her mouth.

Daphne Dolores makes a small noise in her throat. Her hand presses the back of his neck as they kiss.

Her love for him is complete and true. Lord Pierrot knows that of her. He knows it so well that he no longer reflects on it. It is not in her nature to love a man and afterwards, cease from loving him.

Lord Pierrot rolls up his ruffled sleeves, pushing them back from his long, slender wrists. His hands are narrow, his fingers taper. He wears a ring with a large, square, black stone. He wears it at all times, and never takes it off, not even with a woman. He has excused it to them, to Daphne Dolores and to all those who came before her, as a sentimental attachment, a betrothal gift from his wife.

Lord Pierrot begins to undress Daphne Dolores.

She stands quietly on the rug as he reveals her body to the night.

Daphne Dolores is white and slim as a boy. Her hair is cut short, and layered as closely to her head as the fur of an otter. Lord Pierrot runs his hand over her hair and kisses her throat. She shuts her eyes and lifts her chin with pleasure.

Her shoulders and hips are narrow, Daphne Dolores, her stomach flat. She has no breasts to speak of. Her nipples look like wounds in the dim light. It is scarcely conceivable now, but thus his wife, Lady Dove, used to be, ah, long ago, in the first days of their marriage. Lord Pierrot goes down on one knee to remove her stockings. With his lips he brushes her pubic hair. He is consumed with desire for her.

Rising, Lord Pierrot pulls at the buttons of his gown. Beneath it he wears neither shirt nor undergarment. His chest is narrow and hairless. He kisses Daphne Dolores as he tugs his arms from the sleeves and forces down his baggy trousers.

His penis is slender, and elegantly curved. It lifts in the dark like some strange nocturnal plant of Triax, seeking for the moon.

Lord Pierrot directs Daphne Dolores to take hold of it, and she does. He gasps in pleasure.

Later, when pleasure has had its fill, Lord Pierrot lies back against the pillows with Daphne Dolores nestling in the crook of his arm. She lies lightly upon him, for which he is grateful, for the night is very hot, and they are both somewhat sticky.

Up in the rafters, something catches Lord Pierrot's eye: a small mass darker than the darkness. It is sure to be a nest of the skylings, which persist in infesting his eaves. Every year at this time it is necessary to send an automaton to pluck out the nests of the skylings and cast them into the lake. These nights Lord Pierrot shares with Daphne Dolores are numbered; they are precious and few. The squawking of baby birds must not be permitted to disturb the making of love.

'You're very quiet, my love,' says Daphne Dolores.

Lord Pierrot kisses the top of her head.

'What are you thinking of?' she asks him.

'I'm thinking of you, my delight,' he tells her. His voice is high, and quavers. It seems to lose all its virile resonance after lovemaking. Lord Pierrot has remarked it before, and wondered whether anything can be done about it. 'I'm thinking of you,' he says. 'And how perfect you are.'

It is a lame, trite answer, he knows. Nor is it altogether true. Lord Pierrot is in fact thinking of his wife, Lady Dove, and wishing she were away from home. But what a gross error of tact it would be even to mention this to his mistress, as they lie together in the afterglow of passion. Lord Pierrot is nothing if not fastidious. It embarrasses him to utter falsehoods and platitudes, though Daphne Dolores has an inexhaustible capacity to receive them. She rejects nothing, not if Lord Pierrot gives it.

He gets out of bed, leaving her lying there. He finds his accordion on the floor and, dusting it reverently with the palm of his hand, remembers his plan to delight Daphne Dolores with a serenade or two. He opens the door and sits there, on the step, looking out at the night.

Now that he has drained the cup of passion dry, the melancholy fit is upon him again. Lord Pierrot plays once more the slow, sad tango.

'What a mournful tune, my love!' exclaims Daphne Dolores.

Lord Pierrot looks round at her, seeing only a dark shape in the dark house, out of reach of the moonlight. The lodge is full of the musky scent of her. Lord Pierrot lays his accordion aside.

'Would you have me always happy?' he asks her.

'For my sake,' she tells him.

'Ah, that I might do everything for your sake,' he muses, sorrowfully. 'Then would you be mistress indeed.'

Lord Pierrot wishes his wife might be sent away, just for a while, before the end of summer. He has an aunt, in the north-west. She and Lady Dove have always got on wonderfully well together. They play bezique, and compare their illnesses.

While the accordion finishes its tango Lord Pierrot cups his chin in his hands and watches the golden moon of Triax climb above the trees along the lake shore. The heat blurs the sky about it to the violet of a fresh bruise.

The moonlight creeps through the open door, finding Daphne Dolores where she reclines, naked and pale on the tousled sheets. When the instrument falls silent, Lord Pierrot speaks in Latin, telling her that his melancholy is but natural, under the circumstances. '*Post coitum*,' says Lord Pierrot, '*omne animal triste est.*'

'You have said that to me before,' says Daphne Dolores. 'I remember it. I wish I could be learned, and know such things.'

'So you could, my dear,' replies Lord Pierrot, 'so you could, if you would first grow to my age.'

'Oh, now you will complain of your years, and talk of decline and the inadequacy of flesh,' says Daphne Dolores at once, protesting, though in gentle merriment. 'I shall not allow you to remain in this mood,' she declares, and she rises from the bed and comes to him where he sits in the doorway. Stooping, she embraces him from behind, stroking his cooling flesh and kissing his ear and his neck until he begins to rouse again.

'No, Daphne Dolores,' says Lord Pierrot then, and with a touch he deters her, disengaging her arms from about his neck. He nods his long head in the direction of the lake. 'It is time I returned to my lady.'

At that Daphne Dolores casts herself upon him and clasps him to her once again. 'Stay with me tonight,' she pleads. She twists her fine fingers into his soft white hair.

Lord Pierrot is surprised at her forwardness, though flattered as any man would be. Usually she is more modest. He felicitates himself for having roused a new passion in her tonight. Her love for him, which he would have sworn was complete, is growing yet.

He detaches her hand from his hair and brings it to his lips. 'Alas,' he says. 'I may not. Women,' he tells her, 'are creatures of the heart; but men must bend the knee to duty.'

The truth is that Lord Pierrot is grown old, as they reckon these things on Triax, and amorous exertion, especially in the season of heat, leaves him not only melancholy but also exhausted. But this is neither the place nor the time for truth; only for the voice of regret, in words of parting.

Bidding Daphne Dolores a gallant farewell, Lord Pierrot closes the door of the lodge, straightens his cuffs, and steps carefully in the dark down past the black rock to the sandy margin of the lake. He goes to board the little boat that will take him back to the shore.

It is a boon, Lord Pierrot's little boat, a device of his own invention quite indispensable for these nocturnal trysts. As it rows itself noiselessly across the honey-coloured water, Lord Pierrot is able to take his ease and recoup some of his dissipated energies. He looks around at the torpid, sultry night. In the reeds not a lizardfish, not a dabchick is stirring. The whole world, it seems, is still; still as if all Triax were barren, and the secret ways of life not yet pieced together there.

Lord Pierrot congratulates himself on the satisfactory conclusion of another night's dalliance.

Back indoors, Lord Pierrot sheds his clothes and hands them to a waiting automaton, which trundles away to launder them. They will be fresh and dry by morning. Belting a poplin robe about him, Lord Pierrot steps into the shaft and allows it to carry him up past the dining hall, past the libraries and laboratories, to the upper floor where both he and his wife have their apartments.

He looks in on his wife, the Lady Dove. She is still awake. She lies propped on a great many pillows, reading a volume of the collected correspondence of a grande dame of another age. Here, on this benighted outpost of the empire where the Pierrots keep their family seat, few letters reach them, and Lady Dove must make do with these printed relics.

She looks at him over her glasses. 'What time is it, Pierre?'

She has her bedside console, and need only ask the house intelligence; but she prefers to ask him. Lord Pierrot stifles his irritation, making an effort to construe this habit of his wife's as deference due to his authority in the household. He tells her it is half-past eleven, or a quarter to one, however they reckon these things on Triax. 'Time you were asleep, my dear,' he tells her, and pats her on the shoulder. Lady Dove needs a great deal of sleep. She has grown colossally fat since he found it expedient to remove her ovaries. The slightest exercise fatigues her.

'And you, Pierre, are you not going to bed?' she asks.

'Directly, my angel,' says Lord Pierrot; but first he will stay and converse with her awhile, as is only mannerly. He looks around for a chair, but they are all laden with clothing, books and female impedimenta that Lady Dove has been too weary to put away. Lord Pierrot averts his eyes from a pile of her enormous underwear. He sits gingerly on the narrow margin of the bed that is not occupied by the flesh of Lady Dove.

'I have been taking a stroll in the grounds,' he tells her, 'by the light of the moon.'

'Moonlight is not good for the brain,' declares his wife at once. 'The radiance of the moon is unsettling. It tends to unbalance one.'

Lord Pierrot strokes her great hand consolingly. 'I find it more calming these days than the heat of the sun,' he tells her mildly.

Lady Dove is full of opinions on what is and is not healthy. Her capacity for them has grown as her bulk has swelled, and as her own vitality has declined. This stricture against moonlight is typical, mere feminine superstition. As a scientist, Lord Pierrot would like to dispute it, but as long as he allows her to remain in error, he can be sure Lady Dove will leave him to pursue his nocturnal excursions uninterrupted, for fear of moonlight.

And Daphne Dolores knows never to come near the house. So all is well. He embarks on a trivial anecdote, the story of an amusing but entirely logical error made by his automatic lepidopteron, which has been unable to grasp the subtleties of Triacian taxonomy. 'There it sat, solemnly mounting and labelling an entire drawer of bluebottles!'

Lady Dove lies like a torpid hippopotamus, breathing hoarsely through her open mouth. Her heavy eyes never leave Lord Pierrot's countenance, though he does not assume she is attending to his anecdote. She is simply watching his mouth move. Meanwhile, covertly, he is studying her. Unintentionally, automatically, he compares her cumbersome flesh, her stale and suffocating bosom and lank hair with the fragrant delights he has tasted so recently in the arms of Daphne Dolores.

He remembers when he first set eyes on Lady Dove, at a gala concert on Artemisia to celebrate the opening of the new Trans-Galactic Passage. She was a delicate flower then, a rose in bud adorning the arm of her papa, Lord Panteleone, while he was but a subaltern in the ranks of science, a rising young buck of some promise in the Innovation Corps. Now he is Lord Pierrot, master of the tango and the heavy night, yearning madly for the moon.

'You seem tired tonight, Pierre,' says his wife. 'You drive yourself too strenuously.'

Lord Pierrot looks sharply at her. It would be unlike her, unworthy of her, to resort to innuendo.

'Science is a hard taskmaster,' he replies, blandly.

'I hope you are not overdoing it,' she says. 'You will make yourself ill.' He thinks she sounds a trifle disgruntled, but Lady Dove has returned her attention to her book. Lord Pierrot bids her politely good night. He kisses her pendulous cheek, quickly, and goes to his own room.

As he bids the intelligence turn out the light, a second poignant memory occurs to him, unsought, of that time when Dove and he made a foursome with Gerard Pomeroy and Mona Twisk to sample the innocent pleasures of the gardens of the moon. Those golden days. Behind the marshmallow kiosk his Dove had unbuttoned her glove and, almost unprompted, relieved him of an importunate erection. His astonishment and pleasure were alloyed, a little, with alarm at her expertise. How could his dainty treasure be so know-ledgeable about the male organ? How did she know what to do? Not, thinks Lord Pierrot to himself, that she had to do very much. In acts of venery, he commends himself as he falls asleep, he has always been prompt, very prompt.

Next morning, when Lord Pierrot awakes, he directs an automaton to throw open the window. The green land of Anise lies veiled in haze. This day promises to be just as hot as all its immediate predecessors. The heat can affect a man, playing upon his blood. Lord Pierrot thinks again of his memory of Dove, of her unexpected dexterity. It is bitter to him now. When did he and his wife last enjoy the pleasures of concupiscence? How many years is it since he has seen beneath that billowing nightgown?

Lord Pierrot winces inwardly and turns away from these unhappy reflections. Already he is suffused with longing for his paramour, for Daphne Dolores. He must meet her again tonight. He orders breakfast in the Magenta Room, with the french windows open onto the terrace.

It is nearly an hour before Lady Dove makes her ponderous appearance. She drops, panting, into her reinforced chair.

Lord Pierrot is courteous, even solicitous. He waves away the butler hovering with its scalpel extended and cuts Lady Dove's grapefruit himself. 'My poor precious,' he murmurs, 'how was your night? Was it comfortable at all?'

'Not a bit,' answers Lady Dove, and proceeds with a catalogue of symptoms and grievances so anatomically detailed that Lord Pierrot's disciplined scientific objectivity is almost overborne. Swiftly passing beyond sympathy into squeamishness, he withdraws his attention, and recovers equilibrium only by most meticulously buttering a muffin.

'I was thinking you might visit Aunt Penthesilea, my darling,' says Lord Pierrot, 'in the north-west. It is cooler there.'

'Your aunt is on a cruise,' says Lady Dove. 'To Percival's Star. She has gone to take the waters on Syringa. I told you so. You never listen to me, never.'

She mashes her grapefruit clumsily with a spoon.

Lord Pierrot looks at her in rising anger. His wife is being petulant. She believes she is the one who should have been taken on a restorative cruise to Syringa, as if that or any other fanciful 'therapy' might make any dent in the arsenal of her ailments.

Lord Pierrot regards his wife, her wet lips drooping over her breakfast dish. He is on the point of retorting that he too could wish her halfway across the galaxy; but he maintains his dignity.

'What a shame,' he says, and finishes his muffin in three quick bites. Slender as he is, Lord Pierrot has always had a robust appetite.

He attempts a new, neutral subject. 'The skylings will be hatching any day now,' he observes.

Suddenly, for no apparent reason, Lady Dove drops her spoon. It falls from her fingers and clatters among the crockery. She gives a small, convulsive quiver, but no sound.

To his horror, Lord Pierrot sees that she has begun to cry. There she sits, silent and still as a great bolster, while tears well up in her tiny eyes and slither down her mountainous face.

Embarrassed by this unprovoked effusion, Lord Pierrot blots his lips hurriedly with his napkin and flees the table, leaving his kedgeree almost untouched.

He spends the day in the laboratories, where his privacy is guaranteed. While the brilliant primary of Triax moves pane by pane across the stained glass windows, dappling the apparatus with rainbows, Lord Pierrot tends his vats. They are coming along very nicely. Suspended in their rich brown soup of nutrients, the fibrous lengths of pale pink matter slowly twist and thicken.

In his laboratory Lord Pierrot is accustomed to be happy. He will talk to his specimens, and fancies they reply, mutely, waving their rosy fronds. He will sing to them: no melancholy tangos here, but snatches of songs of love.

His homunculi gather chirping and chuckling around Lord Pierrot's feet. They like to fetch him the curious, wriggling things they trap behind the wainscot at night. On any other day one might find them skipping along after as he glides from vat to vat with flasks of concentrate and slips of litmus paper.

Alas, today his mood is quite ruined by this disgraceful display of his wife's. To break down! At the breakfast table! And for no reason at all.

Sensing their master's displeasure, the homunculi retreat, cowering beneath the cabinets. Lord Pierrot slumps on the couch, fingering his black ring.

At dinner that evening Lord Pierrot is relieved to find the table laid for one. Lady Dove, the intelligence informs him, is indisposed. She will dine in her room. There will be no need for him to attempt polite conversation, to conduct relations with his wife as though her shameful outburst of the morning had never happened. Instead he can concentrate on the pleasures of the palate, a fitting preliminary to the pleasures of other senses, other organs, he will shortly be enjoying in the company of Daphne Dolores.

Night falls swiftly in the land of Anise, on the planet of Triax. The moon rises and blesses the park with its golden glaze. The heat does not subside. It grows, if anything, more oppressive. Thick clouds begin to mass in the sky.

Lord Pierrot lingers a moment on the terrace, breathing deeply of the rich scents of hibiscus and false phlox. It is night, and the melancholy fit is upon him. He gazes into space, remembering other nights on other worlds, fresh, piquant worlds at the frontier of science.

On his way through the hot gardens, Lord Pierrot composes a poem on themes of ripeness and decay. Once he looks back towards the house, and sees the light at his wife's bedroom window. He sighs.

A blundering sourmoth flies into his face, battering him with its dusty great wings. Lord Pierrot brushes it aside without anger. Tonight, nothing can disturb his mood. He is feeling acquiescent, resigned to his age and the passing of time, accepting his place in the grand scheme of Nature. He can afford to be magnanimous, to his poor, suffering wife, and to the ignorant little creatures of the dark and stifling night. He puts the sourmoth into his poem.

Arrived, at last, at the lake, he summons his little boat and rides out across the gilded water. He sees the light burning in the window of the lodge, and yearns towards it. How he envies the simple life that Daphne Dolores leads there. That, he decides, is all one really wants: a lantern and a humble wooden bed; a loaf of bread and an accordion. What need has an old man of more? He could let all the rest go, the great house, the laboratories and libraries with all their oppressive weight of ambition and responsibility, history and posterity. True peace is to live simply, in a little house by the water.

Lord Pierrot lands and climbs on his father's rock. He stands with arms akimbo, looking towards the door of the lodge. He waits for his paramour, Daphne Dolores. She always hears his boat and comes running. He waits; but she does not come.

Something is wrong. Perhaps she is ill. Perhaps she has been stolen away.

Lord Pierrot climbs down again from the rock. He goes to the lodge and stands outside, listening at the door. Should he knock? At the door of his own property? What if he does, and alerts some brigand, some beast of prey lurking within, poised with fell intent over the swooning form of his beloved?

Courageously Lord Pierrot reaches for the door and flings it open. The lamp is burning, and she is there, Daphne Dolores, lying naked on the bed. She is, as always, alone.

She smiles at him, a fetching smile. 'Welcome to my house, Lord Pierrot,' she says.

'Daphne Dolores!'

She reaches out her arms.

'Come to me,' she commands him.

Moving like one in a dream, he crosses to the bed and embraces her. She clutches him in a grip of desire. How urgently she caresses him. He hears her breathing shallow and quick. He feels her heart pounding in her breast as if with an emotion too large for that narrow cage.

'Daphne Dolores, my treasure!'

Lord Pierrot wonders if she is unwell.

Daphne Dolores laughs. 'Do you like my surprise?'

'But you are naked,' he says. He feels a twinge of annoyance at this: she knows it is always his pleasure to undress her when they meet. She sets him at arm's length and looks into his eyes.

'I am pretending this is my house,' she says. 'I am mistress here. And you are *my* suitor.'

Her manner is intense, Daphne Dolores, her eyes amused at his discomfiture. Lord Pierrot has never seen her like this before.

'I want you,' she says. Her voice is deep, suddenly, and thick with passion. 'Now.'

She tears at his clothes, straining seams, snapping buttons from their threads.

Lord Pierrot is alarmed. He tries to restrain her hands, but desire lends her strength. She fights him, attacks his gown again. He falls sprawling across the bed, laughing feebly. But he is not amused. He is an old man, and not accustomed to such violent handling. And from a woman! One of his women! 'Gently, my pet!' he cries. 'Gently!'

She takes no notice. She lunges at him, throwing herself on top of him and kissing him fiercely.

Something must be wrong with her. The heat has unhinged her. They are such sensitive creatures.

Lord Pierrot pushes weakly at her, at Daphne Dolores, striving to rise; but she pushes him in return, turning him over on his back and clambering upon him. She grasps his baggy trousers, dragging them off and hurling them into a corner.

This is not love, that sweet, sad, tender enchantment, Lord Pierrot thinks to himself as she tears off his gown; this is brute lust! What can he do? With all his women he has always been able to retain control, even in the giddy toils of desire. Daphne Dolores seems to have gone quite mad. Mad, it is true, with passion for him, for Lord Pierrot; but mad nonetheless.

He is almost unmanned by dread, repelled by her undignified abandon. Pinned beneath her writhing body, Lord Pierrot closes his eyes and thinks of her as she has always been before: soft, tender, yielding.

Daphne Dolores fastens her teeth in his nipple. Lord Pierrot cries out in protest. But she laughs and twists around above him, seeking every moment a new and more gratifying position.

Lord Pierrot thumbs his ring.

She sees him.

At once she rises up, straddling him in a way that makes him catch his breath. She seizes his hand, and tugs at the ring.

'My dear!' gasps Lord Pierrot.

'Off!' she cries. 'Off with it!'

'No!' He covers the ring with his hand.

Daphne Dolores pauses, looking down at him with a wrathful gaze. 'I hate it. I hate everything that reminds me of her,' says Daphne Dolores.

'It was never hers,' Lord Pierrot says at once. 'What I told you was untrue.'

Daphne Dolores arches her brows. Her curiosity is piqued. She keeps hold of his hand. She requires an explanation.

Glad of the respite from these exertions, Lord Pierrot gives her one. 'The ring was never a gift from Lady Dove,' he says, somewhat hoarsely. 'It is a family heirloom. A device of my great-great-grandfather's. He was a man of many enemies.'

With a flick of the secret hinge he shows her, concealed beneath the square black stone, a needle steeped in a swift and fatal poison. Concocted by the first wearer, that poison has been improved by his subsequent heirs. Against it there is no appeal.

Lord Pierrot tells her of the apprehensions he suffered outside her door. 'One sweep of my hand, my love, and there he would lie, your assailant, paralysed and dying at your feet!'

Daphne Dolores examines the ring, the needle beneath the stone.

'And have you ever made use of it?' she asks, speaking low.

'Experimentally,' he tells her. 'On suitable local creatures.'

She laughs again. In her present mood such macabre prospects amuse her. She flips shut the ring and, before he can prevent her, ducks her head and lightly kisses the square black stone.

She looks at him from under lowered brows, her lips still touching the ring.

'On suitable creatures,' she repeats.

Then she is upon him once more, and there is nothing he can do while she has her way with him.

Lord Pierrot senses at last the stirring of desire. There is something splendid, he recalls, about a woman towering over him thus, in an access of hunger and power. Unnatural? Is it truly so? There may be many things in Nature, he thinks; many hidden things. And did not Lady Dove excite him thus when they were wed?

She reminds him, Daphne Dolores, of his wife when she was young. They all do, all his women. He is prone, Lord

Pierrot, to such sentiments. He thrusts into her with rekindled appetite. The old voluptuary is not defeated yet.

But even while she grinds and rocks upon him, yelping and growling like an animal in rut, the scientist in him considers: was there no warning of this last night? No sign, no prior indication of this unprecedented frenzy?

Lord Pierrot has always prided himself on the accuracy and good order of his memory. Even as they rise together towards their climax he recalls how Daphne Dolores disparaged his serenade, and opposed him when he made reference to the melancholy matter of his age. And yes, he remembers now how she revealed her hatred for Lady Dove, trying to keep him from his lawful place beside his invalid wife. She clutched him by the hair! And he thought nothing of it!

It was love, Lord Pierrot understands as Daphne Dolores falls upon him in her sensuous spasm. Love, that delusive, obliterating passion: only love could make so experienced, so wise a man so blind.

Daphne Dolores lies lathered and gasping on his chest. But Lord Pierrot, he is not yet spent. He heaves at her, stroking distractedly at her hair. She lifts her head, Daphne Dolores, from under his hand. She lifts her hips, and withdraws.

'My love!' cries Lord Pierrot, aghast.

She kneels up once more, straddling him, toying with him. Her eyes are languid now, her movements satiated.

Yet he is not done, Lord Pierrot.

And nor, it seems, is she, Daphne Dolores.

She speaks. 'Take me up to the house,' she says.

'But my sweet!'

She ignores his protest.

'Take me to the house,' she says again. 'Let me be mistress there.'

Lord Pierrot is astounded. This is absolutely counter to

the first rule, that she must never interfere in his domestic arrangements. Daphne Dolores has abandoned all sense of place and propriety.

Then he smiles.

Is his spirit dead, his blood quite cold? Is he not still Lord Pierrot, the libertine of Fomalhaut, the rakehell of the Innovators? And is she not Daphne Dolores, creature of his passion?

He flings his arms about her slender waist. 'Yes, my love, you are right. Let us be wild! Let us be free of trammelling checks and consciences! Let us go where love bids!' He chortles. 'Oh, my darling, my mistress, I must say: how cunningly you teach me!'

Together the lovers scramble from the bed and out into the clouded night. Barefoot and naked they run down to the rock where the dependable little boat has moored itself. They climb aboard, Lord Pierrot sitting astern with Daphne Dolores sprawled between his shrunken thighs. He gives the command to steer for the shore.

As they ride, Lord Pierrot looks behind them. The moon is still hidden, and all the stars.

He strokes the short, soft hair of Daphne Dolores. Perhaps she will be calmer now, more docile since slaking her lust. No – she turns energetically in his arms, nuzzling forcefully at him, almost upsetting the little boat. 'Will you take me to the house?' she asks again.

'To the very heart of the house,' he promises.

They cross the lake. Lord Pierrot passes by the boathouse and puts ashore at the abandoned grotto. Leading Daphne Dolores by the hand he scales the bank, and slips between the statues of the Astral Graces, each of which wears his mother's face. Along crazed paths, between straggling rhododendrons the couple hasten, circumventing the garden by an obscure route that brings them out at last on the croquet lawn. The east wing looms ahead, its windows glittering darkly.

Suddenly Daphne Dolores stops. Lord Pierrot knows she remembers his instruction, that she is never to come near the house itself. She stands naked and panting on the croquet lawn, seeking her lover's face in frenzied, mute appeal.

'Come, my darling,' Lord Pierrot bids her in a secretive tone. 'Let us within. We shall baffle Lady Dove with our boldness.'

All at once he hears a dreadful sound.

'Pierre! Pi-erre!'

It is his wife. It is Lady Dove, materializing as if at the merest mention of her name. She has left her bed and come blundering into the garden in her nightgown. Lord Pierrot hears her now smashing towards them through the undergrowth, bellowing for him like a panic-stricken heifer.

Does she suspect? Has she seen them? Or is she sick, and roaming in her sleep? Perhaps, of all things, her premonition has come true: the full moon has unsettled her brain. It is a night for the madness of women.

Lady Dove is coming nearer. Lord Pierrot sees her monstrous shape bobbing in the darkness beneath the shade of trees.

Silently giving thanks for the iron self-discipline, the blood and breeding of the Pierrots that enable him to keep his head even through the ordeal of such a night, Lord Pierrot puts his fingers to the moist lips of Daphne Dolores, commanding her to silence. He points across the croquet lawn to the flowerbeds. They will confuse Lady Dove. She will not think to seek them that way.

Daphne Dolores drops Lord Pierrot's hand. She sprints away across the Triacian grass, Lord Pierrot panting after.

Trampling the blooms so carefully laid out by Lord Pierrot's horticultron, they burst into the arbour leaving Lady

Dove behind, still stumbling through the shrubbery. Arriving at the door of the conservatory they hear a faint, disconsolate moo, a distant sound of breaking branches.

Inside, the house begins, without asking, to raise the lights. Lord Pierrot countermands it. Daphne Dolores does not notice. She hardly pauses to admire the glories of the Sirian frescoes. She kisses Lord Pierrot vigorously and pulls him into the gloomy passageway and along the hall, where the butler rolls out to greet them.

It scans them with a brief burst of invisible light. '*Good evening, sir and madam,*' it says, in its buzzing voice. '*May I take your coats?*'

Daphne Dolores laughs uproariously, heedlessly. Her laughter echoes in the rafters.

'Let us go up, my love,' Lord Pierrot bids her. 'To my chamber.'

Again she contradicts him, her blue eyes shining with joyous anticipation. 'No, dear heart,' she insists, 'to your laboratory! Did you not tell me that Lady Dove never sets foot there?'

With a private, wistful smile, Lord Pierrot congratulates her on her stratagem. 'An excellent choice, my precious!'

Ignoring the attentive automaton, they jump into the shaft and float up to the level of the laboratories.

Here too Daphne Dolores strides ahead, as if she knows the way. She was here once before; perhaps, unconsciously, in some infant part of her brain, she remembers it. She sweeps through the catalogue room, where all knowledge lies sleeping in banks of deep cold drawers. In the mechanatory, beneath the great bleached skeletons of Lord Pierrot's first automata, she runs her white hand carelessly across the rack of obsolete implements, the tarnished rods and serried claws that recall his years of service in the Innovation Corps. She does not spare a glance for the cabinets of the salon zoologique with their stiff, staring specimens of every kind of fauna, natural and otherwise, as they reckon these things on the planet Triax.

Pierrot is pleased to follow her. Her haste gladdens his old and disappointed heart. He is grateful that, in the dark, she fails to notice the lines of mannequins above her head, encased in glass along the wall. Each is clad in some cast-off of the younger, slimmer Lady Dove; yes, even back to the yellow sundress and matching gloves that she wore on their trip to the moon. It would not do to let Daphne Dolores see those clothes; nor the figures that wear them. They might disturb her.

'Ah!' cries Daphne Dolores then. She has reached the last laboratory. She stands amid the vats, gazing about in wonder and delight.

Behind her, Lord Pierrot slips into the curtained alcove for a gown. As he plucks one from the hook and wraps it around his nakedness, the homunculi stir in their nest of rags. Lord Pierrot hastily silences their querulous cheeping, dropping a cloak over them. He steps back into the laboratory.

The stained glass windows are black and opaque in the occluded night. The only light in the cluttered chamber is a faint glow of phosphorescence from the things in the vats. It highlights the slick bubbles of alembics and retorts, the dusty brass barrel of a giant microscope. There is a lingering scent of formaldehyde and rotting orange peel.

Lord Pierrot sees Daphne Dolores padding barefoot from vat to vat, trying to discern what each holds. Some are mere seeds yet, little spatters of darkness in the broth. Others are burgeoning, dendritic: a tubular stem with floppy branches above and below. Daphne Dolores has reached one so far grown as to be spinning a slick integument about itself, like a protective cocoon. Its members are well defined.

The largest tank stands alone in the corner beneath a sagging bank of shelves. The waters of that one, Lord Pierrot knows, are empty.

As Daphne Dolores goes to peer into its slimy depths, the moon of Triax suddenly heaves itself from behind a bulwark of cloud and sheds light into the laboratory. All the coloured panes flare up at once like a curtain of cold jewels.

Daphne Dolores turns about. She catches sight of Lord Pierrot standing there in his white gown, and cries out in pleasure.

'My love!' calls Daphne Dolores. 'You have become a very harlequin!'

Lord Pierrot looks down at himself and chuckles. He is illuminated, as if by the rainbow-coloured primary of an unknown world, daubed from head to toe with carmine and gold and viridian. All down his gown the smears of acids and enzymes show up as harshly as though they were stains of rust or blood.

From beneath the coloured window comes a cry. '*Pierre!*'

Lord Pierrot crosses the floor and cautiously peeps out. Lady Dove is there, still tangled in the bushes, swiping blindly at the moonlight with her huge arms.

Daphne Dolores laughs.

'Will you not take care of her?' she asks.

'Take care of her?' repeats Lord Pierrot.

'Release her from her misery.'

She nods at his hand, at the fatal ring.

Lord Pierrot looks at his ring as if he has never seen it before. He marvels at the audacity of Daphne Dolores, at the daring and ambition she has concealed from him all this while. Her spirit is a match for his own. He sighs.

He opens the ring, inspects the reservoir. 'Let us be sure,' he says. 'I should not wish her to suffer even a moment.' He closes his eyes, suppressing a shudder of emotion, of potent memory; and opens them again.

'I have some fresh distilled. On that shelf up there, in the corner.'

Daphne Dolores turns to look at the shadowy ranks of vials and flasks that have bowed the shelves. Lord Pierrot, feeling behind the couch, fetches out a slender staff of glass a yard long, with a brass ferrule. A homunculus scrabbles briefly from under the valance. He shoos it back out of sight.

Daphne Dolores leans across the vat, stretching up to the bottles. She cannot reach. She lifts herself up and puts one knee carefully on the rim. The coloured light streaks her tiny buttocks.

'Oh, I can't get it,' she complains. 'Come and help me.'

Lord Pierrot comes and stands behind her. He puts one long, thin arm around her naked waist, hugging her body to him as if to steady her on her precarious perch. Her flesh is warm in his embrace. With the other arm he reaches over her shoulder for the flask. Their faces are very close together. Daphne Dolores turns her head and kisses Lord Pierrot on the lips.

'*Pi-erre!*' moans the stricken woman beneath the window.

Daphne Dolores gives a little laugh and slips her tongue between her lover's teeth.

Lord Pierrot thrusts forward with his shoulder.

Daphne Dolores is small and slight, like all his women. With a cry and a splash, she topples into the tank.

The questionable fluid at once froths pink, surging high and closing avidly about her delectable limbs. It spatters Lord Pierrot's motley gown, and he steps quickly backwards.

In the spume he catches a final glimpse of Daphne Dolores, bobbing up: her startled eyes, her open mouth. He raises his glass staff, plants its brass tip between her breasts, and thrusts her down.

From her little ears, her nose, her perfect lips, bubbles

flurry. Lord Pierrot waits patiently until they cease.

Whispering, the homunculi scuttle from their corners and come to stand around him in a flock, holding hands and craning their necks. They lift one another up to the glass.

Lord Pierrot does not rebuke them. The moment is too solemn. Wiping the staff on his sleeve, he turns away and opens the window, admitting a wave of hot, dank air.

Lord Pierrot sighs. The melancholy fit is upon him once again, as always when he has made the great renunciation. One by one he raises them; and one by one they become unstable, unreasonable, and have to be stilled. Must it be ever thus?

He gazes out of the window into the thick and tangled garden. By the light of the yellow moon of Triax he sees his wife, Lady Dove, standing below, her nightdress in tatters, twigs and leaves in her hair. She looks up and recognizes him. A scowl crosses her bloated face. '*Pierre!*' she shouts.

Fatigued, unhappy, Lord Pierrot orders the intelligence to send his taxidermatron. Then he goes out through the salon, passing beneath the line of his daughters, going to seek forgiveness once again of Lady Dove.

II

VOICES

Every writer needs lots of help to get started, and I needed more than most. At the wobbly, precarious outset, when I understood nothing at all, no one was kinder to me than Brian Aldiss, who selflessly gave me hours of his time and made some decisive interventions on my behalf.

I remember Brian saying once: 'Novels are fine – you can wander around and lose your way in a novel, and still have lots of room to get back on the track. Short stories – ' He lifted his jaw and opened one hand in a gesture both fatalistic and pugnacious. 'Short stories you have to catch on the wing . . .'

This is probably the only story I've ever caught in flight, rather than assembling in my customary laborious fashion. It took no more than a couple of days to write, pretty much as it stands now, and subsequently became the first grown-up story of mine to reach print, as runner-up in a competition organized by The Fiction Magazine and Faber & Faber. At the award party Frederic Raphael and others told me how wonderful it was and that I should write many more like it.

I've never been able to, of course.

Miss Otis Regrets

1

HERE WE ARE, looking at each other through the window: she in her room, I in mine. I assume she is looking at me. She waves. I wave back.

Nothing here is what it seems; then again, it may be. Why not.

Not mute: at least she is not that. She gives me that much to work on. Her voice, every sound she makes, comes to me through the loudspeakers. When she speaks all the instruments jiggle. The tape spools burr; the dials flutter. Similarly, when I speak, my voice is carried into her room. I assume she hears me. This is communication, but only I have a microphone with a switch. Such is our relationship, I fear. I resolve to give her a switch on her side too, just as soon as we find out what she can operate. These early good resolutions rarely achieve anything in the long run, you will find, but it is not better not to make them. This is our first day together.

I want to say that this is not my speciality. I am not much of a linguist or a phonologist or whatever, though my military training did include some cipher work. But all the equipment is here and any of us can become proficient with any of it through the learning tapes, and I am the most verbal of us, I suppose. So they tell me. Certainly I am one of the least busy now that we are so far out of direct radio contact with Earth. That may also be why I want to keep some kind of written record of the investigation, even though everything we do here is impartially recorded and stored for general access.

Perhaps one day I shall be able to present it to her for her to study *my* words during this period of forced intimacy. (Another fair resolution.) Of course, she may be doing so already.

2

What is the condition of speech? 'The willed production of complex sound-patterns of a high degree of organisation and repetition.' This is not of much use as a definition. Pattern and organisation and complexity are in the ear of the beholder, and 'willed' is as arguable as it ever was. Probably I ought to call up some Chomsky at least, but I fear too much meta-language will deafen me to the real thing. From observation, then: the Otis make sound aplenty, with a statistically significant incidence of repetition. The most vocal and repetitive of them are the ones we have decided to call female.

That looks outrageous written down, so I have asked Gordon how he would put it. He said that the Otis appear to show anatomical differentiation of a sort that may well be sexual. All the Otis heal swiftly, but one 'sex' also seems to undergo encystment and regeneration without prior injury, perhaps on some periodic scale. These are the ones we are accustomed to call 'female'; they are also, and incidentally, generally more vocal than the 'males'.

Which is probably just as outrageous and no less analogical.

If we had given the job to Myra would it all have bothered her as it does me?

As usual we outnumber the female crew members by five or six to one. I still say it is ridiculous, and dangerous too, to have sexual bias to contend with, on top of everything else.

This one is our most vocal specimen. No doubt she'll put us right as soon as she can. Chirp, chirp, she goes.

3

I test her for: skin tension and conductivity, fluid pressure and internal osmosis, temperature, electrical activity, dilation and contraction, sensitivity. I measure the muscle tone of each sphincter, play her own voice back to her and measure everything again. Gordon and Marco have developed a special adhesive gel for my electrodes, an appropriate disinfectant for my waldo probes. But the Otis's allergies and immunities remain unknown.

I began by having music playing while I worked, as I habitually do, but now I turn it on only when my microphone is off. I explain this to myself and others scientifically, as the reduction of superfluous stimuli, but it is primarily a piece of absurdity. Over-protectiveness on my part. How can I tell, say, what is music to Miss Otis and what is not? Perhaps she is singing to me all this while.

Will I know her scream when I hear it?

4

Miss Otis and I have three things in common:
  Life.
  Assignment to each other.
  The window.

Otherwise:

Miss Otis is a ragged square, about four by four. She looks like an outsize pillowcase partly filled with luminous petroleum jelly. As she habitually stands, on one corner bent under her, there is a line of orifices, four in all, along her lower right-hand edge, fringed with irregular muscular projections. Two of these are capable of expelling air and shaping it, much as human lips do to whistle. Her colour is off-white, noticeably phosphorescent, occasionally varied with marbling of silver or a delicate china-blue. Her skin is smooth and clammy, apparently featureless and actually extremely complicated. Receptors for sound, for light, and for other portions of the electromagnetic spectrum, as well as some that respond to stimuli yet unknown, cover her from apex to foot on both surfaces, entirely without apparent system. She bobs and weaves and climbs the walls with a slow, supple restlessness that seems always about to defy gravity. She ripples and pulses intermittently. She whoops and moans.

The Otis decay to slime within seconds of death. Surgery is immediately fatal in every case: this despite their phenomenal healing ability. No one can account for this. X-rays produce blank plates. The computer has assimilated all Miss Otis's measurements and responses into one multi-dimensional profile like the ward of some cosmic key. On no axis does it compare with any human or animal profile; nor does it fit any known or inferable lock.

Miss Otis chirps. I am in despair for Miss Otis.

5

Clifford says: 'There really isn't any point in taking any more time over this one. No offence, Anton, but you know I've been against this project from the start. Everyone who was round this table last month will remember – well, let's take a look at the minutes for last month, the month before, was it? You'll see I spoke against Anton's project and only let it go through under protest, with the proviso that it's a secondary project, nothing to do with the expedition. If the Otis were civilized, or if they were savages, if they were wild animals even, anything that actively helped or hindered us, then of course we'd have to learn to deal with them and learn quickly. As it is, Anton's using valuable computer-time and equipment we could use elsewhere, and where's it got him? Nowhere! It's perfectly obvious we ought to cut our losses on projects that don't pan out and concentrate our resources on the ones that do. The Otis are perfectly happy to leave us alone. Fine, well, let's leave them alone, fair enough.'

The vote went against him again, I am relieved to report, and later Bernardette said: 'Oh, Anton, don't you realize he's shitting coprolites? Surely. If your Otis-English phrasebook proves their tootling is actually protest songs about his open-cast mining, he's not going to be popular back home. Granted, your beasties don't look too het up, and they do float around doing sod all, all day, but that doesn't mean they're not intelligent, nor does it mean they don't have rights or principles, etc. etc. – I'd have thought you should have been pushing that line at the meeting, but still, no need really, eh? Everyone's on your side anyway, either because they reckon they're humanitarians or because they reckon they're academics, like Niels. But they're all going to go and play with something else if you don't come up with the odd result soon, dear.'

Sometimes it is hard to work out what one's friends are saying, never mind the bland Miss Otis.

*

6

Today Miss Otis is saying nothing at all. Not a peep. In every other respect she seems as normal. The Tao teaches us that without silence there would be no sound. Existence is defined by void, like the white space between the words on this paper, between the letters too of course. Understanding is a critical process, distinguishing between signal and noise, figure and ground, meaning and meaninglessness.

Her silence today indicates that Miss Otis's sounds are not automatic but intentional, a willed production, just so.

May I assume that?

Is it to presume to assume so?

If I assumed more perhaps I might reach more conclusions.

Only when we assume the presence of meaning do we find meaning. Only by imposing pattern can we distinguish pattern. Tomorrow (assuming Miss Otis is back to normal) I shall begin to teach her English.

7

Food.

First I let her go three hours past her usual feeding time. She showed no reaction, discomfort or any other. She is tooting her customary tone-deaf toot.

'Food,' I said. I turned up the volume on the intercom. 'Food.' I said it many times. I said it especially when she wandered near the trough, and most loudly when she stepped in it. 'Food.' The Otis seem to live on a sticky alginous scum that forms readily on stagnant 'water' and in damp places. They absorb the scum through the lowest orifice, and through the soles of their 'feet'.

Food. This made no visible impression on her. Eventually I let a little of the slime trickle into the trough. Miss Otis sucked it up at once. 'Food, food, food,' I chanted. My plan was to repeat this partial delivery many times, until the slime was all gone, hoping in this way to keep her attention on the lesson. Unfortunately after that first small portion she ignored the rest and showed no further inclination to eat.

This made me wonder whether I might not be overfeeding her. Perhaps she is pining. When removed to unfamiliar environments or overcome by grief, terrestrial creatures frequently lose their appetites. Or by love. Yet she has never done other than eat heartily, hitherto.

I made up a tape loop and had the machine relay it at a powerful amplification, processed to the higher timbre and frequency range of Otis speech, for bursts of two-and-a-half minutes with two-minute intervals. I darkened our rooms but for a spot directed at the algae trough. I heated the soup slightly to enhance its rankness. After a few days of this intensive exposure Miss Otis will scarcely be able to remain unaffected.

8

Food. Water. Air. Man. Woman. Bush. Stone.

Today Miss Otis lives in a treasure-house of sights, sounds and smells, essential and artificial. I have bribed and cajoled Marco into developing the requisite chemistry to produce my sensory pageant in her alien atmosphere. Clifford will find this out and crucify me at the next meeting, but I do not care, I must have them all, all the elements and radiances of two worlds, and the machinery to convey them, to her, to her. Films and transparencies flash, holograms creep in and out of emptiness, vacancy blooms at the creating words. Food. Water. Air. Man. Woman. Bush. Stone.

Hoot. Chortle. Ahh. Moan. Whoop. Miss Otis waltzes melodically through my multi-media, her own pale lustrous flesh the screen for my educational extravaganza. Was ever suitor, since 'The Twelve Days of Christmas', so lavish?

Over and under and through it all the soundtrack is woven, the incantation of the names, my own voice garbled up into a chirp for her better understanding.

9

In the night, waking all in perspiration from an urgent dream to a more urgent thought: could there be, somewhere in this prodigality of worlds, a language *without nouns?* Our tyranny of things and names, proper and common, figure and ground – but what if the Otis speak in shades of verbs, all time one continuous present, an infinitive, a participle? *Being* . . . What if my prisoner has been carolling conjugation while I have been drumming her into materialism, just as my ancestors thundered the startled African out of her green thought into the grey suit of Christianity? Mopping my brow I have risen to make this solemn memorandum. As soon as it is day and I can coax some more programmers out of the breakfast room I must intensify the cramming. Primary sensations: hot, cold, wet, dry. Emotions: anger, calm, fear, yes, but love too . . .

I must don breathing apparatus and pressure suit and go into her chamber, like the sailor who loved the mermaid. I must place my gloved fingers on each of her sweet and secret vents and caress it to pliability, to mucilaginous excitement; I must manipulate it from sighs to sounds, and from sounds to sense.

As I step feverishly into the control room I find the tape I forgot to turn off last evening running tirelessly round and round the heads and Miss Otis flattened across the loudspeaker grille like a slab of raw pastry, pale and barely pulsing. Has my robotic representation abused her delicacy, stunned the nervous quickness of that creamy hide? Have I talked her insensible, or worse? I snap the controls off, the viewing light on. 'Miss Otis! Speak to me! Tell me you live, and forgive!'

She trembles. I cry again.

At the sound of my proper voice in the sudden quiet she rises through her heavy atmosphere and floats across her cell like a pregnant kite. I press my lips to the window, our window. With the cumbersome precision of a dream she spreads herself tight across the glass, quivering in recognition. I hear her moo of salutation.

10

'No, of course they're not.'

'Well, we won't be certain until we've been here another year or two. But it seems unlikely, highly unlikely.'

'Anton will tell us. Anton! Come and tell us about your creatures.'

Gordon is not treating this as a joke. He continues in his dependable, placatory tone. 'They may have three sexes, or even more; we really don't know. The differentiation we've found may not be sexual. We've not done a lot of work on them and frankly, we're stuck for a basic model, especially since we haven't come across any other fauna.'

'Well, Anton?' says Russ. 'You're shacking up with one of them, aren't you? You can tell us: is she a Real Woman?'

I make my voice neutral, ashamed to dishonour Miss Otis

with this juvenile conversation. 'It's not for me to say. As Gordon has told you, it is most likely the Otis do not have sex as we know it.'

Russ cracks a grin, but restrains his jocular prurience, repressed perhaps by the presence of Niels. I try to get back to Gordon's level of urbanity. 'They do not seem to reproduce in any terrestrial fashion. Only they regenerate themselves.'

'Yes, I've heard that,' says a man whose name I do not know. 'Do you mean to say they're immortal?'

I look at Gordon. He says: 'Apparently, yes, though we've seen some of them die from different causes. All of those were what we've been calling males. The females regenerate far more quickly and efficiently; but we don't know how many times. We don't know anything, really, without proper long-term observation, in the natural habitat.'

'They can of course be killed,' I add, seeing that he has not been honest enough to mention the fatalities under his own scalpel.

Gordon looks at me coolly.

'I see,' says Niels, 'you've called the ones that regenerate female because you think the new Otis may be the offspring of the old, is that it? Well, now, this is very interesting. Are the regenerated ones discrete individuals, or are they, literally, born again?'

'Who can say?' I say lightly, hoping to forestall a theological dispute. As multi-denominational padre to the expedition Niels feels he has been called to construct the interface between science and faith. In his universe there are no aliens, only sheep not yet enfolded.

'Has your pet borne herself again, Anton?' smiles Myra.

'Not yet since we captured her.'

She casts her gaze upwards. 'I think that must be so wonderful! To live forever, like an amoeba, only in the same body!' She twists stray hair around one finger. 'All mothers share their identity-experience with their babies, you know, but actually to be one!'

Bernardette chips in. 'If you ask me, that's a load of sexist horsepiss, dear, and I'm surprised you can swallow it.' (She isn't.) 'The only reason anyone thinks these creatures are female is that it was a man who suggested it. Well, look around you, dear: we're outnumbered six to one. Who do you think the aliens are on this mission? The men can't cope with us in here so they project us out there. I shall tell Anton's pet: Know your enemy, I shall say.'

She nods at me rudely. I often find Bernardette's bluntness of expression discomforting and quite uncharacteristic for a psychiatrist.

'Yes, Myra,' says Laszlo. 'You might as well say that the Otis's physical immortality is a classic sign of male arrogance. It's the triumph of ego over death!'

Myra smiles her ineffable smile. 'Oh, no, Laszlo! If his Otis were a man, Anton would be in no doubt about it. Women are much more subtle, more mysterious . . .'

The man I don't know butts in again. 'Well, wait a minute: that peculiar song of theirs, that's what you're studying, isn't it?'

I nod, impatient to get back to it.

'Is that an identity thing, you know, what's the word, like birdsong – territorial?'

'It seems not to be. The repeated elements are common to all the Otis, regardless of location, or of sex.'

Russ hears his cue again and leans forward. 'I still say you should put a male in with your female, Anton, and watch them very closely. You could learn a thing or two.'

His tone disturbs me.

'Watch out, Russ,' says Bernardette. 'You've got him worried now, boy.'

'I am sorry,' I reply. 'I cannot indulge this levity. Miss – my specimen is not a plaything. She is a sensitive creature, highly strung.'

In my mind's eye I see her, eclipsing these indelicate gross faces: highly strung indeed, her skin stretched tight as a drumhead, resonant to my amplified plosives and fricatives, tremulous under my gauntlets.

11

I do not enjoy hearing Bernardette and Myra speak in that way. I like to think I am a rational man, and so, since there are fundamental physiological differences between the sexes, I think it most probable that there are fundamental psychological ones too. But to attribute qualities to each generally, as, men are more dynamic, women more stable, this is what Bernardette calls stereotyping, and taking the cultural for the natural. I think it improbable that all human psychology is conditioned, yet I do not trust Myra's Jungian mysticism. If there are fundamental psychological differences between the sexes, is it probable that they are exactly those described by her quaint mythology? Could it be so easy, that we must take the old wives for our authorities? If so, how may we then distinguish and extirpate the sexual discrimination that still moulders through society?

There is no switch on Miss Otis's microphone, no handle on her side of the airlock. De Sade would have approved. She is the victim of my tyranny, captive, subject to continuous observation and arbitrary interference, pierced by my electrodes, suffering a purgatorial discipline from which she can redeem herself only by learning to express herself in my language. I have her hooked up to the computers once again. The screens flicker with an interminable confetti of signs, letters and figures as my machines strive to convert her cries and whispers into human notation. This is the most intimate violation. All the while the tapes revolve, scourging her with her master's voice, each repetition another stroke on her quivering flanks.

As I enter my chamber Miss Otis rises and presses herself against the window, agog. She is a willing victim; perhaps she will one day write her own version of this journal, a new *Histoire d'O*.

12

Strange premonition. My fancy did not err.

It may be as the old Marquis taught, that there is a unique consent between the torturer and his victim.

Miss Otis has spoken her first word.

She shows no indication of learning to express herself in English yet, though her understanding is radiant to one who knows her countenance as I do. But the VDU, tossing the gargantuan word-salad garnered for it from the memories of all the machines in the dome, has frozen on one blinking turquoise titbit. Screening her output for strings repeated more than randomly, comprehensible in English, and commensurate with its index of her hypothesized mental and physical states, the computer has isolated the first element of Miss Otis's vocabulary:

'Sorry.'

13

Clifford looks at the word in the centre of the screen. '"Sorry"? How do you like that, eh, Anton? The brute's apologizing to us for wasting our time!'

'*Qui s'excuse s'accuse*, Clifford?' Bernardette shrugs. 'You've done a good job, Anton: well done. You'll be famous. They'll want to write it up for *Time* magazine. "Guilt: The Alien Condition." Papa Freud would be proud of you both.'

She takes the geologist's arm and they walk out together. I call after them: 'If I have a result, how come it's still a waste, according to you?'

One of the cybernetic engineers looks up from his microscope. 'No, actually, that was an interesting comment of Clifford's, don't you think? She communicates her apologies for being unable to communicate.' He gestures at the screen. 'It's a self-cancelling sign.'

'I'd have said it was pretty obvious,' says Laszlo. 'She's sorry she's here, that's all. Cooped up̄ like a leopard in the zoo.'

'No, no,' I insist. 'I've isolated the sound-group that corresponds and here, you see? It's one of the Otis's most frequent groups, even in the wild. And why assume that she means sorry for herself? There's sympathy in that "sorry" as well as pathos. Well, don't you think?'

'They are all sorry,' says Myra gravely. 'All sorry we came. An inauspicious conjunction.'

Myra must be the only stellar navigator qualified in both astronomy and astrology. Her head is bowed.

Niels is impressed. 'A binding ethos built upon the principle of inadequacy. Fascinating. Absolutely fascinating. The dialect of the confessional.' He gives a wry smile. 'The old "science fiction" writers used to dream up Paradise planets without Original Sin. We seem to have hit on one whose inhabitants are still enacting the Fall.'

The last of them is Gordon, who has been standing at the back all this while with his hands in his pockets. He comes forward and looks glumly at the screen, as one who confirms bad news to himself. 'QED,' he says, in an odd, gruff voice. He prods the computer with the toe of his boot, as if he'd prefer to kick it. 'Okay, Ant, shut it down and we'll get the gear sterilized.'

I gaze at him in amazement.

'You've got your result, haven't you?' he growls, heading for the door. 'I can tell you, I don't envy you having to show your working.'

14

Sorry.

Miss Otis.

Sorry.

Miss Otis.

Sorry.

Miss Otis, I forgive you.

Sorry.

Perhaps Bernardette was right and we do share our neuroses with these wailing women of another world. Perhaps this female sense of guilt is the sexual absolute, ubiquitous, in the heavens as it is on Earth, where we gave it social establishment in China and Japan, wrote it down in *Ancrene Riwle* and *Paradise Lost*.

Sorry.

Or did we create it with those books, and are the Otis just another sexist race?

Sorry.

Miss Otis. Miss Otis, was it me? Are you abasing yourself, or did I humiliate you?

*

15

Miss Otis falls silent. The VDU blinks blank. Her temperature drops sharply. A tough white carapace begins to form about her body.

We make haste to carry her to the cavern where she must spend the next three months. With difficulty we hang her among the others, up in the stalactites. The fumes of the underground river simultaneously preserve and nourish them, is Gordon's theory. I have brought a votive candle to light, but he warns me that in their present condition Miss Otis and her companions are likely to be highly inflammable.

I shall wait for you, Miss Otis, and be the first to greet you when you emerge.

Or your daughter, when she emerges.

Or some other woman, heartbreakingly familiar but quite unknown, a stranger with your face.

I can change too. I promise.

Next time it will be different.

It was Relate, actually, the marriage guidance charity, that rang me out of the blue and asked me to be responsible for a collection in my street. Caught off guard by the candour of the request, I said I would. Only afterwards did I start to think 'Why?' and get annoyed with myself, and them. I decided I had to get something out of the incongruous and unwanted chore, even if it was only a piece of fiction which probably no one would ever publish.

The result was the first of my stories to be broadcast on BBC Radio: always a special ambition of mine. I listened to Geoffrey Whitehead reading it on the transistor in Susanna's kitchen while I was doing the washing up; which seemed just about perfect.

The Suffer the Children Man

THE PHONECALL HAD been completely unexpected. 'I'm calling from *Suffer the Children*,' said a young man calling himself Steven, or Simon, or something. 'We're looking for someone to deliver and collect twenty charity donation envelopes in your street.' Clive had been doing nothing, as usual, staring at the telly. He was so surprised that he said yes.

He started regretting it the moment he put the phone down. *Suffer the Children* was not a charity he really wanted to support. Looked at realistically, there were too many children in the world already. There were too many people in the world, and they all kept having children, and always would, whether you supported them or not. If the envelope with the decorative waif on had come through his letterbox, Clive would have given it back empty. He probably had done, before now, many times. And if he wouldn't give them money, why on earth had he agreed to work for them, free?

As the weeks went by, Clive began to dread his task. Passing the gates with their broken latches, the wintry strips of garden with their displays of torn crisp bags and cigarette ends, he thought the houses in his street had never looked less charitable.

He started dreaming up ways to get out of it. Clive was good at excuses; he liked to concoct really impressive ones. 'I'm really sorry,' he would tell the *Suffer the Children* people, with a laugh. 'I won't be here. I'm going to America next week, to make a film. I had no idea.' And then, with great sincerity: 'I *am* sorry.'

He never made the call. Why agonize about it? Delivering twenty envelopes. Collecting twenty envelopes. How arduous could it be? It would be easy, surely, collecting for a cause you didn't care about. It wouldn't matter whether people gave or not.

Clive didn't know anyone in his street, though he had lived there for years. He wondered if they knew him.

At last his collector's kit arrived. Forty-four envelopes, each with its design of a wispy infant in tasteful shadow; a page of instructions; a bank credit slip for the money; and a sort of warrant, which the instructions called a 'badge of authority', though there was no pin.

Forty-four envelopes. That was annoying. Right, thought Clive, I'll do half and no more. That's twenty-two, that's more than twenty. Then he felt ashamed. If you're going to do it, do it. He put an elastic band round the bundle and went out, to do it.

There were different kinds of letterboxes, Clive discovered. Some were low, as if for letters delivered by dachshunds. Some were up high. Perhaps they were for airmail. Some, when Clive pushed them open, proved to have mouths full of stiff bristles that resisted flimsy envelopes. Others concealed a small guillotine: an inner flap on a spring.

Here was a letterbox with no flap at all, in a front door shabby with neglect. No light showed through the hole. Above it was a piece of notepaper stuck with tape. It said: 'POSTMAN: please do not leave parcels on doorstep or with neighbours.' Clive read it twice. Nothing about charity envelopes. He dropped one through the lifeless slot.

At another house, the front door was open. Someone was coming downstairs, carrying a box. First two feet came into view, then two legs; then a box, with two hands wrapped around it. Clive put their envelope on the doormat and left, before the face appeared. He didn't want to meet anyone. He didn't want to have to say hello, or explain his business. He hadn't even got his badge of authority. The instructions said you had to wear it when you were collecting, and he wasn't, was he? He was delivering.

The last twelve numbers in the street were a block of flats. There were no letterboxes, only bells. The street door was locked. One of the bells said TRADES. Clive pressed it. Nothing happened.

He left it at that. Thirty-two deliveries. It would do. He would collect them on Sunday morning, when most people would be at home.

On Sunday when Clive woke up it was already ten. He tried to hurry to get up and get dressed and find a pin for the badge and a bag for the envelopes and a pen to write down where no one answered, but by then it was nearly noon, and if there is still a sacred hour in the week when the privacy of the British household cannot be disturbed, it surely must be Sunday lunchtime.

He set out at two, on the dot.

The first house was a dingy old red-brick detached. Clive felt strangely exposed, crossing the forecourt, as if he were up to no good; as if his bag had a bomb in it.

He rang the doorbell. The door opened at once, disclosing a smiling aproned woman and a smell of baking bread.

'Sorry to bother you,' said Clive, politely. 'I'm collecting for *Suffer the Children*. I left you an envelope, a couple of days ago?'

'Oh yes,' said the woman with pleasure, and produced the little envelope from a handy shelf. The envelope was sealed and weighty.

They won't all be like this, Clive thought.

They weren't. Some people were out, or didn't answer. Others said they'd lost their envelopes, or thrown them away, as if the lack of an envelope meant they couldn't give anything.

As a connoisseur of excuses, Clive was not impressed. He started asking these people who'd been unable to hang on to their envelopes: 'Would you like to make a donation?' Which was more, actually, than he had undertaken to do. He started to feel good about that.

'Sorry to bother you. I'm collecting for *Suffer the Children*?'

A stout black woman in a crumpled nurse's uniform regarded him heavily. 'I don't know where I've put it,' she said. 'Sorry.' Her hair was tousled, her head hung down; her eyes were puffy with grief or sleep. Clive was about to go, but she was saying, 'You'll have to wait a minute.' And after he had, she came back with a pound, which she gravely held out to him.

Next door at Number 22, an elderly man in a cardigan drew himself up and said, 'Ah, now I'm glad I've caught you.' His cardigan was neat, his sparse hair was combed flat across his scalp, he wore a tie. It was as if he had been standing on the doormat ever since his envelope arrived, spruced up and ready for this moment.

'You've taken this round over from me,' said the occupant of Number 22, in a tone of self-satisfaction. The Done Our Bit Club, thought Clive. He himself would be joining, very soon.

'This isn't a charity I normally give to,' the man explained, pointing to Clive's badge, 'because it's not a cause I particularly support.' Nor me, thought Clive, though he thought perhaps it wouldn't help to say it aloud.

'I don't normally support it,' continued the man, 'but I did do your job last year, because I felt I should like to contribute something. Then I resigned, and I should like to tell you why.'

Clive was patient.

'It was a matter of principle,' explained the abdicator. 'I didn't mind delivering the envelopes and I didn't mind picking them up, although it's not pleasant work.'

'People have been very kind so far,' hinted Clive.

'What I object to,' declared the man, oblivious, 'is when you've collected the money and counted it and taken it to the bank, you have to send the paperwork in *at your own expense*. Which is completely wrong,' he concluded.

'They don't give you a pin for your badge, either,' said Clive.

The man frowned. He held up a finger. 'Now, another thing,' he said.

'I don't know if your round includes that block of flats down the end.'

That's right, thought Clive. Nor you do. 'I couldn't get in,' he said.

'The sort of people who live in there,' said the veteran, 'you might as well let them get on with it.'

'I shall feel justified in doing so,' said Clive.

His duty done, the man heartily wished Clive luck and closed the door.

Clive rang the bell of Number 20.

'Now there's one more thing I should ask,' said Clive's predecessor from behind the closed door of Number 22.

Clive looked at the door.

It opened again.

'Did they just phone you up, out of the blue?'

'They did,' said Clive.

The man looked triumphant. 'There you are, then,' he said, and shaking his head closed the door once more.

There I am, thought Clive. Where am I? Number 20. He rang the bell again.

There was no answer. *20*, added Clive to his list.

The bell at Number 18 summoned a man effortlessly holding back an indignant little dog with his legs. 'Sorry to bother you,' said Clive. 'I'm collecting for *Suffer the Children*. I left you an envelope, a couple of days ago?'

'Sorry, mate,' said the man. 'I'm just the builder.'

That, Clive thought, was quite a good excuse. The plaster dust on the overalls was a particularly nice touch. Even builders, Clive supposed, carried small change; but there was a limit to how far you could go in this pursuit of patronage for the hungry young.

The last house Clive had to visit was the one with the notice for the postman. Someone had left a parcel outside. It had been raining in the night, and the ground was still damp. Not a good sign, thought Clive, looking at the parcel; but he knocked anyway.

After some time the door opened reluctantly on a chain to reveal a two-inch vertical section of a pale yellow woman in a pale blue dressing gown. She looked harassed, what there was of her. Clive could barely hear what she was saying as she started to shut him out, but he understood it to be *No, no, no*.

'Wait a minute,' he said, picking up her parcel.

She started to speak more loudly, with anguish and aggression, new versions of *No, no, no*. The door was almost closed.

Clive pushed at it. The woman's refusal grew almost desperate. Through her toothless letterbox Clive shouted, 'This is *yours*!', and rammed her parcel into the closing gap. The woman saw it then, and pulled it inside, and banged the door shut. There was the sound of bolts being shoved home.

On the way back up the street Clive looked at his list of No Replies. Fourteen. Nearly half. It hadn't seemed that many. Mentally he composed a note to the officials of *Suffer the Children*, to enclose with his bank credit counterfoil, his unused envelopes and his badge of authority: 'Before you ask,' he would tell them, 'no, I never want to do it again.'

On Wednesday evening he made his round of defaulters. It was cold, and raining again, on and off, in an unconvincing fashion. One man searched busily among the papers that lay around his hall. He looked like a badger digging in piles of dead leaves. 'We must've had a clear-out,' he concluded. 'Sorry.'

'Would you like to make a donation?' Clive asked him.

'No, thanks.' It was funny, how people would thank you for pestering them fruitlessly.

At the last, nine doors remained unanswered. It would have to do. 'Before you ask,' Clive wrote, returning his counterfoil and badge, 'I never want to do it again.'

It was all such an anti-climax, really, he wished he hadn't agonized about it. Rather, he wished he'd had the sense to say no in the first place. He'd consumed five hours traipsing back and forth in the cold, and several more worrying, and all for what? To secure for hundreds of thousands of starving children overseas the sum of thirteen pounds eighty-five pence.

Clive put a stamp on the envelope – nineteen pence, second class, in honour of the man at number 22 – and went out to post it.

On the way back, he saw a woman walking towards him, quite big, black, a few years older than him, maybe. He took no notice of her.

As they were passing, the woman said: 'Hey, you.'

Her voice was musical, amused, though her face was tired.

Clive recognized her. She was the tousle-haired nurse with the heavy eyes.

'You're the *Suffer the Children* man, aren't you?' she said.

Clive said he was.

'How you doing?'

Thirteen pounds eighty-five, thought Clive. Can't tell her that.

'All right,' he said.

'Well, that's good,' she said.

They looked at each other.

'I'm not really the *Suffer the Children* man,' said Clive. 'I don't work for them or anything.'

Her mouth twitched.

'Well, then,' said Clive, shifting his feet.

The stout woman laughed at him. 'Well, then,' she echoed, mockingly, pretending to slap him on the arm. 'You coming down the pub or what?'

We've all done this one: dialled a wrong number and got into a ludicrous loop with the person on the other end. Our increasing tendency, officially encouraged, to assume that we and a chance-met stranger will have nothing in common, nothing to give each other, is, as Connor here reflects, one of the less heartening characteristics of a dizzyingly fissile culture. Fear of unspecific harm rushes in to fill the gap. The Republic of Ireland is one of the places I've found where this tendency has yet to take hold. (Colorado is another.) The title of this story was given to me by a friend of Gill Alderman's in a tiny bar in Cork, before I even knew that's what it was.

Always carry a notebook.

Talking Through the Wind

CONNOR PICKED UP the phone and pressed out the number he kept pinned up on the notice board.

The phone rang, once. Then a woman's voice said:

– Hello?

Connor frowned.

– Is that the dairy? he said.

Already he knew it wasn't. Though she'd answered straight away, the woman sounded puzzled, as if it was an unusual thing for her to have to do; as if it was completely unexpected that the phone should ring.

She didn't sound like someone working at a dairy. She sounded to Connor like someone in her own home. There was a silence around her that was a silence of shag pile, of discarded slippers, yesterday's newspaper folded to the TV page, souvenirs of Malaga on the shelf unit. He could hear her putting down her duster and sitting on the edge of the settee to answer the phone, her thighs at a sharp angle in tan nylon.

– No, said the woman. You've got the wrong number.

– I'm sorry, said Connor.

He looked at the piece of paper on the notice board. It was no bigger than a bus ticket, yet it had three numbers on it. Two of them were crossed out. The first was the number the dairy had had when Connor came to live here, several years ago. Then the dairy had been bought up by a bigger dairy, and Connor had crossed out the old number and written the new one underneath it. Now the new dairy had closed down the old depot, and there was a third number, which Connor had managed to squeeze in underneath the second. That was the number he was calling, or trying to.

The woman Connor had reached was about to hang up. He could feel her getting ready to remove the receiver from her ear and place it back in its rest. She would give it a squirt of polish and a quick rub with the duster, and that would be that.

– Just a moment, sorry, said Connor. Is that –?

He read the third number off the little piece of paper.

– 734876?

– You've got the wrong number, the woman repeated, firmly.

– Ah, I know that, said Connor, and I'm truly sorry to be disturbing you. But is it 734876? Because that was the number I meant to dial, 734876. Have I dialled something else, now, by mistake?

– I don't know what you *dialled*, the woman said, as if this was a complete irrelevancy, like the shape of his nose or what he'd had for breakfast. You've got the wrong number.

She was stern. She was warning Connor not to dispute the fact.

– This isn't the dairy.

Connor pressed on.

– But it is 734786, he said swiftly, hoping to induce her to confirm or deny it.

He looked again at the paper on the board; touched it with his finger, smoothing it out where it had curled.

– Sorry, did I say 734786 then? 734876 is what I meant.

This time there was no reply. Connor could hear her disapproval mounting, her Tudor Rose lips twisting into the shape of a little fishhook.

– Because if it is, said Connor, ploughing ahead hopefully,

if it is 734876, and that is what I dialled . . . You know, it's funny we still talk about *dialling*.

It was a thought that had just struck him.

– I don't know when the last time was I *dialled* a number, he said.

– Just now, the woman told him. You dialled the wrong number.

Her resistance was impervious, her patience like iron. She thought she was speaking to a foreigner or an idiot of some kind: someone incapable of understanding plain English.

– Ah, but I didn't, you see! said Connor brightly. That's my point. This phone doesn't have a dial, it has little buttons that you press.

Connor swung around and leaned his hip on the table where the phone sat. He drove his hands deep in his pockets, hunching his shoulder up to hold the receiver to his ear. It was very bad for your back, holding the phone that way, Connor's friend Sandra had told him, and she would know, because her boyfriend was a physiotherapist. You could get a special plastic thing now, that would sit on your shoulder like an obliging parrot, and hold the phone to your ear for you without jeopardizing your posture. It was wonderful, the way people kept thinking of new things to invent.

– I bet yours is the same, isn't it, said Connor. They're all like that nowadays, with little buttons instead of the old-fashioned dial. Really we ought to say *I pressed your number*, oughtn't we?

There was another tiny but significant silence. He was losing her. He was. He could hear her looking at her fingernails, checking the clock on the wall, thinking about her coffee.

– Computers, now, said Connor wildly. If you use one of them at all, you know they say *Hit any key to continue*. Or *punch*. Punching a button! That's Americans for you. The little devils are so sensitive you hardly need to tickle them, let alone punch them.

– The buttons, I mean, he explained quickly. Not the Americans.

He could hear the interrupted houseworker summoning her forces.

– I have no intention of punching anybody, she said frostily. I'm not a violent woman, as a rule. I'm merely trying to inform you that –

– I understand, said Connor immediately. I've got a wrong number. Only could you please tell me just one thing, if you'd be so kind. Is that in fact 734876?

The upholstery of the settee creaked. His unknown interlocutor was hardening her attitude. This was a subject on which she was not to be drawn.

– Because if that isn't your number, Connor went on with some force, then the mistake I made was when I dialled. Say I *dialled*, he added, in a spirit of generosity and co-operation. Let's assume, for argument's sake, what I did was dial.

– I'm not arguing, said the woman. There's nothing to argue about.

– But if it *is*, now, said Connor, talking over her. If 734876 is your number, then I dialled it right but I've got it written down wrong. What I've got written down, in that case, is your number, d'you see, instead of the number I meant to write. The dairy number.

– You haven't got the dairy number, she pointed out. This isn't the dairy.

Connor reflected.

– I'm just talking through the wind here, aren't I?

– I'm sure I don't know what the weather's got to do with it, said the woman tartly. You've got the wrong number, that's all. That's all I'm trying to tell you, if you'd listen. I should think you could hear that, however windy it is.

Connor bared his teeth, as one who contemplates a tricky or unappealing task. He scratched his cheekbone with the tip of his finger.

– No, he said. I didn't mean is it *windy*? It's a thing they say in Ireland, *talking through the wind*. It means wasting your breath. It's what you say when the person you're talking to –

He broke off. *Isn't listening to a word you're saying*, he had been about to say; but that seemed rude. She was listening to him, in a sense. She just wasn't telling him what he needed to hear. A simple yes or no would do.

In need of inspiration, Connor looked out of the window. It was quite windy out, in fact. The sun was shining brightly and a wind full of character and vigour was worrying the leaves of the lime tree over the road. Connor realized that was the first time he'd looked out of the window today.

– It's quite pleasant here, actually, he said. And it is windy too, what do you know? If you're thinking of doing some washing it would be a grand day for drying it.

Or for flying a kite, he thought to himself, but he didn't say that. He'd already managed to give her a good impression of a stupid person. He didn't want to go compounding it with the image of a feckless one, with nothing better to do with his time than go kite-flying. He had had a kite once: a big blue and yellow one. What had happened to that? It must be around somewhere, he was pretty sure. It was probably in the hall, behind the coat stand, with an assortment of lost umbrellas and carrier bags and yellowed newspapers and exciting offers from long-extinct mail order companies and gloves sadly severed from their intended partners.

Connor scratched his head.

– I'm sure we can crack this, he told her. If we both put our minds to it. You see, you don't have to tell me your number, if that's what you're worried about.

– You're right, said the woman with conviction. I don't.

– I don't want to know your number, said Connor. I'm not interested in your number. It's not your number I'm interested in.

He took a deep breath. It was like trying to calm a nervous animal. He imagined looking resolutely into her eyes. They were green eyes, defended by bold rings of mascara.

– All you need to tell me, said Connor, is, is your number 734876?

– I thought you said you didn't want to know, she said. There was a gleam of triumph in her voice. She had caught him out now. She had persevered in her defiance, and forced him to expose his base duplicity.

There was something amiss, surely, thought Connor to himself, in a society which bred such suspicion in its members that when they found themselves in a chance situation, an unexpected encounter with a stranger, their first thought should be not, *Indeed, indeed, hello, and how are you today?* but *How am I to protect myself from you and the harm you will undoubtedly try to do me?*

He reacted that way himself often enough. The importunate drunk at the bus stop, the peculiar woman in a hat and three cardigans who hung around the launderette, the toddlers in the checkout queue that decided he was an ideal recipient for their rudimentary social skills and bits of half-sucked chocolate – how zealously he avoided their unsought attentions.

– A simple yes or no would do, said Connor, with a touch of desperation.

– Yes, you've got the wrong number, said the woman crisply. No, you haven't got the dairy.

There was a kind of flourish in her tone. She was pleased to have parried another thrust.

Connor contemplated her answer.

– Ah, now, but that doesn't help me, d'you see? he said regretfully.

The woman sat up straighter on her settee, taking control of the situation.

– You're beyond help, she told him, rather offensively. Hang up and dial again.

– But I might end up with you again! he said. If you're 734876, which is what I've got written down here in front of me – if that's you, d'you see, and not the dairy at all . . .

It was then that the other possibility occurred to Connor, the third one. A dreadful possibility it was. He was overwhelmed by it, by the sheer appalling cosmic awfulness of it.

– There again, he said gloomily. There again. The other possibility is, I might have written it down wrong *and* dialled it wrong. Written down 734876 instead of 734786, say, and then *dialled* 734867, made two mistakes you see, and then –

He fell silent.

– And then, she said.

– And then, said Connor.

– And then what? she said.

Connor considered.

– And then we'd neither of us be any the wiser, he said sadly. At this point. At this moment in time. We'd neither of us know what to do, how to proceed . . .

Her voice became quiet and kind, almost maternal.

– You hang up and dial again, she advised.

Connor clenched a handful of his own hair.

– But what shall I dial? he demanded. Shall I dial what I've got written down here on the paper, 734876, and then what if that's your number, I shall be disturbing you again, shan't I, and we'll neither of us be any further on with our separate days and all the several tasks and responsibilities and obligations that comprise them, which do not include and never have included standing here at either end of a telephone line quarrelling ·with each other because actually, in God's own truth, it's not either of us the other wants to talk to at all in the first place?

– 743876, she said.

– Pardon me? said Connor.

– I think you want 743876, she said.

She spoke judiciously, as if she had divined that number by some manner of calculation from the various permutations available; or from the sound of his voice, or the clouds in the sky and the wind in the yard and the way it blew her washing about.

– 743876, said Connor dully.

– Yes, she said.

Connor put the telephone back in its cradle as gently as anyone might restore a sleeping baby bird to its nest.

– Thank you very much, he said to the silent phone.

Then he picked it up and pressed 743876.

– Fairfield Dairies, said a woman's voice. Hello? Fairfield Dairies? Hello?

This is another true story. It happened to my friend Stella Hargreaves, who is not a bit like the poor woman I'm so patronizing about here, honestly. That hat, for one thing. That was mine, actually, in another life. So there.

I'd have called this woman something else if Stella hadn't been the perfect name for her. That's what I shall tell them, anyway, when they come to take away my artistic licence.

Them That's Got

IT WAS SEVEN O'CLOCK in the evening. Stella had already finished her dinner and done the washing up. She didn't always eat so early. She could eat any time she liked, really. There was only herself to please. But today was Wednesday, and there was a band on at the Kingsfield Arms, playing the blues.

Stella didn't know the name of the band that would be playing, or anything about them. It wouldn't be anyone she'd ever heard of. But Stella liked the blues. The blues was so strong. The blues could get right down into the saddest, grimmest, most wretched heart of the most miserable person alive, and come up singing. It was simple, too. Anyone could sing it.

Stella felt she really ought to sing the blues. She wasn't black, and that was supposed to be a disadvantage. To sing the blues you had to be black, and poor, and born in the Delta in 1920. Stella wasn't black. She wasn't poor, really, compared to most people in the world, although it felt like it a lot of the time. And she wasn't even sure where the Delta was.

Stella got down on her knees to look for her good shoes, which were under the bed. She found one straight away, but the other one had got itself further under, out of reach. It was lying on its side with the fluff and a screwed-up tissue. Stella groped for it, squashing her cheek against the mattress. She didn't think it mattered where you were born. Things were tough all over, wasn't that what they said nowadays?

Stella levered herself upright with a grunt and sat down on the edge of the bed. It was a double bed, still, though there was only her in it, single. She had been married once, but that hadn't been much. He was a quiet man, living only for his allotment and his dinner on the table when he got home each day from the carpet shop. Stella had been stunned when they finally told her about him and the young woman from the chemist's three doors down. Everybody had known, except her; everybody had seen them, walking about in broad daylight, and heard what they got up to in the stock room in their lunch hour. Stella hadn't felt angry, or betrayed, not that she could remember. What she remembered was being surprised and disappointed, like the way you feel when you cut open a hot baked potato you've been looking forward to and find there's a big black rotten bit right in the middle.

She had divorced him, quick as a wink. That was a mistake, it turned out. You only got sympathy if *he* left *you*, apparently. That was the rule, in those days. If you had a bad man, you were supposed to put up with it and soldier on; for the sake of the child, people said. A babby needs a father, they said, as if any kind was better than none.

Stella put the dusty tissue in the wastepaper basket and the shoes on her feet. She went and got her warm coat out of the wardrobe.

Nancy. There was her wedding picture on the chest of drawers. She had married a car mechanic called Gerald and moved to Gateshead. She would phone, once in a blue moon. They were always going to come and see her, Nancy and Gerald; but they never did. She wondered sometimes whether they were ashamed of her, her own daughter and son-in-law. A lot of people had been ashamed of Stella in her lifetime. There had been no community outreach, no social security for single parent families; not in her day.

Stella went slowly and heavily downstairs and put on her hat. It was a funny sort of hat, Stella's, made of a kind of multi-coloured crochet stuff that someone had gone over and over until it was as stiff as a piece of carpet. She had had it for years, and it kept your head warm and never blew off, even in the strongest wind.

Stella inspected herself in the hall stand mirror. Little wisps of her hair stuck out from under the hat. Her skin was yellow and blotchy. Her nose was piggy, and her eyes bulged like a person who's been hanged. It was years too late to worry about things like that.

Mississippi, thought Stella to herself as she waddled down the road. The Mississippi Delta. Fancy living in a place no one in the world can spell, let alone remember.

In the Kingsfield Arms there was no one she knew. She didn't go in there much. She only went in when there was a band, and then only if she knew they'd be playing the blues. She counted out the price of a pint of stout, and took it carefully off to a table by herself.

The band was setting up on the little stage. The Blues Bandits, they were called. Stella had never heard of them. There were four of them, all blokes; in their thirties, she supposed, too old to make the grade now, but not quite old enough to understand what they were singing about. Stella gulped her pint. She should talk! She had been at school when she'd got started on the blues.

The lead guitarist had cherry-coloured Doc Martens and a huge paunch. He kept saying 'One, one,' into the microphone and holding up his thumb to the man on the p.a. The drummer had a ponytail and a black singlet, and a sort of black leather dog collar with silver studs all round. The bass player had a red polo shirt and glasses. He looked more like a scoutmaster than a bluesman.

Stella drained her pint and went and got another before

the crowd came in. She had to wait because the barmaid was too busy letting a couple of boys chat her up, but she didn't complain. She remembered Nancy when she had been that age. She remembered when she herself had been. She'd never been the sort of girl boys chatted up. More the sort they smirked and made remarks about as she passed by.

The Blues Bandits finished the sound check and disappeared. The pub started filling up, slowly. They looked like a young crowd. All crowds looked young to Stella, these days.

At half past eight the Blues Bandits reappeared. 'Good evening, ladies and gentlemen,' boomed the lead guitarist, and leered into the crowd. 'We are the Blues Bandits, and this is what we do. One, two, three –'

The Blues Bandits started to play.

The lead was quite good, Stella reckoned, but not as good as he thought. The other guitarist, not the bass, the one in the middle, she could never remember what you called it – he was the singer too. He was obviously the only one who could sing. He wasn't very good at it. He snarled and curled his lip and jabbed the mike about, trying to sound passionate, but he just sounded weak and whiny. Anyone could sing the blues, but you had to sing them properly. Stella was sure about that.

She found she had finished her second pint without noticing. She shuffled out to the ladies' to get rid of some of it, then back to the bar to queue for a third.

The Blues Bandits were doing their version of Robert Johnson's 'Crossroads'. The singer got the verses muddled and kept grinning at his mates and the audience, trying to apologize while he was still singing, and getting in a worse mess.

Stella got served and went back to her seat. Someone was

sitting in it. She didn't make a fuss. She worked her way closer to the stage and found a place to lean, against the fruit machine.

The Blues Bandits were playing Billie Holliday now, 'Ghost of a Chance'.

> I need your love so badly
> I love you oh so madly
> But I don't stand a ghost of a chance with you.

He really wasn't very good at all, their singer. Stella shut her eyes and swayed from foot to foot, taking great gulps of beer. In her mind she could hear Billie Holliday singing it herself, the way it should be sung, with that little curl in her voice that could be cute and lazy or pleading and desperate, all in the same line.

> But what's the good of scheming?
> I know I must be dreaming
> For I don't stand a ghost of a chance with you.

'Thank you very much, ladies and gentlemen, you're a lovely audience,' the lead guitarist bellowed before the applause had ended. He grinned at everybody as though the gig was a triumph and he was having terrific fun. 'Don't go away, we'll be back in half an hour.'

The Blues Bandits walked close by Stella on the way out. They smelt of sweat and cigarettes and hot metal, like the men that were out in her street every Saturday and Sunday morning, messing around with motorbikes they never rode anywhere.

Stella finished another pint. She wondered vaguely how many she had had now. She looked around for someone to talk to. They all seemed to be talking about football or TV. Stella didn't understand football and she wouldn't have a TV in the house.

Somebody bumped into her, a man, on his way to the gents'. He put his hand on her arm and gave her a sarcastic sort of smile, as if it had been her fault. 'All right, love?' he said.

'All right,' said Stella.

The band came back to scattered applause and whistles. 'Thank you very much,' shouted the lead guitarist, his mike feeding back on him. The Blues Bandits rolled their shoulders and fiddled with their amplifiers.

Stella blew her nose. With exaggerated care, she put her empty glass on top of the fruit machine and pushed right the way up to the stage. It was only a couple of feet off the ground, and Stella was not a small woman, but the lead guitarist took a while to notice her standing there in front of him, trying to catch his eye. He bent down to her.

'Yeah?' he said, importantly.

'Are you going to do any more Billie Holliday?' she asked. She had to say it twice because the crowd was noisy.

'Billie Holliday?' said the lead. He looked at her, summing her up. His eyes strayed to her hat. 'Ron,' he said commandingly. 'Ron!'

The singer leaned over at an angle towards them. The lead pointed to Stella. 'We've got a request here,' he said. He seemed to think something was amusing.

Stella said it again, carefully. Her tongue was already starting to feel a bit thick and uncooperative. 'Are you going to do any more Billie Holliday?'

Ron and the lead looked at each other. In the background the drummer belched and did a fast, ragged drum-roll.

'"God Bless the Child",' Stella said, persisting. 'Do you know that one?'

'"God Bless the Child", yeah, we can do that,' said the singer.

'Can I sing?' asked Stella.

They stared at her. The lead muttered something under his breath and fingered a chord, hiding a grin. The singer spoke to the drummer. They all looked at Stella, perspiring in her warm coat and multi-coloured hat.

'You want to sing, love?' said the lead loudly. He was grinning openly now. 'All right,' he said, 'all right. Up you come, then, darling!'

He put out his arm for Stella to hold on to. She clambered awkwardly up onto the stage. The lead guitarist put his arm around her shoulders and gave her a rough squeeze.

'Know the words, do you, doll?'

Stella smiled coyly at him, as if she was enjoying the attention. The crowd clapped and cheered, seeing her up there, and there were wolf-whistles and laughter all around.

Stella pulled up the mike lead in both hands so it wouldn't trip her up. She saw the landlord standing with his hands on his hips, watching her sceptically.

She was on.

The lead cut into a sleazy, boozy intro, all exaggerated slides and frilly bits. He was making a meal of it, warming up for a good laugh. Then suddenly he was in, and there she was, Stella, singing the blues.

It wasn't hard, actually, 'God Bless the Child'. She'd chosen it to make it easy for herself because she'd already had a few, and she wasn't as spry as she used to be. But then no one ever said Billie Holliday was a clean-living girl. It was her voice they loved, and her heart, and the things she told them. All those things were true.

Now it was Stella's voice that was telling them: not in the Delta, maybe, but in every corner of the bar; and it went right through them and into their blood like a neat shot of whisky.

She knew it would. It always shut them up when she started to sing. She sang it the way Billie used to sing. That was what made it easy. What you did was sing just behind the beat each time. It was nice, a very relaxed way of singing. You let the band do all the work.

The Blues Bandits were up to it, just about. She made them wake up and scramble a bit. They were horrified. She knew they would be. Then they started to get into it.

For their part, like the denizens of the Delta, the patrons of the Kingsfield Arms were happy to hear their worst experiences confirmed. Them that's got shall have, while them that's not shall lose. Yes, wasn't that a fact? They were with her now.

By the second chorus, so was the band. Stella stumped forward and swayed out over the audience. She told them, relations give crusts of bread and such. You can help yourself, she told them; but don't take too much. She swung back and smiled lovingly at the lead guitarist. 'Yeah, sing it, sister!' he shouted, but he was looking as if someone had just bitten him on the bum.

She wrapped it up, simply and neatly, and held the high note.

The crowd went mad.

The other guitarist sat down on the stage, nodding his head and banging the floor and grinning like an idiot. The drummer threw his sticks up in the air and caught them by the handles, over and over again. The bass player was smiling a silly smile. He had teeth like a goat. The lead guitarist swaggered across and put his arm round Stella again, and prised the mike out of her fingers.

The crowd were still whooping and cheering, and clapping up a storm. Stella stood there and looked at the far wall.

She never knew quite what to do during the applause. It wasn't the applause you did it for.

When he could make himself heard, the lead said mournfully, 'Well, I don't think we're going to be singing any more tonight,' and everybody laughed. Then he asked Stella her name, and he thanked her, and he told the ladies and gentlemen to give her a big hand, which they did once again.

Stella clambered down off the stage. There were hands outstretched everywhere, helping her, claiming her. Everyone wanted to shake her hand, to give her their seat. Stella sat down hard, puffing and blowing, and took the pint someone was holding out to her. She tugged her hat more firmly on her head.

If they'd asked her, she would have sung again. She would have happily stayed on for the rest of the set, if they'd wanted her to. But she never asked them twice.

Afterwards, with a towel draped round his neck, the Blues Bandits' singer came and straddled a chair backwards and shook Stella's hand across the table, still grinning, with admiration now.

'How long have you been doing that?' he wanted to know.

They always wanted to know that. 'Since I was seventeen,' she told him.

He decided to get technical with her, musician to musician. 'You do have much the same range as Billie Holliday, you know,' he told her, as if he thought she might not know. 'I suppose you sing along with her records, do you?'

Stella sniffed and took a big swallow of her stout. She drank deep until she could drink no more; then she stood it down on the table with a bang and wiped her mouth with the back of her hand.

'I don't sing along with anyone,' she said.

III

MISSING PERSONS

I first became aware of Robert Aickman with his post-humous collection Night Voices, *though I instantly recognized 'The Trains' as something I had read twenty years before, probably, when I would devour anthologies of fantastic tales like fruit from a tree, without really noticing that the stories were all by different people, or caring. In 1985, however, I was completely swept away by his particular dark, bitter, deeply mysterious vision of ordinary life as a tenuous sham, a frail membrane that we erect to shield us from the monstrous truth of death and its irresistible hand-maid, sex, with which we are all helplessly, self-destructively complicit. For some time thereafter I seemed always to be writing either a novel about a woman who survives or a short story about a man who falls apart.*

'The Wish' was one story that benefited greatly from exam-ination at Milford, the annual week-long workshop for professional writers of sf and allied trades. Rachel Pollack was there, I remember; Gwyneth Jones, Lisa Tuttle, Richard Cowper and John Clute. To see the story refracted through such gifted eyes was invaluable, as always. Fascin-ating too, how many people have been moved, then and since, to quarrel with or rejoice in points on which the text itself is quite silent, or at least ambiguous.

The Wish

THEY WERE GOOD to Steve, when he got over there. They fixed him up with a car and put him in an apartment, rent free, for the first month. The apartment was very big; too big, really, for one. He had left all his stuff in storage, and what he had brought with him was lost in this open-plan cavern. He hung his suits at one end of the louvred wardrobe. There didn't seem to be very many of them. The other end was completely empty, nothing in it but a little spiky twig, a bit of Christmas tree lying forlorn on the white melamine. Steve closed the door again.

The kitchen looked more like a spaceship. Baffled by its keypads and readouts, Steve went out, nodding vaguely at the whiskery old man who was always in the lobby and so must be, he supposed, some sort of concierge. The car was some minutes away, in an underground car park. There was a moment of panic while he searched for the strip of plastic that would open the grille; then he ventured out into the unfamiliar city.

It had been raining. The roads and pavements were slick with wet gold. High overhead in a glistening battery of adverts and animated signs the foreign traffic signals flashed inscrutably. Steve cruised cautiously for an hour. The radio offered nothing but stupid polkas and jerky electronic noises he thought were morse until he realized there was someone singing. He got lost trying to follow a railway line and had to drive through mile after mile of shuttered factories and boxy estates. At a dingy takeaway he asked for directions. The woman spoke no English. She bellowed through the kitchen hatch. A man's voice answered unintelligibly, but no one emerged. The woman stood frowning and pulling at her lip.

Annoyed, Steve pointed to something in the hot cabinet, some kind of sausage, and flung a couple of coins on the counter. This had the effect of jogging her memory, or else she was just trying to get rid of him. At any rate, when he finally arrived back at the flats it was much later than he'd meant to stay out, nearly midnight, and he was in a bad mood. The sausage was cold. The grease had soaked through the bread and the paper before it congealed. It was unappetizing, but there was nothing else. He put it in what he supposed was the microwave and went off to have a shower. Later he sat in the kitchen, a towel about him, eating sausage and drinking fizzy beer by the blue light of the control panels. Below, the city gleamed and growled.

On the whole he was not lonely. One or two people at the shop were friendly enough, in a noncommittal sort of way, though the man who had made all the arrangements, who had met him with the car at the airport and driven him into town, had never appeared again since. Paulus, in whose charge he had been left, seemed to have no use for him at all. He gave him a catalogue and sent him to the stock room, to familiarize himself with the range. Steve suspected Paulus was less than delighted to have a superfluous foreigner dumped on him by head office. Nobody said another word about the management training course he'd been promised. They were a shifty lot, he reckoned.

The boy at the sandwich bar nearest the shop had an English girlfriend. He would like very much one day to visit London, Buckingham Palace, Piccadilly Circus. He told Steve to call him Matt, and practised his English conversation on him, every lunchtime. Matt was a cheerful, irritating sort of bloke Steve would probably not even have noticed and would certainly have ignored if he had, back home. There were compensations, though: a free cup of coffee, once in a while; and Matt would let him boast about life in England, which none of the shop people wanted to know about. Supercilious and smelling faintly of good aftershave, they heard his anecdotes, then started chattering, nodding to each other and laughing. Steve knew they were sending him up.

One day Matt invited him to a party.

'My girlfriend and her friends. She would be so happy for you to come.'

'I'll think about it.'

Steve was imagining students and hippies, red light-bulbs everywhere, washing-up bowls full of coleslaw. It was on a Friday night, and he had to work the next day. But out of desperation, he went.

It was somewhere in the north. The area was more affluent than he had been expecting. The house was narrow and cramped, with old furniture they'd tarted up. All the lights were on and some sort of coloured people's music was playing very loudly. There were children running around shrieking and, in the front room, an elderly couple sitting very upright on a sofa, smiling politely at everyone.

Matt, when Steve found him in the crush, was depressed. He had had a row with his girlfriend. Now would not be a good moment to introduce Steve. Matt excused himself, and disappeared.

There didn't seem to be much in the way of alcohol. Determined to make the best of a bad job, and stuck for someone to talk to, Steve drank most of his own bottle of wine. He was already a bit smashed when he noticed the woman.

She was wearing a long embroidered skirt, old-fashioned, and her hair was a mess, frankly; but she had a nice face, long and rather pale, with huge eyes. She caught him staring across the room. He smiled, and she looked away at once. A few minutes later, he caught her looking at him.

Later Steve went upstairs, searching for the loo. He listened carefully at every door, dreading bursting in on some amorous couple. Then he found the bathroom and had a piss. There were weird pictures everywhere, pictures of little children, with snakes and all sorts. He wondered how the people had the nerve to put them up, in smart steel frames too, as if they were art or something. Hurrying out, he bumped into the woman, who was waiting to go in. He thought her smile warranted hanging around on the landing for her. He rehearsed the phrase, and when she emerged, greeted her awkwardly. She replied in English.

'Were you waiting for me?' she asked. Her voice was clear and low.

Steve winked.

'Very well,' she said, calm as anything. She did not smile.

Steve wondered if his intentions had been misunderstood, but then decided she was probably the cool sulky type. He would soon warm her up. He held up his glass in mute enquiry.

'Yes, please,' she said.

Steve lifted a hand. 'Wait here,' he told her, went downstairs, and struggled through the mob to the kitchen. When he came back she was still there, leaning against the wall. He leant beside her, his back to the stairs, shielding her from the constant flow of people in and out of the bathroom. Much later he remembered what he was about, and offered to steer her into a vacant bedroom, where they would be more comfortable. But she said: 'I must go home.'

'Where do you live?' said Steve at once. 'I'll drive you.'

'A long way. Right up in the mountains.'

'No, really, I'll drive you.'

'I should like that,' she said.

Steve hadn't felt so excited since he was a teenager. He found his coat; but she had come just as she was, apparently, in the white peasant blouse that hung so nicely over her little breasts. Steve put his hand on her breast as they sat in the car, and kissed her. She did not resist, or respond, really, apart from smiling slightly, which was not in the least discouraging, but he felt a bit daft, and took his hand away. He was well in, anyway, obviously. He felt on top of the world.

'I live in the mountains,' she said again. 'Many kilometres away.'

Steve reflected that he had been talking to her for an hour, and that her name was Linzl; but he knew nothing else about her, or what they had talked about. Yet he was not drunk any more. In fact he felt supremely clear.

'How did you get here, then?' he asked her.

Linzl seemed to misunderstand him. 'I always come,' she said.

Steve noticed that she seemed to relax the minute they got out of the suburbs and onto the highway. Fields began to appear either side of the road. The mountains were ahead, dark shapes shouldering towards them over the dark hills.

'Now you will see our country as she really is,' said Linzl.

He drove boldly with one hand, and put the other on her knee. Again, she did not require him to remove it. The women here were all right, Steve decided.

It was indeed many kilometres. The road began to climb. They passed through a little old village with a wooden church and a hump-backed bridge. It was the sort of place you see on Christmas cards, with horses pulling a sleigh, and children in mufflers skating on the river. At the moment, there was not a sign of life. Everyone must have been fast asleep.

After that it was all thick pinewoods. For the last mile there wasn't even a road, just a steep, stony track that the first decent rain would wash away, probably.

'However do you get up and down without a car?' asked Steve, wrestling with the foreign transmission.

'I don't go out often,' she said.

The cottage was wood and stone, quite small and low, with a mossy roof. Steve got out of the car and stood under the stars, enchanted. There was even a well. It had a stone wall and a little mossy roof of its own, just like in a kids' picture-book.

'A wishing-well!'

'It is for water,' said Linzl.

But Steve insisted, no, it was a wishing-well. 'It's got to grant me a wish,' he said.

'You must throw in a coin,' said Linzl. 'For a wish to come true, of course, you have to pay.'

So Steve threw in a coin, one of the small ones, and held his breath until he heard it hit the water, wishing he could stay there with her forever and not thinking himself foolish at all.

'Do you know what I wished?' he asked her, lasciviously, tucking an arm around her.

'You must not speak it,' she warned him. 'It is not lucky.'

'I'm lucky, all right. Tonight I am. Aren't I?'

Linzl opened the front door. It was not locked; nor was there any gate or fence.

'You go in,' said Steve. 'I've just got to – you know. Commune with nature, ha, ha.'

He went up behind the house, to the edge of the clearing, where there was a dead tree, an ugly great spike sticking up at the beautiful sky. The branches had mostly broken away, though the trunk seemed solid enough. He ought to carve his initials on it, he thought, so they would be here always, after he was back in England, after he was dead and gone, probably.

Steve zipped up his fly and went back indoors, through a tiny flagstoned kitchen to a room crammed with lumpy furniture and hung with thick rugs. Linzl was sitting at the table with a candle, reading a small book.

'Hello,' said Steve.

She looked up and saw him. She pushed her hair back with one hand, closed the book with the other. For a moment it was as though he'd disturbed her, as though she'd been reading for ages and had forgotten all about him. Then she said: 'Sit down, please,' like somebody's receptionist, and pointed to an upright, uncomfortable-looking armchair.

Steve sat.

'You will want a drink.'

She reached to the top of a dresser and took a decanter and glass from among the clutter.

'Aren't you having one? Cheers, then.'

It was a small drink, of something thick and clear: some sort of brandy, Steve thought. It seemed natural to knock it back in one.

Linzl got up then, abruptly, took the candle and went into another room, leaving Steve in the dark. He sat fingering the tablecloth. It was thick material, red as blood. The brandy burned in his throat.

'Linzl? What are you doing?'

She said only: 'Be patient.'

The bloom of the candle came out through the half-open door and wavered among the hangings. Within, Steve could see small pictures in oval frames, and a brown frieze of dried flowers, leaves and feathers. He could not see Linzl, nor hear a sound.

'Linzl, don't leave me all alone!' he said. 'I'll get scared.'

He laughed. 'I'm coming in,' he called, but did not move.

'Come in now.'

She had taken off all her clothes and got into bed. She was half covered by a faded golden quilt. She lifted her arms to him. Stirred, the candle made the shadows of her arms swoop up to the roof.

As he pulled down his jeans Steve caught sight of himself in a long mirror with a veil half over it. He seemed to have a peculiar expression on his face. He looked back quickly at the bed, at Linzl, who was worth looking at, oh god, she was beautiful.

The mattress was horsehair, and worn to a cosy hollow. It was like making love in a nest, Steve thought. It felt strange – it felt *healthy*, sort of, which puzzled him and amused him hugely. And then he had neither time nor wit to feel puzzled or amused, only terrified and delighted.

In the morning he woke to Linzl's face leaning over his, her hair falling on his cheek. The sun was shining brightly.

'Good morning.'

'Good morning, Steve.'

He smiled with satisfaction, remembering. 'How about last night, then?'

She kissed him, and got out of bed.

'Come back . . .'

Linzl shook out her hair, then reached for her gown.

'Oh, don't put that on,' he pleaded. But she pulled it tight in front and belted it securely with the sash.

'Would you like tea?'

'Tea . . .'

Steve sat up. The room was just big enough for the bed, with narrow shelves and poky cupboards on every inch of the wall that wasn't covered with some sort of curtain or other. There were little birds carved on the edges of things, and heart-shaped holes. It was exactly like something from a fairy story. He heard Linzl outside, cranking at the well. It was incredible that people still lived like this. But then Linzl was incredible.

She came back with a tray, and a teapot wrapped in fur. Steve coaxed her back into bed. They sat cuddling while the tea brewed.

'You really like it, don't you, Linzl?'

'Yes,' she said.

'I've never had a woman who liked it the way you do.'

After a while he said: 'Was I good? What did you think?' When he failed to get an answer to that, he asked: 'Are they all like you, here?'

'I am not exceptional, I think,' said Linzl. By day her eyes were a slightly distracting blue. Steve tugged at her gown.

'Take this off and I'll show you if you're not exceptional.'

She demurred.

'Go on,' he said, kissing her. 'Just a quickie. You know: quick.' Something occurred to him. 'What time is it?'

It was already eight. The shop would be open in half an hour, half a world away.

Any other morning Steve would have been appalled, and angry with himself. But the world had been different then. He grinned and blew on his tea. 'I'll phone in sick. It's not as if they need me.' He swallowed a mouthful and hopped out of bed, rummaging for his underpants. 'Where's your phone, Linzl?'

'Telephone? There is no telephone here.' She spoke as if he had asked something stupid. Well, perhaps he had. After all, there was no mains water. She was pretty much cut off out here. It must be horrible in winter.

Linzl sat in her robe of midnight blue, her face and hair pale against the fat white pillows. She looked different too, this morning, older somehow, but even more wonderful.

Steve got dressed, gazing at her, grinning like an idiot, he didn't care.

'Stay right there. I'll drive into the village and phone, and I'll be right back.'

Outside the forest was soft and encroaching. The air was like dusty amber. The car would not start.

'It won't even turn over.' He sat on the bed and drank some more tea. 'What am I supposed to do? How long does it take to walk to the village? Do the buses run this far out?'

Linzl said: 'You came a long way last night, Steve. It would take you a long while to get back again.'

'To hell with it,' he said. He felt very frightened, and very bold. 'Linzl, I love you. I don't want to go home ever, not to the city, not to England either. I want to stay here with you. Please, please, please take that dressing gown off.'

She took it off.

They made love in the morning, and again in the afternoon. Steve wanted to go up the mountain, into the wood, to make love in the open air, but Linzl kept him to her bedroom, though it was cooler there. In her bedroom, with all the fur and wood and the sombre autumn colours, it was as if it were late September already, the summer over and done.

At some point Steve noticed his watch had stopped. Everything seemed to break down out here.

'Linzl? What time is it?'

She was getting out of bed. She went and took a large towel from a chair in the corner. He hadn't noticed the chair before, under the towel. It was vacuum-formed plywood, a bit modern for her. In fact he was pretty sure there was one exactly like it in his kitchen, in the apartment.

'Where did you get that chair, Linzl?'

It was irritating, the way she would just not answer sometimes. It wasn't as if she didn't understand him. He would have to do something about that.

But what was he thinking? He had to get up and start walking into the village, to get things sorted for tomorrow. He would have to get started soon.

Linzl dressed herself in a voluminous apron and went around with a besom. She cooked a soup with zucchini, which he had never liked before. She painted melancholy swirling patterns with Indian ink and sat staring at them for hours. He believed she was a fabric designer.

'Don't you need a phone, in your line of work?'

'It is not necessary to speak to anyone,' she told him.

And that was another day gone.

It was getting ridiculous. He had to go back. He couldn't just stay here forever. Nevertheless, though it didn't bear thinking about, he knew he could. An illegal immigrant. It happened all the time. Linzl's lifestyle didn't seem to require money, and anyway he had his chequebook. He could drop a line to his Mum and Dad, to let them know he was all right, and then just – disappear. No, this was daft, he *had* to get started, he'd get up in a minute but now all he really wanted to do was sleep.

He was woken by a shrill, hostile buzz from somewhere just above his head. His hand had found the button and turned it off before he realized it was a small square digital alarm: his own. Or one exactly the same. What a coincidence. It looked an unlikely thing for Linzl to own, but Steve couldn't believe he'd been so drunk he'd brought his own alarm clock here with him and then forgotten all about it until now.

The room was in darkness. By the clock it was a bit after four. In the morning, that must be. Linzl was asleep beside him, warm and firm and very real. The alarm had not woken her. Steve wondered if perhaps it had not gone off at all, and he had only dreamed it had. He felt restless. He wondered if Linzl would be cross if he woke her.

He heard a siren go keening past. They could hear the traffic quite clearly up here. He'd not noticed that before. He lay and watched the headlights sweep across the ceiling. *This is impossible*, he told himself, *we're half a mile up the mountain*. There was no traffic on that back road, anyway.

That was the last time Steve felt any fear. The sound of the cars was curiously comforting. He drew close to Linzl, shaped himself against her back, and fell fast asleep once more.

When he next woke, the birds were singing. It seemed to be a perfectly normal morning. What day was it, though? He wasn't at all sure. Linzl was gone from the bed. He called, but there was no reply.

Steve dressed, determined to pull himself together. There was sunlight in the clearing. His car was completely covered with a film of sticky dust. He turned the key and, when nothing happened, did not know whether he was pleased or not. He sat sideways in the driver's seat and ate some small wrinkled apples he had found in the kitchen, after a search through drawer after drawer of meticulous collections of dead things no one could possibly eat, not even here. He knew he should start out at once on foot, but could not go before Linzl came home. He ran inside more than once, thinking he heard the phone; but of course she had not got a phone.

He went for a piss, by the dead tree. If he was going to be here for a while, he'd have to find something to do, to make himself useful, to keep himself awake. Something like, like cutting down this tree. It was dead, wasn't it? And it wasn't big.

He found an axe on the wall behind the back door, and a log-saw, though they were both very rusty. It felt great, hacking at that old tree with no one there to know whether he was doing it properly or not. He had it down and almost chopped in half when Linzl appeared suddenly. She was wearing a cape with a long pointed hood, and carrying a rush basket of ragged black mushrooms.

'Where did you spring from?' He wiped his forehead. 'Look – I've got your tree down for you.'

'Why?' she asked.

'Why? For firewood!'

'That is kind of you,' she said; but he could tell she didn't mean it. She was just being polite.

Later, in bed, Linzl said: 'I liked that old tree standing there. On clear nights in November it looked like a giant claw, gripping the moon.'

Before Steve could marshal a reply, she was asleep.

Next day he heard the sound of an engine and ran outside, thinking someone had arrived on a bike, or, absurdly, that Linzl was trying to start the car. She was dismembering the tree with a chainsaw. Steve wondered where that had come from. He knew there was no use asking her.

She worked all day, splitting the logs and nailing the slats to a frame. It became a long box: a sort of kennel, Steve supposed, looking out of the kitchen window. He wished she would come in soon and make a cup of tea.

At that moment she came, sunlight and sawdust in her hair.

'Are you thinking of getting a dog? You really should, you know, out here on your own, I mean, a girl like you.'

She stood in the doorway. 'Go and lie down,' she said.

He was confused for a minute, thinking about the dog kennel. 'What?'

'Go and lie down,' said Linzl, smiling as he'd first seen her smile, upstairs at the party. 'I'll come to you.'

He went into the bedroom and undressed. They always

seemed to be going to bed, but he hadn't had a decent night's sleep since he got here, not just because she was insatiable, but because of the dreams: strange, shadowy dreams that felt like being awake, but couldn't have been, because of the things he thought she was doing to him, and he was doing to her.

In the middle of the night Steve got up and went outside for a piss, by the stump of the tree. It was quite light in the clearing. They had so many stars here, it was impossible to tell where you were. They glimmered among the trees, and on the roof of the kennel. Steve squatted down to look inside it. It looked all right: plenty of room, really.

In every audience, there's always one. When the time comes for questions, they stick up their hand and ask: 'Where do you get your ideas?' From you, I answer. From you and you and you. From everywhere in general and nowhere in particular. Fiction of any kind is a response to the world and all there is in it; sf is no exception.

I'm not terribly interested in the phantom of originality. What I'm interested in is the way existing things collide and combine. One idea will not necessarily give you a story. Two, be they never so banal or ancient, very well may.

This story is the offspring of two ideas. The first was given me by Pete Crowther. Pete is one of that small and precious band of archangelic fools, the Anthologists, who continue to knock on the Gates of Hell, which is to say the doors of publishers, to persuade them to do another one. For his book Tombs, *Pete was determined there must be a story about a derelict spaceship. He had gone so far as to commission one, but the writer had come back with a perfectly suitable story about something else instead. Could I, Pete asked, write the missing story?*

The very specificity (not to say cheek) of the request intrigued me. As anyone knows who has put their nose into Seasons of Plenty, *I am nowhere so much at home as on a nice derelict spaceship. I didn't have a story, though, until a chance phone conversation made me consider the second idea: an idea which has been out there, roaming loose around the world, for centuries.*

Station of the Cross

TEN MINUTES EAST from Copono Base, along the perimeter road, there used to be a place called the Lone Ace Bar. It was never a lively establishment. The first time I went in I remember there was only one customer, a man in a red shirt drinking at the bar. I wondered if he might be the lone ace. Above his head there was Korean freefall wrestling on a big flatscreen with the sound turned off. Squat men in purple and yellow leotards were tumbling about in perfect silence. The drinker paid them no attention. When I took the stool beside him, he paid no more to me.

The barman was the bald, neckless, stolid type, inviting no confidences, impassive to what came. I ordered whisky and glanced at my neighbour. He was in his sixties, I supposed, heavy set, a working man reduced to fat by idleness. His hair was thick and greasy. He sat with his elbows on the bar, his head sunk between his shoulders. He looked as though something invisible and heavy had taken up residence on the back of his neck.

Outside the smoked windows a regulation perfect day was blazing towards its close. The palm trees hung dark and shaggy. A spaceport bus droned distantly by.

I had driven a hundred miles to sit all day in an air-conditioned basement, toiling through flat plans and elevations, stuff so old and academic no one on the net even had it. My head was full of diagrams and marque numbers, the names of defunct design teams. I had no money, nothing in prospect but a burger and a bland hotel, and in the morning another day of the same.

'Another?' I said the word aloud, addressing my neighbour at the bar.

'Sure,' he said. His voice had the indifference of the terminally disappointed. 'Sure I will.'

The glasses were filled. I saluted my new acquaintance with mine. 'Lenny Cassler,' I told him.

He raised his head far enough to show me a pair of vague, uninterested eyes. 'Tourist?' he said.

'I'm here to do my research,' I said. 'At the base here.' I nodded in its direction.

He stuck out his bottom lip a quarter inch and poured whisky into it. He didn't seem to be about to do anything more sociable, so I tried to interest him. 'I'm working on engineering design trends in orbital modules of the sixties,' I said. The title of my dissertation rolled quickly off my tongue.

It rolled straight past my new friend. The lifeless eyes surveyed me. 'You're an engineer,' he said.

I shrugged one shoulder. 'Some day, maybe. When I qualify.'

He nodded, once. 'College boy,' he said.

'That's me,' I agreed. 'Are you at the base?'

He didn't seem to hear the question. 'College boy,' he said again, with the somnolent air of the ruminative drunk. 'What are you studying?'

'Engineering design trends –'

He interrupted me. 'What is that, what do you call that, history?'

I said we did.

That seemed to amuse him. He caught the barman's eye. 'History!' he repeated.

The barman smiled like an iceberg.

I felt I should defend my field, not invite mockery. 'Things move fast these days,' I said at random.

'Too damn fast,' my companion said lugubriously. 'Too damn fast. My days of moving fast are over,' he told us both, and smacked the bartop gently with his palm. 'History,' he said.

I took the invitation to ask him what it was he had done. He confirmed, in a few offhand words, that he had indeed worked out of the base, flying on emergency squads to accidents in low space. It sounded more exciting than history or engineering, but he didn't seem to think it had been any big deal.

I rubbed my eyes. 'I've been looking at orbital plans all day,' I told him. 'Old transit stations, TSK's.'

It sounded incongruous as soon as I said it. I hoped the old patrolman wouldn't be insulted, thinking I associated him with a line that had been obsolete when he was a boy. But before I could speak again, he said: 'We had a callout once to a TSK. TSK 120J . . .' He wasn't looking at me. He recited the number as if it were the name of an old friend, or an old enemy.

'When would that have been?' I asked.

'26 June '64, twenty hundred fifteen EST,' he said, slowly and deliberately.

I blinked at the precision. 'What happened?' I asked.

'Somebody saw a light,' he said.

I watched the old spacer's hand lift his glass to his mouth. For a moment I thought he was proposing to spin me a line. He must have flown hundreds of callouts in his time. How could he remember one in particular?

'A light?' I said.

'A light on TSK 120J.'

I continued to watch him, waiting for the explanation. The way he put it, it didn't sound like a crash. Trespassers, then. Hooligans looking for something beautiful to destroy. I had conceived a great nostalgia for the great days of the TSK. The architecture of early transit stations had a titanic, convoluted grandeur quite unlike the boxy functionalism of the modern compact school. Musing over my graphs and sections and detail cutaways, I envied the fortunate travellers who had threaded the baroque valving of their corridors.

'What was it?' I asked. 'Kids?'

The patrolman hunkered on his stool, ignoring me. He was staring into the illusory space beyond the mirrored shelves where the pretty, coloured bottles stood in line.

I talked because he wouldn't. 'She must have been a derelict,' I said. 'The last K's were decommissioned in '48, '49. All her utilities would have been stripped . . .'

My unnamed companion drank suddenly, almost convulsively, and grimaced. I wondered what it was I was trying to prove.

'You want history?' the man said, his voice low and gravelly. 'I'll give you history.' He made it sound like some kind of unpleasant disease I had foolishly volunteered to contract. He swivelled round, jumped down from the stool and with an abrupt, aggressive gesture summoned me across to a booth.

If I hadn't wanted to believe him already I would have started to believe him then. He had the classic walk of a space veteran, the bow legs and sliding gait of one who has never quite accepted that gravity has renewed its claim in full and for good. With two fresh drinks the barman followed us, then withdrew with a grave nod, a fraction of a bow, like a referee stepping out of the ring before a bout.

I wondered then what I had woken. Some grievance, some obsession. I hoped saying a friendly word to the old-timer wasn't an action I was going to regret. Then I thought, oral witness, Jesus, if only I had a cam, maybe I could make something of it that would impress the examiners. I made up my mind to concentrate hard and not miss anything.

The old patrolman and I sat in the booth, and he gave me history. '26 June '64, twenty hundred fifteen EST,' he said again. 'I'm in the gym, working out with some of the crew. My buzzer goes. Callout, public report to officer on the beat, suspected trespass, transit station K 120J. Routine procedure, Nebulon scoutship, crew of three, top of the roster. Me, Winterman, Captain O'Casey. Light arms, med tent and basic resus kit in case of casualties.'

He spoke in terse, abbreviated phrases, like an asthmatic. What I saw in my head was something infinitely more glamorous than these curt facts, more heroic, a distillate of war movies and cop shows, low angles and fast tracking shots of sexy black pursuit vehicles scrambling into flight. I have played it over and over, stretching it this way and that, taking it apart and building it up again – so many times I can no longer tell the difference between what the old man told me and what I imagined for myself. I seem to see the forbidding appearance of the abandoned station as the investigating ship approaches. It floats, black in blackness, big, like some ill-planned marriage between a football stadium and a chemical refinery. The Nebulon circles it swiftly and warily, in two planes. There are no lights showing anywhere now.

The captain, a big-jawed Irishwoman, matches the spin of the scoutship to the station. She decides they will try the doors. My companion, younger, burly, still glowing from his workout, points out that the doors of the decommissioned orbital are surely sealed. The captain dismisses this. 'If they got in, so can you,' she says. There is music playing in the cockpit, rock and roll guitars accompanying the start of another docking manoeuvre.

In the viewport the transit station swells up to envelop them, drawing them nearer, nearer, until up becomes down and the big clamps bite, locking the scoutship to the space-scoured hull. The trio suit up. Winterman, dark-skinned and slender, shoulders the lofty med pack. They hop out of the lock and jet the short distance to the yellow and black striped maintenance door that the captain selected on their first pass. It opens easily, on weakened hydraulics. Nobody says anything as they step into the lofty hallways of the deserted station.

TSK 120J is a metal mausoleum. There is little gravity, no air, no power of any kind. The investigators play their lights around the depopulated pavement, showing only scuffs and dints. The heavy architecture of the place is confusing. Bends, braces, buttresses conceal every corner, block every line of sight. The team try some doors – anterooms, locked, intact, or long ago vacated, bare as an empty fridge. They pass on, into the pitch black corridors.

Now they are entering the sector where the fugitive light was seen. They search, but the giant curvilinear apartments are bare as caverns in an asteroid. There is nothing here but the detritus of vanished lives: empty drug canisters; a puffy, disintegrating slipper; a tiny nebula of pins and press-studs, forlornly twinkling. O'Casey reaches to pick up a fragment of newspaper. It collapses in her hand like a cobweb.

In vibrations through their suits the trio hear more than feel the hushed traction of the stippled carpet beneath their feet, the click of a joint against the beading of an archway, the whispering thud of a door handle, tested but unyielding. Their light beams only emphasize the darkness. My nameless companion shields the lifesign meter with his mailed hand. Winterman stands down his backpack and crouches, running his fingertips down the main door seal.

I can hear him call. '*Captain?*'

Some yards away, checking a vast cross-tunnel, O'Casey responds. '*What is it, Winterman?*'

'*Captain, this was locked from the inside.*'

Floor plans beamed up to them en route show the system of interconnecting doors that will lead them around the obstacle. Without orders they adopt standard defensive postures, Winterman and O'Casey back to back, scanning the corridor in opposite directions while between them my companion wrenches open the stiff latch on an inspection hatch. Overhead the voluminous shadows hang, vanishing like mist when a beam of light sweeps among them. As the three figures disappear through the hatch, taking all the lights with them, the shadows rush together, clotting in the corridor like honest night.

The team are penetrating the very bowels of the station. They climb along a horizontal shaft, their diminished weight easy on the stapled rungs. One by one they jackknife around a bend in the shaft and disappear. Each hears his own boots scrape and clank.

Now TSK 120J encloses them in its entrails. Blank white illumination shows only blank grey wall, very close to. Sudden mysterious signs, bright as the day they were stencilled, indicate covered stopcocks and junction boxes. I can read those signs, I want to tell them, identify the chevrons, the dots and letters. But I am not with them. No one is.

One after another the team squeeze into a tall, narrow, bottle-shaped chamber where O'Casey orders them to rest. No one will speak, no one state an opinion or question their duty at this point. Their ears are full of the sound of their own breathing. Twenty-five decks of perforated steel are stacked up all around them, and they are many miles from home.

Even here the absolute, unrelenting cold of space has penetrated, eroding every surface, flaking the face of the metal away like scurf. My companion points to a heavy hatch between their feet. It is black as iron and carbuncled with bosses and shielding. '*It's here, Captain,*' the young man says. '*Whatever it is, it's here. Under there.*'

The others look. The meter is alight. It fills their faceplates with its primrose glow.

They kneel, as if at a shrine. My companion breaks out the tools. Soon enough, they unseal the hatch and haul it open.

Across the table in the Lone Ace, the fleshy spacer emptied another glass. The lights in the place had been dimmed, or else I had been keeping closer pace with the drinks than I had meant to. I regarded my companion's face, his thickened, disappointed face.

'He was lying there under the floor,' he said.

I exhaled loudly. I do not know what I meant by it: satisfaction, impatience, derision. I fixed my eye on him and waited for him to speak again.

'He was old,' he said. 'Ancient, ancient. Long white beard, down to his waist. He had this robe on –'

He rubbed his thumb against his fingers. I heard his calluses whisper. 'Coarse thing, like a sack. Brown skin gone yellow. Staring eyes. Sometimes in the middle of the night I'd like to forget those eyes.' The navigator shook his head. 'The way they looked at each of us in turn.'

Without my will my hand floated across the table and clamped hold of his arm.

'What are you saying? What are you trying to tell me? Are you trying to tell me the old guy was alive?'

'He was alive.'

'That's impossible!'

I saw the glistening bald head of the barman turn our way, and realized I was shouting. I let the spaceman go, almost pushed him from me in disgust. He was just a burned-out cop, a derelict himself, shipwrecked in a thousand bottles. He wasn't making any sense. And I, I was wasting my time here listening to his crap. I would be better off watching

TV in my hotel. At least on TV you know it's all made up.

Instead I sat staring at him belligerently, and he at me no less so. With the restricted vision of advanced alcoholic fugue I seemed to see him small and dark at the end of a narrow dark brown tube, and yet at the same time with such clarity, such detail I could have counted every broken capillary on his devastated face. I signalled for a couple more drinks. When they arrived I watched him take a sip, just a sip. His hands moved with the perfect steadiness of supreme concentration. He had had practice. I swayed across the table towards him.

'What happened?'

He gave me a look eloquent of human irony, a challenge to acknowledge the bitter humour of their inadequate, inevitable response to the inconceivable.

'We put the tent up.'

In my mind's eye I see Winterman struggling in the confined space of the metal room to erect the med tent over the hermetic sarcophagus and fill it with air. The Captain is on the radio. My companion is not listening. Inside the tent he tears off his helmet, levels his weapon at the supine figure. He barks a question, a warning.

'The old guy wasn't interested in guns. He reached right up out of that pit. Grabbed hold of the front of my suit. His hand was like something made of wood, like a knot of wood. And his eyes were staring at me like there was something he wanted from me. Something he wanted bad.'

I waited until I could wait no more.

'Did he – say anything?'

The old patrolman nodded slowly. He protruded his lip again. 'He did,' he said.

'What did he say? For god's sake, what did he say?'

He gave me a strange, sardonic look, as though my question had amused him somehow. When he spoke, it was not in English. I suppose I had no reason to expect it to be. His voice was like the rasp of a friction match in the empty bar. '*Od hu khazar?*' he said. '*Od hu khazar?*'

There was nothing I could say.

The old man fights them. He is strong. He has no wish to relinquish the remote cave he has chosen for his solitude. But the law must have its way. My companion pins him at last, and Winterman pumps him full of enough sedative to keep him out for a week. Even then the trespasser lies there and pants. They mask him, cuff him, drag him to the nearest airlock, into the ship that my companion is sent to bring round. At the base a security ambulance rushes the prisoner into hospital, where they check him over in a sealed room, no visitors, electronic locks, armed guards, the works. The medics are up all night, arguing over the preliminary results. The head of Bio Division has a shouting match with the director, demanding to call in experts, but by 07.30 the matter is out of their hands, on other desks, in other bureaus. At midnight the nurse checks the monitors, sees him there safe and sound, respiration, heartbeat, EEG steady if not strictly normal. The next time she looks, at 07.42, the bed is empty. The involuntary patient has found a way to discharge himself.

'I guess he can look after himself,' said my companion. 'I guess you would, if you lived that long.'

I was hot. My head was reeling. My throat was as sore as if I had been the one doing all the talking. I realized I had no idea what time it was. The Lone Ace had closed hours ago. Even the flatscreen was off. I looked across the sick dark green infinite space of the Lone Ace and saw the barman still there, solid and white behind his fortifications. He did not seem to have moved since delivering our drinks. I supposed he had been watching us and listening. I supposed I had been the main entertainment for this evening, my reception for this story he had doubtless heard a thousand times before.

'Did you search?' I asked foolishly. 'You must have searched. Did you search the station?'

But the story was over. My companion had lapsed back suddenly into his non-negotiable silence. I remember babbling a while, raving, I imagine, jeering, I believe. I remember staggering into the bathroom, slipping on the tile, banging my head. I remember being shovelled into a cab, the driver being given my credit chip. I remember waking up in my clothes, smelling like a bum of the third degree and hurting like a stretcher case. It was two before I dragged myself into the library.

My dissertation was accepted in the summer of '97, when I was given leave to supplicate for the degree of Master of Science at the Faculty of Space Engineering. There are the traditional three bound copies lurking on the faculty library print shelves, way down in the archive stacks where no one ever goes. You can get the whole thing, text and diagrams, off the net, if you have the basic access codes. You won't find anything in it about TSK 120J.

Oh, I had poked around for a time, looking for anything that would invalidate the patrolman's story. There was nothing. There was nothing to support it either, except the very lack of evidence anywhere about that mission. Eventually of course I found the number of the bar and called it, but the barman had moved on and nobody was interested in identifying my ravaged interlocutor. After a while they started hanging up when I called.

Then I went at it systematically, from every angle, under cover. Zero. I grew righteous and demanded satisfaction, challenging all agencies and individuals wheresoever to deny the appalling miracle. I attacked the churches. They were obdurate and bland and soothing as always. I attacked the police. They registered my complaint. It was no use. The old buzzard had got clean away again.

Sometimes I think I see him, on a crowded transport, further along the car; or among the people spilling out of a movie theatre on some uptown mall, an old man with a beard down to his waist and a rope around his tattered gown and a wild mane of hair like some ancient prophet. Once I thought he shouldered me aside in the street outside the faculty. He looked like a lunatic professor, condemning me to abysmal grades. I knew he had come to seek me out, to tell me he knew who I was, to curse my quest. As he thrust me aside I saw the great beak of his nose, the frenzied glare of those insatiable eyes. It wasn't him, of course. He would never take his shame anywhere so public.

For the longest time I won't even think about him. Then something happens, some newspaper reference to apocryphal texts, some chance remark in a stranger's conversation, some piece of scripture I hear mangled by a TV evangelist as I sit alone late at night, unable to sleep, mindlessly flipping channels. Then I remember that piece of blasphemously ambulatory antiquity. I see him in imagination as the defeated patrolman described him, sitting upright in his violated vault. Then it is I he seems to grab by the coat with his bony fist, I of whom he asks his one eternal, unanswerable question: 'Is He back yet? Is He back?'

Music feeds my writing, in all sorts of ways. Some songs tell me stories, which I write down. Others give me atmospheres, soundtracks for the movies in my head. Other Voices is the title of a song by the Cure (as well as — coincidentally — an album by the Doors, and one by Paul Young), from an album which supplied many other quotes and allusions to that book, and which includes another track inspired directly by the plight of Fuchsia in Mervyn Peake's Gormenghast. *The music goes round and around, as someone once said; and it comes out here.*

Candy Comes Back

SAMMY IS A SALESMAN. He has a wife he doesn't see for
weeks on end, which worries him sometimes but doesn't
stop him fooling around a little. He doesn't worry much that
he almost never sees his daughter; he has long ceased to
understand her. When anything does worry him, he has
another drink. Tonight Sammy is drinking with a guy from
Seattle who supplies trade fairs for the garment industry. 'I
can take as many as they got to get rid of,' he keeps saying.
'Come on, Sammy, how many they got to get rid of? You
can trust me, Sammy.' The guy from Seattle paws Sammy's
arm in alcoholic fraternal bonhomie. Sammy thinks he is a
pain in the butt. Guy should know he can't commit to anything before he's talked to the boss.

In any case, just now Sammy wants to pay some attention
to his other companion, who is forty-five if she's a day but
is stacked. She is a bottle blonde in a purple sheath dress
so tight Sammy wonders if it came out of a bottle too. She
has a smoker's cough, a laugh like a crow, and legs that
could stop traffic. Right now she has a sour expression on
her face. She wants the guy from Seattle to shut the fuck
up, and so does Sammy. When the broad goes to the john,
Sammy says, 'I hate to cut and run,' and takes out his billfold
to settle up. In his billfold he sees the picture of his daughter,
who is sixteen and cares more about Candy and the Bon-Bons
than about him or her mother. Any boy who wants to feel
his daughter's tits only has to buy her a Candy and the

Bon-Bons record. Candy and the Bon-Bons have made four records already, and Sammy's daughter has them all.

Candy and the Bon-Bons do record hops. They do radio, and residencies. Four shows a day at the Madrigal, five at St William Street; seventeen nights straight in Connecticut and New Jersey. On the road they lie in the back of the truck and stare at the streetlights flipping past through the skylight.

When they get to the theatre they find the dressing room full of dirty bottles. It is under the stage, damp and cold, or hot and airless as a bakehouse. 'I like guys called Rick and Rob and Ray,' says Rona, one night before the show. She cannot be sure that what she says is true, or that it even means anything, really. Then again, who knows?

Cora looks at Rona in the dressing room mirror. Rona looks at Cora. 'The boy I marry will be called Gordon or Galen or Gus,' says Cora. She twists the cap off a stick of lipstick. Her lips, like Cora's, are already as red as poppies. 'He will have to have yellow hair and a wonderful smile. He will carry me in his strong arms. He will work for the record company.' Cora purses her lips and redraws the top one.

'I want a fireman,' says Rona suddenly. 'Or a truck driver. Cora, I want a cowboy.' She hugs herself. Her arms are sleek, and completely hairless. She lets her head loll down. 'I want *somebody*,' she says.

'*Somebody who wants me*,' sings Cora.

'*Somebody who needs me*,' sings Rona, standing up at once.

'*She-do-lang-lang*,' sing the Bon-Bons, '*she-do-lang-lang-lang*.'

The door opens and Candy comes in.

'Hello, girls!' says Candy.

'Hello, Candy!' they say.

'How many kids do you want to have, Candy?' asks Rona.

'We think two would be just perfect,' says Cora.

'A boy and a girl,' they chorus.

'Heaven,' says Candy ecstatically, and she starts to clasp her hands together, but fails to complete the motion. Her hands twitch. The girls look at her, and for a moment nobody speaks.

George comes in, wiping his hands on a rag. 'What is it, Candy?' he says. 'Is it your timer again?'

Rona and Cora gaze at each other in apprehension. Timing is everything. Timing is the most important thing in the world. If your timer goes, you can't even make it as a mannequin, up and down the catwalk in white lace mini-dresses and nylon boas, never allowed to sing a note. And if you can't make it as a mannequin, you are scrap. No, the catwalk is your last hope. Beyond that Cora and Rona can imagine nothing, only deafening black silence.

George is out of the question, as far as potential husbands go. George is not like the girls. He is one of the people who make everything work, along with Sammy, and Spencer.

Spencer is their manager and producer. He has his hand on their master switches. '*Candy?*' says Spencer in the control booth. '*Candy, are you with us? You going to do this one for us, sweetheart? Jesus Christ Almi –*' they hear him mutter angrily, as he switches off his mike.

Spencer works for the record company, Skyrocket Records. Days off he likes to watch demolition derbies and drag racing. When they go to the track his wife packs a lunch of Polish hot sausage and pickled gherkin. She puts mayo on the bread instead of margarine, and packs a thermos of coffee beside the beer. He gets hot for her watching all that mayhem and destruction. Sometimes she gets drunk along with him. Once she blew him right there in the back of the stands. 'C'mon, gang,' says Spencer, 'let's hustle it up now. Got a hot weekend ahead.' He claps his hands and rubs them, grinning at his girls. He wonders if they have the first idea what the hell he's thinking about.

He bets that Candy does. Candy watches you, watches you like she knows you know something, and she wants to know it too. Like a suspicious child. She frets about stuff. Only when she's singing is she completely at peace. She stands there now holding her hands clasped between her innocent young breasts and giving out like a gospel belter. '*And one day I'll see you,*' she promises, fervently. '*One day I'll see you.*'

Candy is fine today. Running sweet. George had patted Candy on the shoulder and flashed them all a grin. 'Just kidding, girls,' George said, loudly. 'Talking to myself. Don't want to pay me no mind.' Rona and Cora had smiled back. They could see George's grin did not reach his eyes. Now George is fiddling with the generator. Candy and the girls are starting to warm up.

'*Running back into my arms,*' sings Candy, with feeling. '*Running back into my heart,*' she sings, '*again.*'

'*Again,*' chorus the Bon-Bons.

'We grew up together,' Cora and Rona tell the journalist. Their new record is in the charts, at number fifty-nine, and Spencer says somebody heard it on Radio WMCA. The journalist is interviewing the Bon-Bons for the local paper. 'We went to high school together,' says Cora.

'All of us,' says Rona. 'I was a cheerleader, Cora was an athlete, Candy was homecoming queen. Boys would buy us Cokes,' she says, smiling, and she clasps her hands around her knee, leaning back where she sits, on the table. 'They'd buy us Cokes and ask us to sing.'

She looks down at Cora, sitting in the chair. Cora looks up at her and they smile.

Candy is supposed to be the leader, the one who talks to journalists, but she is off somewhere. George has taken her off somewhere again.

'Who are your favourite bands?' the journalist asks. He touches his tie and monitors his smile. Never before has he been alone in a small room with two such gorgeous babes. They are almost too good to be true. The journalist is frightened and excited, which is why he is trying to be very professional and cool.

'Oh, we all like different bands,' says Cora.

Rona chimes in. 'Candy likes Dorian and Cora likes the Flapjacks,' she says. 'I like the British beat groups.' She holds her hand up with her fingers stiffly bent, as though she was drying nail polish. 'I think they're just so cute!'

'They have the cutest smiles,' says Cora.

'All the girls are *crazy* about them!' they chorus.

Cora and Rona and Candy would like things one day to be like in the songs. Not the sad songs like 'Crazy Paving Heart' or 'Loving You', just an ordinary nice song like 'He's the One for Me'. Candy and the Bon-Bons imagine that all the girls who buy their records must live lives like that, which they never get to. Candy and the Bon-Bons don't really have lives, not of their own. They never meet anyone they aren't going to say goodbye to in a day or two. They are always working or sleeping and never at home.

Meanwhile they are completely devoted to Skyrocket Records, and to Sammy, and to each other. 'Honey, you're so natural!' says Rona to Cora, while they turn and run on for another bow. Candy smiles and lifts her hands above them both. They all love the audiences, of course, and the audiences love them too.

Onstage they shine, in their blonde bouffant wigs and candy-stripe party frocks over starched petticoats. Rona and

Cora's stripes are pink and white, Candy's are tangerine and white. 'Skyrocket Records have been so good to us,' the girls tell everyone. 'Being on tour is good, you get to travel, see places.' The songs they sing are not about travelling. They are about being true, about knowing the right one and staying forever right by his side. When he goes away, they know they will be sad. But when he comes back, baby, then they will be glad.

Privately, when they have been left switched on and forgotten in the dressing room all afternoon, Candy and the Bon-Bons feel less secure about the prospect of eternal love and happiness. They often feel afraid, abandoned, left out. Sometimes they think about what can happen to a girl if she gets married and is off on the road the whole time. While you're going from town to town singing 'My Wonderful You', your marriage could be breaking in pieces. The Bon-Bons can't remember anyone special, but they know Spencer always likes them to say they are married, or have boyfriends waiting for them back home.

Candy and the Bon-Bons do four shows a day, fourth on the bill. Dorian is the star, the headline. The Flapjacks are second. 'Back home everyone loves the Flapjacks,' Rona is telling the motel manager.

Candy is suddenly there, leaning in listening to the conversation. 'Where?' she says.

'Back home,' says Cora.

'Where we come from,' says Rona.

They stare at her with eyes like headlights on the highway.

'All our school friends think the Flapjacks are really cool,' says Cora.

'What *school friends*?' says Candy suddenly, in a voice of bitterness and scorn. 'We never went to school.' And she starts to cry.

Rona and Cora start to coo. They pat Candy feebly, in distress. What is wrong with her? Has she been drinking or taking some drugs? It upsets them to see her standing there with her battery lead in her hand. The lead goes up her skirt and she is just standing there in the lobby in front of everyone, crying.

Spencer is on the phone. 'Where the hell is George?' he says, craning over his shoulder to watch Candy. 'I don't like what I'm seeing here in this motel lobby, Sammy, old buddy.' He listens a moment, then shakes his head. 'You get out here now, Sammy, then tell me they don't have tear ducts.'

His voice is high and fast. They would almost think he sounded scared if he wasn't so strong, so responsible. Spencer is one of the people who make everything work. He puts down the phone and goes back to the desk. The motel manager stands there with his mouth in a straight line and his eyes going backwards and forwards, side to side. Spencer passes him a ten.

Candy sits in the corner of the room in her stage frock reading poetry. Her head seems to hang low between her beautiful defeated shoulders. She is making the other two edgy, just sitting there. They keep keening quietly, off-key, and pulling their hair with their fingernails. One will start and then it will set the other one off. As for Candy, these days you never know what she's going to do next. Onstage she is fine, never sounded better, storming them with eyes and teeth shining fit to dazzle the front row. Onstage Candy is pure flair, spin, sway, motion. It is during rehearsals and after hours that she'll suddenly throw a tambourine across the room or try to open her wrists with a screwdriver. Or she gets out, and they find her in the parking lot at midnight, her face pressed against the windows of Impalas and Caddies, shading her eyes with her hands. She spies on the couples necking in the back seat, watching them with hollow, haunted eyes like some vampire of the freeways. One night somebody sees her and calls the cops, but the company takes care of it.

Someone has given Candy a record called 'The Times They Are A-Changin''. Tonight in the motel she demands a record player and plays the thing until everyone's just about distracted. 'Can't you *hear* what he's *saying*?' she demands.

'He's a wonderful talent,' says Rona.

'Like some kind of poet,' says Cora.

They nod solemnly and turn back to the TV.

Candy snatches the arm off the record with a horrible ripping, scratching sound. She throws the record player on the floor and starts kicking it. George has to come running and cool her down again.

The next day, the Bon-Bons are up and ready for rehearsal at ten. By eleven Candy still isn't there. No one is.

Rona pulls a wisp out from her hair, twisting it between her finger and thumb. 'She's run out on us,' she says.

Cora agrees. 'She's gone to the West Coast,' she says.

'To San Francisco.'

'Hollywood.'

'She'll never last on her own.' They know you can't go more than twelve hours without a recharge. They've always known that. That is the rule.

'They'll split us up.'

'Maybe they'll send us to Seattle.'

Cora and Rona cling to each other in a stiff clashing froth of rayon and terylene.

The studio clock ticks, and ticks again. Each time it ticks the minute hand jumps, a whole minute all at once, as if the seconds in between didn't count for anything.

Rona says: 'We can go on as a duo.'

Cora says: 'She would want us to.'

Rona says: 'They would want us to.'

But Cora shakes her head. 'No they wouldn't.'

Rona looks at her.

'They wouldn't,' Cora says again.

'How do you know?'

Cora shrugs her shoulders. 'I just know, that's all. If they did want us to carry on, we'd know, wouldn't we?'

'I guess,' Rona says unhappily. She looks up at the empty glass booth. 'I don't know, Cora.'

'They'll be here soon, honey,' says Cora, gazing around at the empty studio.

'I wish Candy was here,' says Rona.

'Let's sing,' says Cora.

'What shall we sing?'

'Let's sing one of the new ones. Let's sing "Teen Supreme",' says Cora.

'With no music?'

'Sure.'

Rona puts her head on one side. 'Well who's going to sing lead?'

'Both of us,' says Cora. 'We'll sing it together, all the way through, like the people will when they hear it. We'll make believe we're singing along with Candy.'

Outside the recording studio cars drive in and out of the parking lot. The studio is right in the middle of downtown, above a shoe store. Thousands and thousands of people walk past the building never knowing they're right next to a place where chart recordings are being made.

'*You're my king,*' sing the Bon-Bons,
'*I'm your queen*
And forever in my dreams
We rule the world of lovers
Teen Supreme.'

*

Next day, Candy comes back, just in time for the Eldorado show. She walks in the door with Sammy. 'Hello girls!' she calls, with a wave.

'Candy!' they cry happily. They stare at her. Her hair is different. Different from the way it always was before; different from theirs. Candy's hair is brown and straight. It hangs halfway down her back.

'We like your hair, Candy,' say the Bon-Bons.

'Look what I've got for you,' says Candy. She opens a brown paper sack and takes out three fresh, warm donuts.

The girls don't say anything.

'One for Cora, one for Rona, and one for me. Mmm!'

'But Candy,' says Cora. 'We mustn't.'

Candy lays a hand on her flat stomach. 'Just this once,' she says.

'But Candy,' says Rona. 'We can't.'

Boldly Candy brings a donut to her mouth, but her mouth refuses to know what to do with it. 'Oh well,' says Candy brightly, and throws the donut in the trashcan.

The Bon-Bons laugh and turning, throw their donuts in the trashcan too. They wipe their fingers on the paper napkins.

'I've had such a time, girls, you can't imagine,' says Candy, holding up one hand.

Lovingly, Rona and Cora take hold of her arms, one each. 'We're just so happy to see you, Candy,' they say. 'We missed you!'

Together they hurry into the rehearsal studio. 'Why don't we start with one of the new ones?' Candy asks them, while she waves to Spencer. 'How about "Teen Supreme"?'

Spencer watches from the control booth. The mike is off. 'Didn't she used to be with the Cherry-Tops?' he says, not taking his eyes off the girls.

Sammy turns his head away, sharply. 'It's Candy,' he says.

Spencer puts his hand to his chin. It's Candy's face; or at least that's the shape of her head. They're all much the same size. What does it matter anyhow? She's got the moves. This is 1964, girl groups are a dime a dozen, there are scores of them working in New York alone.

George comes in and changes Candy's wig. He twists her long brown hair up at the back and puts her old blonde wig back on her head. 'That's better,' says Spencer. He opens the mike. 'Is that better now, ladies?' he asks.

'Much better, thank you Spencer!' chirp the Bon-Bons from the box speaker on the wall. George gives them the thumbs up. Candy beams at Spencer and Sammy, at everyone.

Spencer flicks off the mike and flops back in his producer's chair. He reaches inside his sports coat for a cigarette. 'Thank Christ for that,' he mutters.

Sammy bounces in his seat, laughing, plucking the creases of his slacks. 'I swear you really care for these girls,' he says.

'I do,' says Spencer, lighting his cigarette. 'I do care for them. So do you.'

Sammy grimaces, raising his eyebrows. He looks down at the floor. 'Damn it,' he growls, and punches Spencer on the arm. 'You're right.'

'*She-do-lang-lang*,' sing Candy and the Bon-Bons, '*she-do-lang-lang-lang*.'

Sammy sits in the office at the factory. He sits hunched forward, his hat on his head, his chair pulled tight in to the desk. He is on the phone. 'Put her in the truck with the others,' he says. 'Seattle, yup. What? What you say?' Sammy twirls his cigarette between his thumb and his broad, hard forefinger. 'Stack 'em sideways,' he says, scowling. 'Get more in that way.' He feels gloomy this afternoon. He has a headache coming on. Maybe he drank a little too much at lunchtime.

While the guy on the other end is talking, Sammy stares out of the window, frowning vacantly. Over behind the factory he can see someone standing by the highway with their thumb out. Long brown hair, a girl, he reckons. Young girls hitching rides all over the country these days. He sees them, all over; never picked one up, though he's been tempted. Sometimes it seems like half the young women of America are up and out and on their way to somewhere else. Sammy wonders what the hell has got into them.

IV

OTHER PEOPLE'S HEROES

The other answer to 'Where do you get your ideas?' is another two-word one: Neil Gaiman.

I asked Susanna how on earth I could describe Neil Gaiman. She said several words like lovely *and* sweetie *that personal pride prevents me from repeating. It is one of the more galling facts about the world that Neil Gaiman is not only immensely talented, heroically successful, incorruptibly good and devilishly handsome – he's incredibly nice too. Your author turns away, shaking his scurfy head and scowling.*

Then Susanna said: 'He's the fairy godfather to many good stories.'

Which is true. Neil Gaiman is the Sandman, *dressed all in black, stepping into everyone's bedroom every night to sprinkle our pillows with stories. Why was it that Terry Pratchett, Mary Gentle and I all woke up one morning thinking:* Assassins' Guild? *Where did all those* Midnight Rose *stories really come from? Did we dream that mysterious man in the black glasses, or is he dreaming us?*

I always dream about losing my luggage, or finding old Rupert Bear annuals I've never seen before. I can imagine other kinds of dreams though, midsummer nights' ones, about chasing ever-fleeing women through entangling woods. If you ask me, Desire and Dream really should not be enemies.

Masquerade and High Water

SHERRI STOOD IN the doorway with a mug of iced tea, shading her eyes from the sun. 'You missed the wedding!' she called.

Oliver shut the car door and went up the steps to the porch. 'You had a wedding?' he said.

In fact Oliver had been aware of them all morning, the battered cars and bikes trailing up the road past his house. He had heard the laughter coming from up here, the distorted wail of old Jefferson Airplane albums. It was either a wedding or a wake. He kept away until the celebration died down and everything went quiet. He didn't know why he had come up here now. Just being neighbourly, he supposed.

Sherri was pottering inside and out, picking up. There was enough mess: paper plates smeared with guacamole, empty bottles, half-empty cans. There was always mess at Sherri's house, wedding or no wedding. Oliver kind of liked it. It helped confirm his resolve to keep his place down the road vacuumed and tidy, free of bachelor squalor.

'It was a great wedding,' Sherri said. 'I married Johnny and Turquoise.'

She knew everybody in the hills for miles around, and always assumed he did too. In fact in two years here she was the only one he had got to know at all. It was the solitude he liked – that, and the low property prices that meant he could own now instead of paying top dollar rent on some cracker box downtown. He liked living among the trees, in clean air, with the mountains in the distance. He sat on Sherri's broken-down porch and looked out into the soft dark green of spruce, the shivering yellow aspen. Above his head hung the sign, black letters charred into a slice of birch wood: *Church of the Wild Elk*.

'Want some of this?' She put a big cold bowl in his lap.

'What is it?'

'Melon ginger ice cream.'

Probably half an ounce of hash in there too, knowing Sherri. 'No thanks.'

Sherri half sat on the porch rail in her worn long tie-dye skirt, cradling the bowl. Her arms were sunbrown and strong. 'You know, I had this amazing dream,' she said, dipping her finger in the ice cream and licking it. 'I dreamed I was sitting there where you're sitting, only there was this big white cat in my lap. And I stroked it, and it got up and went away, and I looked down in my lap and there were all these tiny little kittens! It was ama-a-zing,' she said, drawing the word out into a whole drowsy musical phrase. 'It was really amazing. Don't you think that was a good omen for Johnny and Turquoise?'

'I never have dreams,' said Oliver.

In his black onyx boat in the form of a sphinx, Morpheus the Shaper and his sibling Desire float across the waters of the buried lake. The air is hot and gloomy. The sailors in their nightwear haul at the ropes, putting on more sail. Eyes closed, they trawl the darkness for the sluggish wind.

The two travellers lie upon cushions. They speak of responsibility. Desire says it is a tiresome illusion. Morpheus does not deny it, but claims it is inescapable in the human realm, inseparable from it as shadows from sunlight.

'People pursue things,' says Morpheus. 'As soon as they have them they run away from them. But what they run away from stays with them, dragging along behind them like an ever-lengthening cloak.'

'Cloaks are nice.' Bright-eyed Desire bites its finger. 'You can wear a cloak and have nothing on under it at all. And you can go anywhere you want like that!'

The water is dark and murky, like an old painting. Desire makes water lilies in it, green and white and golden as egg yolk. Morpheus broods, as he does so often, his long chin resting in his wax-white hand.

Far away across the water, at the Pavilion of Recurrence, the summoning bell is ringing.

'Everybody dreams, Ollie,' said Sherri, fetching him a beer. 'They say you are what you dream. Did you ever hear that?'

'No,' said Oliver. 'I never did.'

'You are what you dream,' said Sherri again, nodding, and smiled her blissed-out smile. Her eyes were pretty. She picked up some butts, an empty corn chip box. She came across a shawl and draped it round her shoulders, despite the warmth of the afternoon.

Oliver glanced at her. She couldn't be much older than him, though she had a grown up daughter somewhere running around. They always had dressed like grannies, the Earth Mother types, in long dresses and scarves and twenty pounds of beads. He did wish she wouldn't call him Ollie.

Sherri was a nice Jewish girl from New York, originally. She had come out here to clean out her headspace. Her house was a legally consecrated church, tax exempt. She had told Oliver she was figuring out a way to write off the hot tub as a baptismal font.

Oliver smiled and drank his beer. Sherri and her congregation. People who had crawled up in here when the sixties turned to shit and never crawled out again. But Sherri was okay. She had helped him the first winter, when he got

sick, and when his Subaru went into that snowdrift she got
somebody for him, somebody she knew who came with a
tow truck and pulled it out and never even sent him a bill.
Sherri was okay, when you had time for her. Sherri wouldn't
do you harm.

Sometimes the Pavilion of Recurrence looks like an Arabian
tent, a finespun marvel of white and scarlet cloth billowing
in a place of sand and mirage. Sometimes it stands to one
side of a grassy river meadow where swans glide beneath
willows and great helms and targets with obscure devices
hang amid the branches of bowed and ancient trees. Sometimes it is made of pellucid white marble, the Pavilion of
Recurrence, with gilded balconies, and the sound of a piano
tinkling lazily from an open window.

Sometimes, like today, the Pavilion of Recurrence has the
aspect of an island monastery, with a bell-tower and a thick
coat of evergreen creeper. The bell tolls slowly, insistently,
across the buried lake.

Inside the Pavilion of Recurrence, as anywhere else in the
Dreaming to one extent or another, whatever is needed is
provided. A morgue, where night after night forensic patho-
logists find members of their families stretched out on the
slab, opened up for dissection, though still pleading to be
released. A school where adults of all ages return again and
again to face unprepared and incomprehensible exams. A
tram that takes commuters on an eternal journey to an omin-
ous destination through unknown yet strangely haunting
streets. A sepulchral second-hand shop, on whose shelves
authors find dusty books with titles that are completely
unreadable, but whose covers bear their own names.

Inside the Pavilion of Recurrence today they are assembling for a dream of masquerade and high water. The bell
calls them in, the figments, the chimeras, the larval entities

that make up the crowd. A raven perches on a sill above the jetty, inspecting them as they disembark. Beneath their long hair they are faceless. Smoke drifts from their unfinished fingers. One carries a tambourine. Others seem to be swirls of paisley and embroidered clothes with no bodies inside them at all.

A foreground character with the likeness of a placid child speaks to the librarian, who is consulting the index of a large book. 'How many more times must we do this?'

The librarian answers, 'Until he ceases to mourn.'

Her voice was harsh, roughened by smoke and bad habits. 'What are you doing the rest of the weekend?'

'I've got some stuff to sort out. Some projections.'

'Astral projections?' she asked, teasing.

'Just the regular kind. Sales and budgets.'

'Shit, Ollie, they really got your feet nailed to the floor, don't they.'

Oliver drank beer, licked his lips. 'The work don't do itself, Sherri,' he said. 'It don't go away.' He found himself saying things like that, *don't* instead of *doesn't*, when he talked to Sherri. It was more appropriate, somehow, out here where people wore beer brand T-shirts and drove around with their dog beside them in the front seat.

'Sure it does,' she said. 'When it goes away, that's when you start to worry.'

He asked her: 'What are you doing these days, Sherri?'

'I'm going into solar,' she said. 'You know that little place down on the mall? They got a sales training program and incentive scheme and everything. You sell enough systems, they fit you one for free.' She braced her arms on the rail and beamed up at the sky as though she could already see the big glass panels erected on her roof, gathering heat from the benevolent sun.

'That would be good,' said Oliver.

Sherri never told you what she was doing, always what she was going to do. She never seemed to do anything, unless it was some crazy scheme, charting horoscopes, designing children's clothes, selling tofu sandwiches out of the back of a truck. House painting, she did sometimes. There was a house across the valley she told him she had painted. It had a huge yellow sunflower on the side.

Sherri always made Oliver think of California, twenty years before. Nearer thirty now. She reminded him of when he had lived that way himself for a time, on the coast, in the days of Donna. It had been possible then. In the summer it was a gas – had they really said that? Something was a gas? The phrase seemed strange to him, as if it could not possibly have ever fit inside his mouth. In the summertime, anyhow, yes, the living was easy: plenty of work, warm nights, they slept on the beach.

In the winter it was different. Then there was no work, it was freezing cold and it rained all the time. You had to hole up in the empty tourist cabins, try to live on what you'd saved from the summer. The two of them had joined a commune, a bunch of psychedelic musicians and their 'old ladies' – Jesus Christ, had he said that too, and called them chicks and talked about freaking out and scoring dope? Living on rice and beans, sleeping in bags on drafty floors, keeping watch for the Russian River to flood. Jesus Christ, he must have been crazy.

Oliver thought about Donna then, almost without knowing he did so; and as he always did, blanked out her features before consigning her to oblivion. He drank his beer.

The figments troop into a small room. The room has walls and a floor of green jade. No matter how many of the figments come in, the room is always big enough to hold them.

In the green jade room the Continuity Girl checks their manifestations for them. The Continuity Girl wears gold bangles shaped like stirrups and a reassuring jacket of russet tweed. She tries to call the roll. 'Parqua . . . Quarpa . . . Apquar . . .' The letters on her clipboard wriggle about.

'Minimum May . . . Dr Scorpio Bongo . . .' The figments are ignoring her. Background characters settle into clusters, comfortably. Absent-mindedly they start to merge.

The raven perches on the librarian's shoulder. It speaks. 'What's the story here?' it asks.

Patiently the librarian adjusts his glasses, dislodged by the raven's landing, and turns over a page. He follows the line of an entry with his finger. 'It looks like a dream about lost love . . .' he says.

'Yeah, well, typical,' says the raven.

'. . . and about a river rising.'

The raven nuzzles its purple plumage. 'I think maybe I've seen it.'

The clustered figures are growing consolidated, like statuary groups. Their fringes are entwining, the patches on their denims running together. The Continuity Girl has not yet noticed. She is dealing with the thing that is Donna, helping it into a dress made of dried leaves and peacocks' eyes.

Over the years the foreground characters have become quite stable. Some of them are acquiring memories; personalities, almost. A little brown thing like a stretched cherub with bat wings and a screwed up, miserable face speaks about the wonderful dress.

'His mother had a dress like that. He remembers her in it, dancing with his father in a state of high excitement. It was at his cousin Mona's wedding, but he has forgotten that. He was three. When they sat down after dancing he got under the table and put his head up his mother's dress.'

A man with the beard of a lumberjack and the face of a

turtle denies it. 'She never had such a dress. No one ever had, not in the human realm. It is a piece of something else that has blown in from who knows where, and been caught between the teeth of the dream.'

A grainy boy in a headband laughs. 'Like getting your shorts stuck in your zipper.'

'You ever seen Texas, Ollie? El Paso? I'm going down to El Paso, going to see Pepper.'

Pepper was Sherri's daughter. Short for Chilli Pepper, Sherri had told him. 'Because she was so red and wrinkly!' Oliver had never met her, only seen photographs. The girl looked half Indian; half something, anyway. Sherri was always taking off somewhere or other to go see her.

'You ought to come along,' said Sherri.

'How's Pepper?' he said.

'She's going to Mexico. She's driving a truck for this wildlife survey?' Sherri always made her daughter out to be a conscientious person – 'really focused' – but Oliver had noticed that whenever she went to see her, each time Pepper was in some new place, doing some different thing. Once Sherri had come back from Wyoming in a beat-up Olds-mobile with a story about her and Pepper meeting two rodeo riders in Cheyenne and everybody swapping cars with each other. Pepper, Oliver suspected, might be a lot like her mom.

Oliver glanced down at his car. It needed the transmission looking at. And there was that little bit of rust that needed fixing before it got any bigger. The little bit of rust had been there since last winter. He didn't want to think about it.

Sherri had left the porch and was doing something indoors behind him. Oliver pitched his voice to her.

'When are you going?'

There was a pause. Somewhere in the distance a dog

barked; then another, and another. All along the valley, at all the houses hidden in the trees, dogs roused themselves on porches and in dustholes and under sheds. One after another they lifted their heads up and added their contribution to the neighbourhood chorus. Whatever had woken them remained mysterious as always, remarkable only to canines.

Sherri reappeared. She was eating ice cream again. 'Oh, I'm going real soon,' she said.

The janitor sits down on the set and lights a cigarette. His team are setting up the redwood forest, giant trees that shoot up hundreds of feet to spread their branches. There are bits of twig all over the janitor's blue bib overalls. He says: 'What I can't figure is, we're here luggin' these goddamn trees around, yeah? But the guy's got trees in the daytime, ya know? So what's he need the goddamn trees in his dreams for?'

The librarian turns a page. 'I think it's the other way round, Mervyn.'

A black dog that has been hanging around has turned into a squat bird with a long beak. When it lifts its wings you can see it has legs underneath like a crab. There are several of the things. They run quickly among the shapeless furniture.

The Continuity Girl flicks back her hair. 'What are those?' she calls. 'I've never seen those before.' Intently she searches her list. The list is getting longer. It slips between her fingers and drops to the floor, unrolling as it bounces away.

'No story is exactly the same twice,' observes a figment with paper lips. 'Even written down and printed in a book.'

'Everything is the same as itself,' says another in a dry, whiskery voice. 'That's philosophy, man.'

'It's not the same story because you're not the same person,' says the first figment.

'I'm the same person, man,' the second asserts. 'I used to be in another dream,' it recalls. 'It was better than this one. It was all about flying and chocolate.'

'You're not the same person because it's not the same dream.'

Circling, the raven glides back to the librarian. 'The Quapras are arguing, Lucien.'

'Sort them out, Matthew, for goodness sake, before they start attracting Delirium,' says the librarian. 'Get everyone to their entrances.' It is like looking after a tour party of forgetful old people, always squabbling and repeating themselves, telling each other the same things over and over.

Sitting on Sherri's porch, Oliver fell asleep.

Once again he is standing in the cabin in front of the enormous closet, watching the clown take out clothes and throw them to the people all around the room. The clothes fly over Oliver's head, very slowly. He is in the cabin, but he can see grey sky beyond the floating Hawaiian shirts and party gowns, where the ceiling should be. The people catch the clothes with happy cries and put them on. They are dressing up as the summer visitors.

Some of the people are familiar. That boy with the snub nose and long curly hair, he is usually there. He called himself Dr Scorpio. He used to take acid and play the bongos all night. Oliver had learned to sleep through the drumming. Dr Scorpio puts on a pair of pyjamas. For an instant the pyjamas are a pair Oliver had when he was a little boy, with blue tugboats on, but he could not be expected to remember that. The clown has huge buck teeth. He is still throwing clothes. Oliver tries to catch some, but they seem to pass right through his hands.

He notices a man with a black beard who used to work at the funfair, and someone cooking food, and someone whose skin keeps changing colour behind a pair of circular purple spectacles. 'Fixing plumbing is Nixon cling,' a face swims up and tells Oliver, who folds his hands in his sleeves and laughs desperately. Donna is there – Donna is always there – in red and green striped trousers, playing the piano. In the cavernous closet a placid child sits, contemplatively stroking the jackets and dresses of the absent guests. 'These clothes are not our clothes,' it says. 'That is why they suit us so well.' Oliver laughs and laughs and laughs.

On Sherri's porch, the sun sifted through the trees on Oliver's still face. Sherri was talking to him about Turquoise and Johnny, but he was very far away.

It is winter in the Pavilion of Recurrence. Oliver and a black woman he saw once on a street corner in Philadelphia are trying to warn everyone the river is going to flood. They are clambering up and down tiers of seats, like in a stadium, in and out of trapdoors, up and down ladders with just little stumps instead of rungs. Far below, the rest of the commune come running across the grass, fleeing from a huge wave of water. Oliver and the woman slide down a chute in an upturned table with a placid child and a man with a fishing pole. Everyone passes around heavy packages wrapped in disintegrating paper. No matter how Oliver tries to hold on to the packages, the paper keeps tearing and the weight slides out of his fingers. The flood bears him away under the enormous trees. Oliver tries to hang on to the leg of the table, but there is no table any more. Donna runs away between the trees, laughing. Oliver is not laughing now. He is upset, or cross. Sometimes he tries to catch her, wading frantically through earth that has turned to water, or sometimes through the air. Sometimes she tries to catch him. They never catch each other, no matter what.

Sherri crumpled the last paper cup into the garbage sack. She looked at Oliver sleeping, wondering how long he could hold on to his beer without spilling it. He had the can propped on his belly. He was getting a little pot there, the years starting to pile up around his waist. Why were all the guys she knew getting fat? Sherri had the strongest urge suddenly to put her hands on Oliver's belly and feel the warm firm mass of it, to squeeze him awake and kiss him in his surprise. She snorted at herself and reeled back a way on her heels. She was still a little stoned. Deliberately she went and got the cloth and wiped the tabletop, softly humming a tune that was going round her head, thinking about the wedding and the celebrations and all. Ollie was nice, Sherri thought, though he always seemed kind of sad, as if he was more alone, maybe, than he really wanted to be.

'Weddings always make me horny,' she told the sleeping man.

In the buried lake at the bottom of the Dreaming the black onyx boat in the shape of a sphinx bumps against a shadowy jetty. Its somnambulant crew begin to reef the sails.

Desire inserts a ripe cherry into its own mouth, and one into its brother's. He accepts it with dignity. Desire smiles. It draws its feet up and looks about. 'I know this place,' it says.

'The Pavilion of Recurrence,' says Morpheus. This spot can be reached from any of their realms. All the Endless have sometime been concerned in the ceremonies staged inside this gray secretive building, nightbound ceremonies of loss or discovery or consecration established and sanctified by repetition.

By the light of pale green torches Morpheus and his sibling

climb the steps and walk directly through the wall into the flooded Pavilion. The wall grows vague and confused, admitting them.

Inside, enigmatic monumental furniture floats about, and vast trees seem to tower out of the thick brown water. A human man is being hounded this way and that by chuckling sprites. The Lord of Shapings points at him. 'This is one encumbered by the cloak of his past,' he tells his sibling. As he speaks you can almost see it, a dim integument of ragged moonlight that clings to the toiler's shoulders, holding him back like a spider's web. He tries to lunge forward through the liquid wood, but the phantasms baffle him easily, driving him astray this way and that.

Desire gathers up a handful of air. It seems to have caught the hem of the human's cloak, to be rubbing the unstable fabric between its fingers. With its free hand it points to a laughing woman hiding behind a tree. 'Who is that?'

'His first true love.'

'How sweet.'

Desire reaches into the dream, which seems to have become very small suddenly, like a toy theatre, an enclosure of splashing, scampering little mammals. It does something to the face of the woman, turning her into someone else, someone older, with long dark red hair. 'There,' it says, straightening up again. 'That's better, isn't it?'

At first, the flux of wood and water is so complete it is impossible to notice any change. Then it becomes apparent the endless recircling rhythm of the piece has been disrupted. Individual phantoms are shrinking, dwindling, turning into sparks that go whizzing away into nothingness. Agitated memories are being smoothed and quelled and laid to rest like ironed clothes folded in sheets of tissue paper. The Continuity Girl waves her arms like a scarecrow in a gale. Already she is coming apart, in a flurry of dark green underwear. An infinite number of golden bangles go shooting away in a cylindrical stream. Meanwhile Lucien is crossing something out in his big book, writing hurriedly in the margin with a long stout jet black feather.

Morpheus fingers his jaw. 'I wish you would not interfere,' he says mildly to his sibling, though anyone who knows his voice well might detect a touch of sardonic amusement.

Desire touches itself then in a way that makes even the Dream King inhale reflexively, narrowing his nostrils and hooding his fathomless eyes.

'Darling brother,' Desire sighs yearningly. 'I never do anything else.'

Oliver started awake to a blare of sound, guitar and electric violin. Sherri had put 'It's A Beautiful Day' on.

He sat blinking on the porch, entirely disoriented. The sun had gone down while he slept, and the sky was a rich thick wash of indigo. Soon it would be black, pricked and blazing, dripping cold silver fire from an inconceivable number of stars.

'Sherri?' he called. He could not hear or see her, and suddenly that seemed to matter.

He heard her footsteps inside the house and turned towards them from his chair, almost spilling the remains of his beer. 'When you going to Texas?' he asked clumsily, before he could see whereabouts she was. It was hard to speak, sleep seemed to have gummed up his tongue.

'I don't know,' her voice said, calm and easy as ever over the surging music. 'Next week, maybe. You want to come?'

He saw her then, looking through the kitchen window at him. The smile on her face seemed to welcome him as though he had returned from a long absence, and not just woken from an unintended nap. Oliver had seen her naked one time, dropped in and found the door open and nobody home, he thought, until he came upon her sleeping out back in the yard in the sun. He had stood and looked at her curved and comfortable body, her lolling breasts with their broad dirtbrown nipples, her plump thighs drawn protectively up. He had stood looking at her a moment or two, and then he had returned to his car, got in, and parped the horn. He had sat and waited until Sherri had appeared with a dozy grin on the porch in her long gown of laundromat grey, messing up her thick red hair with her hand.

'What about the solar job?' he asked, in a mischief-making drawl.

She caught his tone. Lifting a plate from a bowl full of suds she squinted at the sky. 'I guess I missed the sun,' she said. Sherri, Oliver thought, was not afraid of time.

'You want to come?' she was asking him again. 'To El Paso?'

With Sherri driving, he thought cynically, probably they wouldn't ever get to El Paso. Like as not they wouldn't get to Texas at all. They would take her car and it would break down in New Mexico. Oliver could see it now, as clear as if it had been a memory, not a premonition. They would wind up waiting all day by the road in the middle of nowhere, comparing their childhoods, making lists of state capitals and singing all the songs they could think of, and finally a Navajo woman would stop in a truck full of paper flowers and take them fifty miles out of their way to go see some cave paintings and then on to a barbecue at the house of a professional hang-glider, only the directions would be wrong and they would wake up at noon the next day in the wrong town, still drunk, on somebody else's floor, and they would have to come home on the bus in each other's arms sharing a hang-over and he would lie to his manager about the unprojected projections.

'Sure,' Oliver heard himself say. 'Why not.'

Sherri paused, arrested over the dishes. Through the glass he saw her pretty eyes fill suddenly with hope and delight and not a trace of disbelief at all. 'Really?' she said. It was like she was getting excited about something. 'Really?'

'Sure,' said Oliver, and yawned, and laughed. 'Sure, why not.'

I lost a chunk of 1992 to the mysterious debilitating disease known generally as M.E., and medically as post-viral fatigue, neither of which names is particularly accurate or useful. On my slow way back from that desperate, grinding state where jigsaw puzzles are the summit of possible ambition and even the radio hurts, I was glad to have this reviving exercise set me by Ellen Datlow (another of the nicest people in the world, as well as one of the indefatigable archangels): to rewrite a fairy tale in a modern style. Incapable yet of creating anything of my own, recreating something that belongs to all of us seemed ideal occupational therapy.

Though Ellen didn't publish it in the end, I was pleased with my effort and glad when Steve Pasechnick brought it to light in the final issue of Strange Plasma. *The tale I chose is a version of the traditional motif known by folklorists as the Grateful Dead: this one by Hans Christian Andersen, a writer whose work has always seemed to me to have exactly the right proportion of darkness and melancholy to spring sunlight and hope. The style I can only describe as somewhere east of David Byrne, and west of David Lynch.*

The Travelling Companion

JOHN'S FATHER DIED and the landlord took back the rooms. On his last night in the old place, John dreamed of a beautiful woman with hair as yellow as the sun. She was standing at his side in a bridal dress, smiling at him and hugging his arm. He woke up. He wondered who the woman was. She was no one he had ever met, or was likely to.

When he got back from the crematorium, he took the last of the food out of the refrigerator and the last of the money out of the dresser drawer. There was fifty dollars and twenty cents. John left the car for the repo men. Now he had no home, no car, no family, no job. 'Better hit the road, I guess,' said John. And he set out to walk across town.

The first night he slept in a doorway. It was a big old warehouse, used to be a movie theatre. Now it didn't look like it was much of a warehouse either. John found some packing cartons and plastic garbage bags. 'These will make a great bed,' said John.

Nobody bothered him that night. He didn't have any more terrific dreams either. He woke up stiff from sleeping on the cement floor, and with a stiff neck from the wind. He walked on his way. He passed a church, so he went in and said a prayer for his father. John hoped the old man was in a good place. While he was praying, he thought of the woman in the dream, who had married him. He could still remember her face, her body, her hair yellow as the sun. 'I bet she doesn't even exist,' said John.

He went out of the church and saw a beggar. 'Spare change, buddy?' said the beggar, so John gave him the twenty cents.

As he walked, it came on towards night-time, and he started to think about places to sleep. That church today, that had been good. Maybe there would be another church somewhere round here that he could sleep in.

He wandered around a few hours, and found a church with a side door open. He went inside and into a kind of side-chapel. There was a coffin there on a couple of saw-horses. John looked in by the light of the streetlights and saw a dead body. It was a black guy, pretty tall too, by the look of him. 'It's okay by me,' said John. 'If you don't trouble me, I won't trouble you.'

He lay down in a pew, but he had hardly even started to go to sleep when the church door opened and two guys came in with flashlights. They didn't see John there. They went straight to the coffin and started roughing the body up, pulling it out of the coffin and jerking it about.

John sat up. 'Hey!' he called. 'What are you doing? Leave the poor guy alone, can't you?'

Those two men were surprised to see John's head appearing out of the pew. They turned the flashlights on him, and one of them asked, 'What's it to you, boy?'

John squinted and put his hand up to shade his eyes. 'What do you want to do that for anyway?' he said.

'Bastard owed us money,' the man said.

'How much money?' said John.

'Fifty dollars,' said the man.

John took the fifty dollars out of his pocket and held it out. 'Take it and go home,' he said. And the two men thought that was a good deal, so they did.

In the morning a man came in the church and when he saw John sleeping there, he told him he had to move on.

John got up and went out into the street. The city looked kind of different at this hour. It was real early still, there was hardly anyone around. The little six-legged people that live in the walls were still out, checking out the trash on the sidewalks, crawling in and out the garbage. They waved their feelers at John. 'Good morning, little people,' said John.

At last he made it all the way out to the highway. He walked along in the dirt with big trucks swinging past him, spraying him with dust and honking their horns at him. Then a car pulled up, a big beat-up Lincoln convertible. There was this tall skinny black guy driving. He had shades on and a suit coat with an old shirt with a frayed collar under it. 'You want a ride?' said the black guy to John. 'Okay, get in.'

They played the radio a while, and talked about the world. John thought the world was okay, pretty much. The black guy said he didn't know.

In no time they were coming into the next town. They had to brake for an old lady who came out of a house and stepped onto a crosswalk ahead of them. John stared at the old lady. She wasn't dressed like any old lady he had ever seen before, though he wasn't from around there. She was wearing a short tight black number, fishnets, and three black whips, one coiled around her waist like a belt, and one around each arm, knotted just under the bicep. She walked across the road on her high heel boots and then she fell down in the road.

John cried out, but the black guy didn't say anything. John started pointing through the windshield and remonstrating with him. 'She broke her leg, man!' he said. 'You can see it!'

'Well, okay,' said the black guy, as though this was a fairly reasonable proposition John was making. There was traffic pulling up behind them, people sounding their horns. The black guy ignored them. He got out and went and picked up the old lady and sat her in the car, on the back seat. She was in a lot of pain, John thought. The black guy got back in and started the car. 'You have to take her to a hospital,' John said.

The old lady started up, complaining. 'They won't take me at the hospital, I got no insurance!'

The black guy pulled out and turned left, driving round the block. 'You don't need insurance, lady,' he said, and he gave John a little bottle of oil. 'Here, John,' he said, 'put some of this oil on her leg.' So John did, and as soon as he rubbed the oil on, her leg was mended.

'Hey, all right!' cried John.

'We'll take you home, lady,' said the black guy. 'No charge.'

The old lady was feeling her leg, squeezing it with her hands and turning it this way and that, wiggling her foot. 'You gotta charge me,' she said. She started to laugh. John thought she was a pretty tough old lady. 'There ain't no such thing as a free leg,' she said.

'Ah, give me those whips,' said the black guy, looking at her in the mirror. He pulled in in front of the house she'd come out of. 'Put them in the trunk,' he said. 'It ain't locked.'

The old lady unwound her whips and put them in the trunk. She thanked them for mending her leg, and she skipped back indoors like a little girl. They drove on. 'She was a pretty tough old lady, I think,' said John, laughing.

'Sure,' said the black guy.

It was still quite a way to downtown. There were some big buildings there, real big, reaching up higher than the clouds. John wanted to go right up to the top of those buildings and look down at everything. He thought about his father, who was so high up now no building would ever get anywhere near him, no matter how tall they made it.

The black guy stopped the car at a bar on the edge of a lake. In the bar they had a cabaret, a guy came on and did some magic tricks, pulling quarters out of the hair of pretty women. The women squealed and put their hands to their cheeks. John laughed and clapped. There was a man there in the bar with a big dog. When the people clapped, the dog growled. 'I don't think the puppy likes the show,' said John to the black guy.

Then the showman unfolded a puppet theatre and set it up on the stage. There was a blonde lady movie star puppet and a big boss puppet, and a couple of cops, just like in a TV show. The showman made the puppets move about and did all the voices.

But the dog didn't like the puppets any more than he'd liked the magic. He got away from his owner and jumped right up on stage and grabbed the blonde lady puppet in his mouth and snapped her right in two.

John didn't know what to do. He grabbed his friend by the sleeve. 'Are you going to help her?' he said.

The black guy shrugged. He got up out of his chair and went up on stage with the showman. He hitched up the knees of his pants and squatted down over the two halves of the broken puppet. Then he reached in the pocket of his suit coat and pulled out his little bottle, and he put some of the oil on the puppet.

In a minute she was mended. She got up and gave him a shaky bow. Then she started to dance. The showman wasn't even holding her strings. Everybody in the bar gasped and clapped and cheered. They thought that was a really neat trick. The blonde lady puppet danced even better than before, just like a real person. The showman shook his head and laughed, and he said to the black guy: 'What is that stuff? You've gotta put some on the others, man!'

The black guy put some of his special oil on the other

puppets, and they all danced and jumped and chased each other round the stage while the people laughed and clapped.

The black guy came down off the stage and finished his beer. 'Come on,' he said to John. 'We have to go.'

In the parking lot, the showman came running out to them. 'Wait!' he shouted. 'What do I owe you?' He was like the old lady, he insisted he owed the black guy something.

The black guy pursed his lips. He said, 'I'll take those bolt-cutters you got in your trunk.'

John didn't know how the black guy knew the showman had any bolt-cutters, but the showman went over to the trunk of his car and opened it up, and he took out a pair of bolt-cutters and handed them to the black guy. He said, 'Thanks, buddy, you did me a real good turn in there.' Then he went back inside the bar to watch his puppets.

The black guy had been in a hurry to leave before, but now he seemed to have changed his mind. He and John went down to the lake and stood for a while, smoking cigarettes and looking out over the water.

While they were standing there a big white bird flew down out of the sky. It was a swan. It was singing. It came right down over their heads singing a beautiful sad song in a high voice like a woman singing on the radio. Then it threw out its wings and stuck up its head and fell down at their feet, stone dead.

John cried out loud. It was a beautiful bird, big and white and with a beautiful voice, and there it was dead. 'You gonna save it?' he said to the black guy.

The black guy pulled a face. 'It's dead, John,' he pointed out. 'That bird is dead.'

John opened his mouth to protest, then closed it again. What did he know? He didn't know anything.

The black guy was going back to the car. 'Didn't you know it was gonna die?' he said. 'It was singing!' He opened the trunk of the car. 'Swans always sing when they gonna die, don't you know that? Man, what do they teach you white kids these days?' The black guy took the bolt-cutters out of the car trunk. 'Good job I got me a pair of these,' he said. Then he went back and cut the wings off the dead swan. They were really big, those wings, and really pretty, with their shining white feathers. The black guy put them in the trunk with the bolt-cutters, and away they drove.

At last they were downtown. John was having a great time looking at all the big stores, the bright lights, the billboards with pictures of pretty women. 'This is the place to be!' he said.

They came to a major intersection. All the traffic was stopped, there were cops on horses and everything. 'It's a parade,' the black guy said, and John wound his window all the way down and stuck his head out of the Lincoln. There were cheerleaders shaking their pom-poms and guys in black leather on big motorcycles. Then there was a big shiny limo with a beautiful woman riding in it. Her hair was as yellow as the sun.

When he saw her John got very excited. He reached out and banged on the window of the next car in line. 'Hey!' he said. 'Who is she? That beautiful woman in the big car?'

The guy in the next car gave him a straight look. 'That's Mary Golightly,' he said. 'Her daddy owns this town.'

'I'm going to marry her,' John told him. It was the woman from his dream.

'You and every other poor sap down on his luck,' said the guy in the car. He revved his engine. They were still sat there, waiting for the lights to change. 'They have this little system going, Mary and her daddy, for prospective suitors,' said the guy in the car. 'What she does is, she asks you three questions. You guess them all right, you win. You don't guess them all right, she wins. She wins, you don't never guess nothing again. You get me?'

John said he did.

'Nobody ever hears nothing more about you ever,' the guy said, lighting up a cigarette. Then the lights changed and the cops started waving people on. 'Mary Golightly is one crazy woman,' said the guy in the next car, and he wound his window up and drove away.

The black guy looked at John. You couldn't see his eyes for the shades. He said: 'You wanna follow her?'

'Sure,' said John.

He sat back and the black guy made the turn.

The parade was over, but the black guy drove along the road and John kept looking at all the big houses until he saw the big shiny limo parked outside one. There were all these guys sitting around on the grass outside the gates. There was this one guy there, he looked like he'd been up all night, but he was happy as a cricket. He hadn't shaved and he smelled of whiskey. When he saw John climb out of the car he came over straight away, saying: 'What do you want, buddy?'

'I'm going to marry Mary Golightly,' John told him, and he pointed to the limo. 'That's Mary Golightly's car there.'

The man grinned at John like he was his friend, and he slapped him on the back and said, 'Okay, buddy, you know what you got to do? First, you go up to the house and check in with Elroy. Now see, these guys,' he said, waving his arm at all the men lounging around, 'they all come here every day, and they just hang around, trying to get up the nerve to go and check in.'

'What about you?' the black guy asked him.

'Oh, me, I already checked in yesterday,' said the man. He sounded very pleased with himself. 'When you checked in, you have to come back three days running. Every day you have to tell her what the last thing was she thought about the night before.'

'It's impossible,' said one of the other men, scuffing his shoes in the grass. He looked annoyed, as if he thought Mary Golightly was cheating somehow with her husband-finding system.

But the whiskey-smelling man said: 'I figure, what the hell. I got nothing to live for anyway. But if I should get lucky and win her, I've got everything to live for, right? What you get is her and half the city.'

'I don't care about the city,' John said. 'I'm going to marry Mary Golightly.'

The whiskey-smelling man thumped him on the arm with his fist. 'Right, guy!' he said. 'Think positive!' He pointed to the house. 'You coming up with me now?'

'Okay,' said John, and he went up to the house with him. A big man like a quarterback opened the door.

'Good morning, Elroy,' said the man, very friendly. 'Wish me luck, friend,' he said to John; and John said, 'Good luck!' Then Elroy let the man in to see Mary Golightly and try to guess what had been on her mind the night before, while John waited there on the porch. In a minute a bell rang, and then Elroy came out again, wiping his hands. 'Who's next? Are you next?' he said to John.

'Yes, I am,' said John. 'I'm going to marry Mary Golightly.'

Elroy wasn't interested. He took John's name and made sure he didn't have a gun on him or anything, and then he showed him into a room where there was a tired-looking man with a bald head and shades sitting behind a big desk talking to someone on the telephone. There was no sign of the beautiful woman from John's dream. John waited until the man put the telephone down, then he introduced himself. 'I'm going to marry your daughter, sir,' he said.

Mr Golightly didn't seem happy to hear it. 'Sit down and have a drink with me, John,' he said.

'Just a soft drink for me, sir, please,' said John. Then they sat and talked about baseball, and dreams, and one thing and another, until Mr Golightly stood up and shook John's hand and said goodbye to him. He held on to John's hand a while. He said, 'You know what, John? I like you. You're an okay guy.' He put his left hand on John's right elbow. 'Do me a favour,' he said. 'Don't come back tomorrow.'

John smiled at him. 'But I have to come back, Mr Golightly,' he reminded him. 'I'm going to marry your daughter.'

'Of course you are, John,' said Mr Golightly softly. 'Of course you are.' Then he shook John's hand all over again, and sent for Elroy to show him out.

John went back to the car. The black guy was listening to the radio. 'Where you been, man?' he said. 'I been waiting for you.' Then they rode off down the road to find a cheap motel.

John wondered why the black guy was hanging around with him. Maybe he just didn't have anything else to do or any place special to go.

That night the black guy said: 'Hey, man, too bad, this could be our last night together.' He sounded real sorry about it too. He said: 'Let's go get drunk.'

John never drank, really, but he had a couple of beers to keep the black guy company, because he was so friendly, driving him around and all, and pretty soon he fell asleep, right there in the booth.

The black guy drove John back to the motel in his Lincoln convertible, and took off his shoes and his pants, and slid him right into bed without waking him up. He stood looking down at him a moment. 'Sweet dreams, little buddy,' he said, softly. Then he went back to the car. He opened the trunk and took out one of the whips he had had off the old lady, and he tied it round his waist, the way she had worn it. Then he took out the wings he had had off the dead swan and fixed them on his back. He looked at himself in the mirror of the car and said: 'That looks real pretty.' He had cut a couple of slits in the back of his suit coat so the wings would stick out right.

Then the black guy flew back to the big house, and he perched himself up in a tree right opposite Mary Golightly's window, and there he waited. A quarter before midnight the window opened, and who should come flying out but Mary Golightly herself. She had on a slinky dress, red as blood, and shiny black boots right up to her thighs, and a pair of big black wings like a big old bat. Away she flew, downtown, where the big buildings were. The black guy stretched his swan's wings and followed, right behind. She couldn't see him because he was invisible.

As he flew, the black guy untied the whip from around his waist and he whipped Mary Golightly across the back. She really jumped, and craned her head around to look over her shoulder; but of course she couldn't see anyone behind her at all, so she kept on flying.

She flew up to a great big building, and right up to the top, to the penthouse. A muscular little guy in a snakeskin suit opened the door. 'Good evening, Miss Golightly,' he said, with a big grin and a bow, and he ushered her inside and shut the door. But before he got it all the way shut, the black guy had followed Mary Golightly in.

Inside it was all lit with tall black candles. The black guy saw whole peacock tails and stuffed animal heads and black mirrors on the walls. There was an evil magician there lying on a big bed with his boots on. He was dressed in a white fur bathrobe, and he was smoking a water-pipe. 'Hey there, babe,' said the evil magician in a rough voice like a big cat purring. His hair was greased down and parted in the middle, and there was a diamond in one of his front teeth. The room stank of incense and bleach, which the black guy knew was really amyl, and there was a big pink and silver chrome jukebox in the corner blasting out 'Alligator Rock' by Vince LaVerne and the Vipers.

Mary Golightly went and bent over and gave the evil magician a big long kiss with plenty of tongue. 'Let's take drugs and dance,' said the evil magician, and the way he said it, the black guy could tell Mary Golightly was totally under his spell.

In a while the evil magician took off Mary Golightly's black bat-wings, and he started to undress her. Under the red dress she had on some sexy black underwear, and the evil magician took that off too. When he had that off, he saw the whip marks on Mary Golightly's back. 'What are these, baby?' he said.

'Bad hailstorm,' said Mary Golightly, climbing into bed beside him.

'Right, baby,' said the evil magician.

After they had finished, Mary Golightly rolled over. She sat up on the satin sheets of midnight blue, and she lit a cigarette. 'So what do I tell this new guy tomorrow?' she said.

The evil magician snapped his fingers at the little man-servant in the snakeskin suit, who bowed and started to refill the water-pipe. The magician didn't look too interested in Mary Golightly's problem. 'Tell him one of your boots,' he said lazily, pointing to where they lay on the zebra-skin rug. Then Mary Golightly and the evil magician both laughed and started to kiss.

In a while Mary Golightly got up and put on her sexy clothes, and her boots, and her wings, and she flew off home; and the black guy followed right behind her, whipping her all the way. 'Well, hell,' said Mary Golightly, squirming, because no matter how she turned her head around, she couldn't see what it was that was making her smart.

When John woke up in the motel, it was morning. His friend the black guy was already up, sitting on his bed fully dressed. 'You know, I had a crazy dream last night, John,' said the black guy in his slow, easy voice.

'What did you dream about?' said John.

'A boot,' said the black guy, with a smile. 'A long shiny black leather lady's boot. Isn't that something?'

John agreed, it was a strange dream.

'Do you suppose Mary Golightly has any boots like that, John?' said the black guy.

John said he wouldn't know. 'But I may as well guess that as anything else,' he said.

When they came to the gate of the big house John shook the black guy's hand and said goodbye, and thanked him for all his help. Then he went up to the door and rang the bell.

The big man with the quarterback shoulders opened the door. 'Good morning, Elroy,' said John. 'I've come to see Miss Mary Golightly, the way she said.'

Elroy checked him out, frisked him, and then he stood aside and let him in the house, and closed the door behind him. He took him into the same room as before, where Mary Golightly's daddy was sitting behind his desk. This time Mary Golightly was there too, with her hair yellow as the sun. John said hello and good morning to both of them, and they both said hello back, but neither of them looked very pleased to see John.

Mr Golightly lit a big cigar, though he already had one burning in a big glass ashtray. He said: 'This one looks okay, sweetheart, why don't you take him?' He sounded more bored than anything, like a man trying to hurry his wife up in a supermarket. He said: 'Quit this game now, hon, before you get any older.'

Mary Golightly clearly had no intention of quitting her game. All she did was bite a little bit off one of her fingernails and say: 'He has to guess.'

Now when John guessed, and guessed right, Mary Golightly went white. She was horrified, and she was pretty mad. Nobody had ever even come close before. Her daddy, on the other hand, was in ecstasy. He jumped out of his chair and came round the front of the desk to shake John by the hand, bellowing to Elroy for champagne.

'Just a soft drink for me, sir, please,' said John.

When John came back down the drive the black guy was waiting in his Lincoln convertible to drive him back to the motel. He was delighted John had guessed right and survived to the second round of the competition. 'This calls for a celebration,' he said. 'Let's go get drunk.'

Now John never really drank hardly at all, but by the end of the day he let the black guy buy him a couple of beers just to be sociable, and then he fell asleep again, right there in the booth.

The black guy drove John back to the motel and put him to bed again without waking him. 'Sweet dreams, my friend,' he said, softly. Then he went back to the car trunk and put on his wings; and this time he took two of the old lady's whips and tied them round his waist. Then the black guy flew back to the big house, to perch up in his tree and wait to see what would happen tonight.

Round about a quarter to midnight, the window opened, and out flew Mary Golightly herself. This time she had on another short tight dress that was black as ink, along with her shiny black boots and her black bat-wings, and a lot of silver and stuff. 'Very nice,' said the black guy; and he stretched his wings and flew away after her, back to the big building downtown, with the evil magician's penthouse on the top. And all the way the black guy whipped Mary

Golightly with the two whips from around his waist. Mary Golightly jumped and shouted out, but look all she might, she couldn't see anyone behind her, no more than the night before.

When they got to the penthouse the chunky little guy in the snakeskin suit opened the door and smirked and said good evening again, and let Mary Golightly in; but he didn't know he was letting the black guy in too.

Tonight there were even more tall black candles than the night before. There was Jack Sheik and the Rattlesnakes on the jukebox, singing 'Hey Bop-a-ree-bop', and the evil magician was sitting on the bed in a crocodile-skin coat cutting up white powder on a mirror with a jewelled switchblade. 'Hey there, babe,' said the evil magician, grinning at Mary Golightly and flashing his diamond tooth; and just the way he said it made the black guy sure that Mary Golightly was the evil magician's most favourite of all his toys. Mary Golightly went and bent down over him and kissed his ear, and ran her beautiful long fingers over his shiny hair. 'Let's have a ball,' said the evil magician, in a voice soft as fur.

Then the evil magician took off Mary Golightly's clothes again, and he saw the whip marks on her back even worse than before. 'Hail again, baby?' he said.

'Really bad tonight, lover,' said Mary Golightly, as she climbed over him and pulled him into bed beside her.

When they were through, Mary Golightly sat up and stretched, and she leaned back on the silver lamé pillows with her hands behind her head and sighed. She seemed really pissed off.

'Bad day, baby?' said the magician.

'The hick guessed, sweetheart,' said Mary Golightly.

The evil magician could hardly believe it. He sent for the little manservant and had him bring more white powder, and open a bottle of wine or two. In a while he said: 'Okay, princess, here's what you do tomorrow. Tomorrow you tell him, one of your ear-rings,' he said, and he started to play with Mary Golightly's ear-ring, swinging it back and forth with his finger. He said: 'The way he'll figure it is, no one could be dumb enough to have something you wear after they already had something you wear and he guessed it.' And just the way he said it made the black guy sure this was one romance that was not fated to last a whole lot longer.

But Mary Golightly was so deep under the spell of the evil magician she thought he loved her true; and she kissed the evil magician and said he was the cleverest man in all the world. Then when they finished the wine and the evil magician said it was time for her to go, Mary Golightly got up and got dressed, and flew away back home again; and the black guy followed right behind her, whipping her all the way.

Next morning when John woke up, his friend was already dressed and drinking a cup of coffee. 'I don't know what it is about this place, John,' said the black guy, 'but I had another of those crazy dreams last night.'

John was all ears. Yesterday the black guy's dream had been good news for him. 'What was it this time?' he said.

'An ear-ring,' said the black guy. 'Nothing but a shiny silver lady's ear-ring. Is that weird or what?'

John agreed, it was pretty weird.

'I don't guess Mary Golightly would ever wear such a thing as that, do you, John?' said the black guy.

John said you never could tell. 'But I may as well guess that as anything else,' he said.

The black guy drove John to the big house again. Today there were more people than usual at the gate. There were reporters, and even a breakfast TV crew. A young lady pushed a microphone into John's face, and asked: 'Are you the young man who guessed correctly what Mary Golightly was thinking yesterday?'

'Yes, ma'am, I am,' said John.

'Would you like to tell our viewers how you rate your chances today?' said the breakfast TV lady.

'The best,' said John, smiling at his friend sitting behind the wheel of his car. 'I'm going to marry Mary Golightly,' he explained. Then he went up to the house, and Elroy let him in. He took him in the same room as before, where Mr Golightly and his beautiful daughter were ready to hear from him. John said hello and good morning, and Mr Golightly said hello back, and John thought he sounded pleased to see him, but maybe not too sure that John could pull it off a second time. But all Mary Golightly said was: 'Okay, mister, better make it a good one.'

Then when John guessed, and guessed right a second time, Mary Golightly really lost it. She shrieked at him, and she shrieked at her daddy, and she stamped her foot and tore her yellow hair, and she ran out of the room, all the while Mr Golightly was calling to Elroy for more champagne.

'I'll just take a soda, sir, please,' said John, 'if that's okay with you.'

So the third night came, and the black guy had bought John a couple of beers and put him to bed, fast asleep, and then he put on his wings and wrapped all three of the old lady's whips round his waist; and this time he took the bolt-cutters out of the car trunk too. 'You never know when these things might come in real handy,' he said, snipping little pieces out of the cold night air.

Well, that night there was a real storm, with wind and rain and snow and hail, but nothing could hold back Mary

Golightly from the call of the evil magician, so out she flew, through the storm, in a dress as white as the snow itself, and the black guy flew right behind her and lashed her for all he was worth with the old lady's whips, and he whipped that dress right off her back. When they reached the penthouse, the evil magician came and opened the door himself, and he looked up in the sky, holding out his hand palm upwards; and he shook his head, saying, 'Baby, you gotta give that stuff up.'

They had a great time that night, going at it so hard they broke all the mirrors on the walls. The jukebox blew a fuse and all the records melted in a puddle on the floor. But the storm was still raging, and the evil magician was hopped up tight, so when he told Mary Golightly it was time for her to go, he said he'd escort her home. Then he put on his sealskin shirt with the sleeves torn out, and a pair of wings just the same as hers, only bigger and blacker, so the black guy knew where Miss Golightly had got hers from; and the black guy followed behind while Mary Golightly and the evil magician flew back to the Golightly mansion, and he whipped them both good and hard all the way.

It wasn't until they landed on the sill outside the window of Mary Golightly's room and were kissing a last goodnight kiss that the evil magician hissed in her ear: 'Think of my head!' But the black guy was close by, standing on the roof, and he heard; and the minute Mary Golightly had gone in, he pulled out the bolt-cutters and cut off the evil magician's head. He put it in a plastic carrier, and in the morning when John got out of the car to go in the gate, he gave it to him, telling him not to open it until Mary Golightly asked her question.

Well, they were all there that third morning: press, radio, cable, cops and crowds – it seemed like half the town was there, waiting to see if John could make it three out of three, or if he was going to strike out. 'What's in the bag, sir?' the breakfast TV lady asked him; but John just smiled for the cameras and walked on up to the house, where Elroy asked him the same thing.

John patted him on the arm, real friendly like, and said, 'Now you know I can't tell you that, Elroy. It's personal. What's in this bag is between me and the young lady in there,' and he pointed to the door of Mr Golightly's office. And because he seemed like a regular guy, and besides, the boss liked him, and even Elroy liked him a little bit too, Elroy opened the door and let John take his bag in the office with him.

This morning, Mary Golightly didn't look so great. She looked as if she hadn't slept any too good, and she was pacing around her daddy's office smoking cigarettes one after the other just as fast as she could light them. Still John thought she looked more beautiful than ever, because today was the third day, and after today she would be his wife. So when she said he had to guess the third time, he did what his good friend the black guy had told him, and opened up the bag and showed her the evil magician's head. Mr Golightly shouted and Elroy swore and Mary Golightly screamed; and John said, 'Good thing I never showed that to those TV guys!'

The game was over, and John had won. Mary Golightly's daddy thought that was just great. He bundled everyone into his big shiny limo before anyone could change their mind, and off they rode to the courthouse with armed guards and outriders, all the cheerleaders and people parading, whistling and shouting and throwing their hats in the air.

In the car John tried to hold his bride's hand, but she pushed him away, so he sat there with the head on his lap. 'Who is that, sweetheart?' asked Mary Golightly's daddy.

'I ain't saying a thing,' said Mary Golightly, and she put

her hand on her chin and stared out of the window, sulking like a kid.

'Gimme that head, son,' said Mary Golightly's daddy to John. He held up the head so Elroy could see it in the rear-view mirror. 'You know who this is, Elroy?'

Elroy said he didn't know.

Mary Golightly's daddy didn't like the look of that head, whoever's it was. He didn't like the hair-oil, or the little diamond in the front tooth. The whole head looked bad to him, like it had belonged to some guy who was better off dead, for the good of society as a whole, not to mention his daughter. 'Piece o' crap,' he said. 'Open the window, Elroy'; and when they drove over a bridge he threw the thing in the water. Then they drove on to the courthouse and had a real fast wedding like in Vegas, and afterwards a big party at a big hotel.

Now Miss Mary Golightly had said 'I do' and married her hick because she had to, because he'd won her game; but she sure as hell didn't have to be pleased about it. In fact she hated the sight of him. He didn't look to her like he'd be any fun at all. 'You just stay away from me, okay?' was all she'd say.

'Oh, okay,' said John. He didn't mind. He loved her anyway.

'Jesus Christ, this is humiliating,' said Mary Golightly.

What with the party, all the loud music and people congratulating him and asking for his autograph and pushing microphones and cameras in his face, John didn't get to see the black guy all day. Then suddenly, after everybody else seemed to have gone home at last, there he was, sitting on a bench in the hotel lobby, drinking a can of beer. 'How's the lovely lady?' said the black guy.

John smiled and shrugged a little. 'I guess maybe she might come to like me a little, in time,' he said.

The black guy reached in the pocket of his suit coat. 'Here,' he said.

He was giving John a special wedding present. What it was, was three white feathers from a swan's wing, and a little bottle. It was the bottle with the rest of the special oil, the kind that mended things that were broken and made them better than new. John held it up and looked in it. 'You only have really a little bit left,' he pointed out.

'That's fine,' said the black guy. 'That'll be plenty. All you have to do is, when she gets in the shower, pour it over her head, and the feathers too. If she tries to get out of the shower, push her back in. If she tries to get out again, push her back in again.'

John looked at him seriously. 'I can't do that,' he told the black guy, in a low quiet voice. 'Disturb a lady? When she's in the shower?'

The black guy smiled. 'John, she's your wife,' he said.

That cheered John up. He stood up straight and put his hands in his pockets. 'Right! I said I was gonna marry her,' he said, 'and now I have! Well, I guess I'll see you tomorrow, friend.'

'See you tomorrow, John,' said the black guy softly.

Up in the bridal suite, all Mary Golightly would say to her new husband was: 'Don't come near me, I don't wanna see you.' But when she went in the bathroom to take a shower, he slid in sideways after her and sat on the edge of the tub, smiling at her with his stupid hayseed smile. 'I'm gonna call security,' said Mary Golightly.

'I won't touch you,' said John. He looked kind of bashful. 'I just wanna look,' he confessed.

'Jesus,' said Mary Golightly. 'Creep.' She despised him so much she flung her robe right off and stepped in the shower.

The second she turned round, John was behind her,

tipping some kind of oil over her head, and bits of something white that fluttered down into her face like scraps of torn-up Kleenex. 'What are you doing?' shouted Mary Golightly. She screamed and tried to get out of the shower, but John hung on to her tight, even though she was all wet and naked. She had turned into a swan black as coal with eyes of fire. 'I'm sorry, honey, I told a lie,' said John. 'That's not a very good start to a marriage, I know.' And he pushed her back under the water.

Mary Golightly was still struggling. She tried to get out of the shower again. By now she had turned into a swan that was all white, but with a black ruff around her neck. 'Sorry, princess,' said John. 'You're not quite all clean yet. I think you missed a little bit.' And he pushed her back under the water.

Then Mary Golightly came out of the shower, and this time she was turned back into herself, her real sweet self, the way she was before she even heard of any penthouse or any evil magician; and now she was ten times as lovely as before. She hugged and kissed John, right there in the bathroom, and told him he was just adorable, and she thanked him for saving her. And John thought maybe it wasn't such a bad start to a marriage after all.

Next day by the time they got up the party had started again, and it went on all day. John was so happy with his new bride, and so busy with everybody congratulating them all over again, that he never even thought about his friend the black guy until it was late and everybody seemed to have gone home again. Then just as he was passing through the hotel lobby on his way up to the bridal suite, suddenly the black guy was there again, leaning on the wall by the elevators, drinking a can of beer.

'I gotta take off, cowboy,' said the black guy.

'No,' John said, shaking his head, 'you have to stay here. I'm gonna give you a reward.' He thought he might be a little bit drunk. 'I'm rich now,' he explained. 'I own half the city, remember? And it's all yours, buddy. Everything I have is yours.'

But the black guy shook his head and patted him on the shoulder goodbye. 'You already did that once,' said the black guy. Then the lobby doors opened and the black guy went out and got in his car, the Lincoln convertible, which was parked right outside. The top was up, and the windows too, and as it drove away, John waved, though he couldn't see the black guy any more. It looked like there wasn't anybody inside that Lincoln convertible at all.

If it was Brian Aldiss who discovered me, so to speak, it was Mike Moorcock who taught me how. Not that he meant to; not that I went to him to learn. In a way, it was because that wasn't the deal that it worked so well. We'd both have been far too self-conscious otherwise.

Until recently I never talked much to Mike about work I was doing or wanting to do. As much as anything because of the way we met, as student and research subject, what I generally found myself doing was listening to him talk: about his work; about his week; about his current enthusiasm for Roger Rabbit, or Andrea Dworkin, or Margery Allingham. Sitting in the window-seat of his tiny, over-filled study in Barons Court, or in the pub after watching him smile his way through the boredoms and terrors of yet another signing session, I must have absorbed vast quantities of the benign radiation. By the dawn of that unimaginable day when Michael Moorcock left London and went to live in Texas, my debt to him had become quite unrepayable.

Except by passing on as much as I can to the next lot coming up; and in the form of little trifles like this next story. 'Temptations of Iron' is my contribution to the saga of Elric of Melniboné, Swordsman of Chaos, Albino Prince of Ruins, etc. etc. There's probably a world of significance in the fact that the character there who interested me most turned out not to be Ol' Pink Eyes himself, but his stoical and thankless companion, Moonglum of Elwher.

Temptations of Iron

'A SWORD, GENTLEMEN, a Sword!'

'The devil you say so!' cried Sinden Creache, starting forward. His other two opponents, long eliminated from the battle, gave a simultaneous groan and curse from the bench against the wall.

With a flashing white smile, the slender traveller showed his hand.

'The Three, to be precise,' he said.

And with a mocking bow he tossed the rectangle of pasteboard into the centre of the table.

Sinden Creache exhaled noisily. He looked distempered. He twisted his mouth in a sour expression, looking the victor full in the face as he had done but rarely that evening. He confronted the weak pink eyes, the bone-white skin, the hair, no less white. He seemed on the verge of making an accusation, a denial of some kind.

The traveller was unperturbed. He was used to animosity from the human race, unreasoning hostility being a characteristic humour of that upstart kind. His smile merely became a degree or two bleaker.

'The girl is mine,' said Elric of Melniboné.

From his seat in the corner, where he could watch both doors of the bar, Moonglum of Elwher whistled silently between his teeth. There'd be trouble now, one way or another. Then he grinned, his ugly mouth stretching broadly across his weather-brown face. Travelling with Elric what else had he ever had but trouble? Better a quarrel with a would-be welsher who didn't know who it was that had beaten him at tarocco than the ruined prince's displeasure. If Elric had lost the game it would have meant tedious hours of orations about doom and the malevolent gods. Let the stupid merchant try to talk Elric out of his slave. Moonglum's hand slipped to his belt, fingered the pommel of his dirk.

Then his vanquisher had the satisfaction of seeing the recalcitrant Creache turn to the brown figure crouching patiently by the hearth and snap his fingers.

As the slave stood up, looking nowhere but at the floor in front of her, Creache said loudly, loud enough for the whole company to hear, 'Stiis, this is your new master. Go with him and obey him. And may you bring him half the bad luck you've brought me.' Then he swept his cloak about him and strode rudely from the room, his friends hurrying after him.

Prince Elric, too amused by his victory to notice the discourtesy, reached out his long white fingers and touched the young woman under the chin, lifting her face to him.

She was sixteen, perhaps, of about Moonglum's height, and slim beneath her homespun dress. She was dark, her skin brown as fumed oak, her thick hair stained the same deep, burnt red as the palms of her hands. The skin was darkest, Moonglum noted, around her heavy lips and her eyes, which were large, and brown too. They stared suspiciously, sullenly, into Elric's red ones, and did not flinch. She had not favoured her departing master with so much as a glance.

There was no way to know whether she had understood his final order or not. She had made no sound all evening, nor given any sign of comprehension. She was completely mute, Creache had said.

'Stiis,' said Elric. 'Welcome into the royal household of the Bright Empire.' And he grinned mirthlessly.

Moonglum swilled the dregs of mucky ale doubtfully around in his pot before lifting it and downing them in a swallow. He grimaced. 'I remember you decrying the slavers' trade,' he observed.

Elric's eyes never left the face of the slave. Lightly he ran a fingertip along the line of her jaw from the brass ring in her ear to the corner of her chin. 'What is any of us,' he asked softly, 'but a slave? Back and forth across this blighted land we toil under the accursed whips of Law and Chaos, seeking only a little respite, a little place to rest our heads . . .'

Moonglum yawned hugely and deliberately, stretching out his arms and curtailing the monologue. 'Yes, well, that's where I'm going right now, Elric,' he said. 'Are you coming up?'

He was hoping he wasn't. He was hoping he would sit up half the night filling himself with the strongest wine, as he had done last night and the night before. Lodgings in Karluyk were so scarce he and his travelling companion had been obliged to take a single room, and sleep for Prince Elric was not a restful state for anyone else. For Prince Elric, the strongest wines were rarely strong enough.

Elric was gazing into the wide brown eyes of his prize. 'Yes, Moonglum,' he said. 'Yes, I think we shall.'

Moonglum glanced at him uneasily, and at the girl, who stared intently, fearlessly at her new master's alarming face.

The room was on the first floor, at the end of a crooked low corridor. Shadows bounded around as Moonglum entered. The only light was the ailing candle he himself had carried up from below. He looked in the corners and up among the rafters and under the beds before setting it on a dusty three-legged stool that stood beside his bed.

He supposed there would be less work now, if they had a slave. Still, certain basic tasks of housekeeping he would always prefer to do himself. He checked that the windows were latched, and wished as usual there were locks to them. Then, unfastening his belt, he removed the dirk from it and slipped it as delicately under his limp pillow as any pilgrim his amulet.

The young woman stood watching while Elric unbuckled the great sword from his back and laid it under his bed. Then, while her new master pulled off his boots, Stiis curled up to sleep on the foot of his bed, for all the world like a favoured hound.

Moonglum shook his head. He scratched his heavy mop of hair and raising one eyebrow at Elric in inquiry, blew out the candle-end. The room filled with the darkness of midnight and a new moon.

'Pleasant dreams to you, Master Moonglum,' said Elric lightly.

Moonglum dreamed he was riding high in a blood-streaked sky on the back of a metal bird. His perch felt highly insecure. Someone was shouting to him from the ground, and he felt an urgent need to hear whatever it was they were trying to say.

He woke. It was the voice of a man, crying out sharply. Moonglum was half-sitting up in bed with his knife in his hand before he recognized the voice and remembered where they were. It was only Elric, with his customary nightmares.

He relaxed; until another cry, a different voice, startled him.

She was not completely dumb, then.

Moonglum lay still and listened to the unmistakable sounds of sexual congress.

He was amused, and a little surprised. Since Myshella Elric had refrained from women, preferring to get drunk and declaim gloomy poetry instead. The little slave girl had obviously raised his spirits.

Moonglum grinned to himself in the dark. For all her

skin was so dusky, this Stiis reminded him of Shaarilla of the Dancing Mist, the wingless Myyrrhnian who had been Elric's companion when they met. Moonglum had been rather fond of Shaarilla, and often wished Elric hadn't dumped her. Elric had been in a bad mood after Shaarilla. He had tormented Moonglum with it for days.

As the Melnibonéan accomplished his climax Moonglum sighed silently. He turned his face to the wall and tried to pull the scanty covers over his ears. It was uncomfortable to have to listen to another man's pleasure while you yourself lay friendless. Perhaps they would be quiet now, he hoped. Elric was not a strong man, except when the evil force of the hellblade flooded his deficient arteries. No doubt he would fall asleep instantly.

The voice, when it came, struck ice into Moonglum's abbreviated bones.

It was low, every consonant soft-edged and every vowel deep and drawled. There was music in it, and yet it was subdued, as if disease or disuse compelled it to speak in a monotone.

'Melnibonéan, I charge you. I charge you. I charge you. I am your mistress now as you are my master.'

Moonglum cursed and sat bolt upright. He groped for his tinderbox.

The couple ignored him and his candlelight. Prince Elric leaned back on his elbows, more at his ease than Moonglum had seen him in many a day. The slave straddled his midriff, her heavy hair hanging down over his face, and both her hands pressing together on his narrow chest. But for her nakedness she looked more like a child playing a game with a favourite uncle than any kind of enchantress. Beneath the bed *Stormbringer* lay inert as a slug of pig-iron. That was the most reassuring thing Moonglum had seen since he lit the candle. Still he kept hold of his knife.

Elric's voice was nonchalant. 'What charge is this you speak of?'

'I am a princess in my land,' she said. 'I swore to find a champion to lift the curse that is upon Chlu-Melnoth, and never to speak until I had laid that charge upon him, and sealed it. On the barren coast of Samarianth I and all my companions were seized by raiders and sold into slavery. Since then I have watched and waited. Tonight the gods have smiled on me. They told me you were the one, Melnibonéan; and they told Sinden Creache to wager me on a last hand of cards.

'This is your task, champion. There is a demon abroad in Chlu-Melnoth. It cannot be defeated by iron, nor by cunning, but only by the dark arts. It will tempt you to use iron, but if you draw sword, it will eat you.'

She shifted on his stomach, arching her back. This had the effect of thrusting her bottom more prominently in Moonglum's direction. He winced. He preferred women with more meat on them, and he didn't care for all this stuff about demons and dark arts. Still, flesh was flesh. He lay back on his pillow, breathing slowly and staring deliberately up into the cobwebbed rafters.

'Fail me,' said the slave princess, 'and every hand in Chlu-Melnoth will be turned against you. Prevail, and you shall rule at my side. We are not a rich people, but you shall want for nothing.'

Elric spoke drowsily, as though her revelation had failed to make the slightest impression on him. 'It has been many a day since any man presumed to command Elric of Melniboné,' he remarked, 'or any woman either.'

His name seemed to mean nothing to her. 'I knew you for a man of the Dragon Isle, by your features and your accent. The gods marked you out to me. Melnibonéans have the ancient dark knowledge. Melnibonéans have no fear.'

Wonderful, thought Moonglum as he lay, listening to the hypnotic voice continue in the candlelight.

'And if I choose not to go?' asked Elric, as though she had invited him to a party.

'You will, champion. You must.' An element of languid self-satisfaction entered Stiis's tone. 'Since you lay between my thighs you have been dedicated to the task. The royal blood of Chlu-Melnoth has this power.'

'Then I shall follow you to the ends of the earth,' said Elric equably, 'and disembowel each demon you snap your fingers at.'

Moonglum grinned to himself. Elric was in a good mood. As for the girl's power of compulsion, Moonglum doubted very much it would outlast the night. Elric was humouring his new pet. Let him enjoy himself while he could. Gods knew it happened rarely enough.

Moonglum closed his eyes and left them talking as he slipped back into the merciful warm black waters of sleep.

Next time he woke it was what he had been expecting. They were good, quick and silent. Two of them were already in the room, a third climbing over the sill, his shape a dim blot against the stars.

Seizing his dirk, the hardy little outlander rolled sideways out of bed, trying to land lightly on the floor.

They heard him. One of them came for him while he was still crouching beside the bed, drawing his sabre from its sheath. The advantage of surprise lost, he yelled as he swiped at the intruder with his knife. 'Elric, wake for your life!'

Moonglum's attacker was armed with a short sword. As he swung Moonglum ducked under his arm, diving across the room towards the other bed. There was a cry – the girl – one of them had seized her, hauling her out of the way while the third sought to dispatch the Prince of Melniboné with a single swing, grunting, 'Here's your three swords!'

Moonglum's assailant blocked his way. Moonglum feinted high with the dirk and cut low with the sabre. The man chopped downward with his blade – a butchery must have been these northerners' sword-school. He missed completely. Starlight gleamed faintly on their blades.

Elric was awake. Moving swift as a snake, he had rolled aside as the sword came down. The girl cried something in an unknown tongue. There was the sound of a sharp blow on a skull and she fell silent. Her captor began to haul her towards the door.

Elric and his attacker were tangling hand to hand, the man must have lost his sword. Moonglum ducked another savage cut – there was an advantage in the dark, men often underestimated his size – he thrust up with the dirk and felt it strike home. His assailant shouted out and lost his footing. He went down, his head striking the floor, and lay still.

Elric shouted, landing a kick on the chin of his man and pulling free. 'Stiis!' he shouted. There was no reply, save for the dragging of her feet on the bare boards. Elric flung himself back against the wall at the head of the bed, drawing up his feet. Why did he not reach for *Stormbringer*?

As Moonglum reached the bed, there was a flurry of witchlight in the swarming air. Elric's attacker began to whinny and choke. He clawed desperately at something invisible in front of his eyes. Elric had caught him full in the face with some occult glamour.

Two down, one still fighting. Moonglum grabbed the blinded man, who struggled violently, eluding his hands.

Pausing only to pull the man's sword out of the mattress, Elric leapt across the unconscious form of Stiis, his naked body a white blur in the black air, white as the light of the all-seeing stars. The renegade prince menaced the thief with his own comrade's blade. 'Leave her, dog, and face me!'

They were made of something stern, these assassins,

though they had underestimated their quarry badly. The last man wasn't giving up. Backing into the doorway, he held the lolling woman up in front of him, forcing Elric to thrust awkwardly from the side, and parried the thrust ably with a flick of his short blade.

Moonglum could hear Elric panting hard. Passion and fury were a fine fuel, but they would not last the frail albino long. Why did he not take up *Stormbringer*?

The mage-maddened man was still whimpering and clawing at the darkness. Moonglum caught his arm and twisted it up hard behind his back. Levering the man off-balance, he reached up with his knife. He could see dimly the sinews of the neck, standing out like wire in the man's panic. He could see the artery, pulsing like a worm beneath the skin. The dirk went up, in and across. The man jerked like a cut pig, flinging blood across the window, and fell to the floor, coughing and kicking.

Stiis was also on the floor. Elric had cut the man's hand, forcing him to let go of her. Still he was fighting back, and Elric was hard beset. Moonglum could tell exhaustion was close. 'Elric!' he shouted. 'I am here!' He flung himself into the battle, slicing at the man with his sabre, ready to take his cut arm off altogether.

Then the sky fell on his head.

Elric saw Moonglum crumple, saw the first man Moonglum had felled standing over him, the stool in his hands. Gasping now, the thin blood pounding in his temples, the Melnibonéan flung the dead man's sword clumsily at him and threw himself to the floor, grasping beneath the bed.

The men closed in. Both of them had swords now. They lifted them up in the starlight like a triumphal arch.

The hilt of *Stormbringer* fitted itself neatly into Elric's clutching hand.

At once he was filled with a violent energy, like white fire coursing through his veins. His lean frame unfolded. He stood on tiptoe, brandishing the black blade, his white hair crackling, floating in a wild aureole around his head.

The room was filled with moaning, sobbing, a low, ululant cry of longing and despair.

And Elric laughed.

'Do you weep now, you mercenary creatures, you pond-scum, you beetles, you less than worthless things? Do you cry for your misspent lives and your paltry misbegotten pelf? Do you moan for mercy from Elric of Melniboné, White Wolf of the Sighing Sea?'

But it was the runesword which was moaning.

They knew him then. The raised blades fell clattering to the floor. The man who had taken Stiis turned and bolted for the door. The other, trapped by Elric in the angle between bed and wall, dropped to his knees. 'Mercy, Lord Elric! If we had known it was you –'

The keening rose to a high clamour, the song of a desperate vile appetite about to be sated.

Then in black lightning the black sword fell. Elric slew both, dispatching in a trice the mewling man at his feet, then turning with superhuman speed and leaping over the unconscious Stiis towards the man who was scampering down the corridor, clutching his wounded hand and crying out in terror.

Like a javelin *Stormbringer* flew, pulling Elric along behind it in its very eagerness. It lunged into the back of the fleeing man.

The bedroom filled with his screams. An unearthly crimson light blazed in from the corridor, bathing the three forms that lay motionless on the floor, and the fourth, Moonglum's victim, still slowly writhing. A hideous sucking sound came through the doorway.

Stormbringer was feeding.

Elric, brandishing the hellsword as though the room still contained an enemy, an army of enemies, came stalking back in. The blade twitched towards the sprawling Stiis and he shouted. 'No, Arioch, no!'

And the Chaos Lord was in sufficiently lenient or inattentive humour to allow his vassal to wrest the humming sword away from the slim form of the slave princess and plunge it into the breast of the man with the slashed throat.

Moonglum, rousing, his head throbbing, saw the room filled with the sick glow of the drinking sword and turned away in disgust. On hands and knees he crawled over to see if Stiis was still alive. She was breathing. She was unconscious, but not in danger, from her abductors, from her hurt, or from her rescuer. Moonglum found himself feeling grateful she had seen nothing of her new champion's eternal shame.

Moonglum lifted her and eased her back into Elric's bed. The room fell silent. It would be a moment or two before the landlord would dare venture out to see what screaming demons had invaded his inn. He would find three dead robbers, two sleeping guests, a manic albino sitting on a stool and blood everywhere.

'Take good care of my princess.'

It was Elric, sardonic, breathing hard. His eyes glowed like red needles in the darkness. It was obvious to Moonglum that whatever power of enchantment the slave claimed, Elric's hands were already at the disposal of a higher – lower – possession.

Elric righted the stool and sat on it, watching the last traces of gore as they vanished into the gleaming surface of the black blade. Moonglum's head was spinning. He patted his friend on the shoulder and stumbled back to bed, back into unconsciousness.

In the morning they sat in the yard on three of the shaggy

local horses, watching them bringing out the bodies. A small crowd stared at the cloaked and hooded albino with a mixture of awe and detestation. Elric ignored them. The morning smelt of dung and sour beer.

Moonglum's head ached. 'Will you not kill the merchant who sent these?' he asked.

'Let him live,' Elric said, 'for my greater glory.' And he smiled wintrily around, acknowledging the crowd with ironic majesty.

Moonglum looked askance at Elric's slave, not letting her see him looking. The princess appeared to have suffered no ill-effects from her attack: not even a bruise, Elric said. It was as if she did indeed have gods who protected her. She had found a jerkin of deep green worsted to throw on over her slave's dress and tied a silk kerchief of Elric's own, green too, about her neck. Sparing barely a glance for the sack-draped heap of drained bodies, she shortened the rein and turned her face to the north-east.

'Come, El-ric.'

'Your Highness.'

Moonglum looked concernedly at his friend's face as he rode past. It was unlike Elric to carry a jest so long; or at all, really.

They rode up to the high plains country. The ground was stony, the roads negligible. Flocks of drab brown birds rose from the meadows as they passed, sweeping up into the air like a thrown cloak and settling again immediately after. On the skyline, yellow and black barns slid gradually into dilapidation, while crippled windmills signalled forlornly into the sky.

They rested in a shed at an abandoned stockade. Moonglum lit a small fire for Elric's potion. While it was brewing, Stiis sat on Elric's lap. She kissed his mouth and murmured into his translucent, pointed ear. Endearments or incantations, Moonglum was not allowed to hear.

They rode on again shortly after noon. Down in a gully a man was digging with a heavy spade. He looked suspiciously at the travellers as they rode by above him, then bent again to his unprofitable labour, not even sparing them a greeting.

They slept at lonely inns, at farms, once in a barracks of shepherds. Hospitality in these parts was given grudgingly, and reckoned down to the last farthing. Stiis had, if anything, less tolerance even than Elric for such dealings. Moonglum thought she would have had her tame wolf skewer any who impeded her mission by so much as hesitating over the porridge. Impatiently, she urged them always onwards. Elric recited interminable epic poems in the Old High Tongue of Melniboné. It was all one to her, as long as he kept following.

Moonglum grew disgruntled. He had gone right off Stiis as soon as he knew she was not what she appeared to be. He got Elric on his own. 'I don't know what you see in her,' he said.

'She does not want me for my sword,' said Elric.

'Well, yes, but –'

Elric interrupted, gesturing delicately to his own breast. 'She does not know who I am,' he said, with pride. 'I think you cannot imagine what that means to me, Moonglum. Where should I find another such?'

Everywhere, Moonglum thought. Not everyone was as preoccupied with the doomed lord of the Dragon Isle as he was himself. There were other legends. Instead of saying this, he hitched up his breeches and scanned the desolate terrain: broken fences and cabbage fields. 'Lucky if you can find anyone out here,' he said.

They rode over a bridge guarded by a stone carving of a troll, or perhaps a real troll turned to stone.

'Tell me of this demon,' Elric said.

'It lives in the earth and is conversant with the dead,' said Stiis obscurely. 'Its shape is loathsome, its arms grip like the devil-fish. When it moves, it moves very suddenly, like a spider. It will devour several people at once.'

Elric merely nodded. Probably he had heard of it. Probably he knew some elemental that ate them for breakfast.

Moonglum reckoned he was having the worst of it on this trek. He was bored. His feet itched for city streets, his ears for human voices. When anything moved he grabbed Elric's arm and pointed excitedly. 'Look! A coyote! Look at that!'

Stiis ignored him, while Elric gazed dreamily. Gods knew what he could see out there. He was sustaining himself with herbs and chipped roots, pinches of powder from a small pewter box. *Stormbringer* he had swaddled like a newborn infant, binding the sword into its sheath with strips of woven stuff, then wrapping the whole thing in sack and binding it again. He slept with Stiis in his slender arms, and for once his sleep was quiet.

Moonglum scratched beneath his cap. He disbelieved in all of it: demon, princess and kingdom, all in one parcel together. He had never heard of any of the names. What was more, there was something devious about the route she was leading them. She consulted the stars more often than the ground. Yet though he mistrusted the cause and feared the outcome, for this reason, that the tortured prince seemed to be at peace for once, or thereabouts – Moonglum kept his own counsel.

'Tell me again of Far Chlu-Melnoth,' Elric bade her, mildly. His face was gaunt in the mornings, and he gasped sometimes while riding, as though plagued by old wounds; but still the runesword stayed wrapped on the packhorse, like a piece of baggage.

'*Far?*' echoed Moonglum, aghast. They sat on a high bluff with bleak grey downs beyond, eating roadbread and dried apples. There had been no sign of habitation for days.

'Not very far, little man,' said Stiis patronizingly. She considered him Elric's manservant, and it annoyed Moonglum every time he failed to convince her he was a free agent.

'*How* far,' he asked, adding for Elric's sake as much as her own, 'Your Highness?'

Stiis lifted her brown face to the sky. 'Soon we shall be there,' she said confidently. 'Can you not smell it in the wind?'

Moonglum sniffed obligingly. He could smell grass and horses and themselves. The wind was cold as ever, and as uncommunicative.

Elric touched Stiis's hand. He often seemed to be suing for her attention these days, as if he felt he depended on her in some way. To her he never spoke impatiently, let alone imperiously. Moonglum thought he had never seen him so passive. It was somehow unpleasant, like the moment between a bad cut and the pain.

'Stiis? Will you speak?'

Stiis shifted in place, drawing herself a fraction away from his tremulous white hand. She looked away across the downs and spoke at random. 'The horses of Inaurim are fleeter than the sharks in the sea. In Samarianth a woman once put her hand to the ground and picked up a diamond as big as a vulture's egg. My tent is large enough to race three horses around inside.'

Horses featured prominently in these descriptions, Moonglum had noticed. He had also begun to feel the absence of palaces; cities; houses of pleasure; buildings of any kind whatsoever, apparently. If he got one more inkling they were travelling as aimlessly as a fly on a windowpane, damn Elric's tranquillity, he would challenge her.

Then they were compelled to make a detour to find a

particular ingredient for the albino's increasingly elaborate infusions.

Stiis was displeased. There was nothing of the slave about her now, nor of the infatuated lover. 'Have I found Melniboné's only weakling?' she demanded, in a temper.

Haltingly and distantly, Elric explained these simples were feeding his magical powers. 'When he gets like this,' Moonglum interjected quickly, 'it means he's getting stronger and stronger. On another plane.' He paused then, wondering whether there was any truth in what he had said; and why he was defending him to her. He was sure the pair of them were no longer making love, though they shared a bed. Waking one foggy midnight, and drawn from his blankets by an eerie noise, Moonglum had come upon her standing naked on a knoll and laughing at nothing visible. Perhaps she had been sleep-walking. Perhaps that was it.

Another day, at no particular point, Stiis suddenly kicked up her mount and rode ahead at speed, around a clump of black trees and out of sight. When they caught up with her, she had the horse at a stand facing back down the track towards them. She was smiling, beaming. 'This is my land.'

Moonglum eased himself in the saddle and surveyed the waste all about them. Low gorse and raw rock, gritty yellow dust that clung to fetlock and mane, a pale hillside topped with dun-coloured trees – he saw no people, no tents, no horses; in short, no kingdom. He would have laid money they'd never left Ilmiora. He signalled to Elric with his eyes; but Elric was gone. His face looked starved as a shoulder blade, the skin taut from his cheekbones down to his long white teeth. His slanted eyes stared myopically over Moonglum's shoulder. 'There's nothing here,' said Moonglum loudly. They both ignored him.

They rode on, seeing no one, no sign of life all day. Somewhere about mid-afternoon, the princess led them down an escarpment to a black gash in the hillside. Moonglum understood it was the mouth of a cave. There was no smell, no spoor, but perhaps being a demon there wouldn't be. In Elric's company Moonglum had seen demons enough to last him several lifetimes and still he felt he knew nothing.

Stiis told them both to dismount. Elric roused himself. With vague but steady hands he unstrapped the sacking bundle from the packhorse and thrust it into Moonglum's arms. He did it as if it were an action he had been rehearsing long in his mind.

Gingerly Moonglum received it. He was more than reluctant, he hated handling the evil thing. Elric had once told him, 'Be wary of this devil-blade, Moonglum. It kills the foe – but savours the blood of friends and kin-folk most.'

It felt like a sword tied up in a sack. It didn't crawl or burn or start to sing. Still it gave him the creeps. 'What am I supposed to do with this?' he asked, his voice jerky and high.

'Keep it for me,' said Elric, and his voice was low. For a moment Moonglum felt a flush of relief, Elric had some plan, some secret purpose; but then the albino added, 'No matter how I beg.'

The princess signalled to Moonglum. 'Make fire,' she said.

Moonglum started to get angry. 'I beg your pardon?' he said, warningly.

'He will need a torch,' said Stiis.

Moonglum exhaled noisily. He set the unwelcome bundle down on the ground and groped for his box.

No sound came from beneath the earth, though it was a while before he had enough fire to light a brand. More than enough time for Moonglum to make his mind up.

Stiis held the torch and led Elric into the darkness. She looked glad to think her kingdom's pain would soon be over.

Moonglum waited a minute. Then he picked up *Stormbringer* and followed.

The ground went down steeply inside the cave, the tunnel following a fault between two kinds of rock. It was low, and twisted, but did not branch. It was not hard to keep track of the torch, or to stay out of sight. When the princess stopped suddenly by a large boulder, Moonglum drew back and flattened himself against the wall.

'Within is the demon's lair,' he heard her say. She sounded tense, excited. He looked. They had their backs to him. Stiis was ushering Elric before her through a natural doorway in the rock. She followed him in. Moonglum ran quickly to the boulder and ducked down behind it. He set his long bundle on the ground before him. Then, holding his breath, he peered round the boulder.

The doorway led into a cave several paces across and taller than a man. There were bones, strewn bones; accumulations of dirt and withered vegetation and rags that had been clothes; some metal that glinted among the rubbish, coins and jewellery, it might be, whose owners were no longer in a position to use them. Here there was at last a smell, the smell of something that was brutal if not exactly a brute; but it was faint and stale, as though the creature had not been here for a long time.

Maybe some other champion had seen to it. Maybe it had got tired of waiting and died of old age.

Maybe it was lurking.

Elric stood in the centre of the cave with his arms spread, as though about to begin an incantation. He turned to look around him. Moonglum ducked back out of sight. He heard Elric say, 'Where is your demon, princess?'

And the princess say, 'Here, prince!'

Then the light changed. A fierce glow of no true fire flared up around the boulder. Moonglum grabbed the hilt of his sword, then let go of it. He stood up, gazing into the cave.

There was a demon in there. It was pale, and wet, and

tall, its blunt head leering down over the unarmed Melnibonéan. It had large hooved feet, but no legs to speak of,
and great flat fins for hands. But even as Moonglum watched,
the fins folded moistly in against its flanks and were no more.
It changed shape as he watched, horrified, growing a beak
and a spray of fat tentacles. They shot out and gripped
Elric tight, drawing him into its body. Absent-mindedly, or
parodically, it sprouted a pair of breasts.

Then it spoke. Her voice was pinched, coming from the
rigid mouth. 'At last I can shed that feeble form!'

Stiis was nowhere to be seen.

Glistening mandibles extruded suddenly from either side
the beak, sluicing Elric's white head with smoking drool.
The tentacles were crushing the Melnibonéan's face into the
soft, scaly body. Whatever spell he had been about to utter
would never be spoken; and nor, in a second or two, would
anything else. His head was sinking into the demon's flesh.
It had legs too now, lots and lots of legs.

Moonglum swore, his gorge rising. He clutched his sword,
his knife. In agony, he hesitated. The creature had woven a
maze of lies as tortuous as the passage to this cavern. How
was he to know the right thing to do?

His hesitation lasted no more than a heartbeat. He had
no magic, no power but the power of steel. He drew sabre
and dirk together. If the curse was true, let it be proved on
his own body. Let the thing eat him, if there was a chance
it would let go of Elric of Melniboné.

Even as he started around the boulder, something rose up
from the floor and hit Moonglum painfully across the knees.
While he was hesitating, *Stormbringer* had taken its own
decision. With a screeching sound of ripped leather and sack,
it sliced straight through sheath, swaddling and all, and flew
into the inner cave, into the pinioned hand of Elric.

At that the demon crowed with great glee.

Stepping inside after the flying sword, Moonglum looked up and saw the girl's head and torso reappear, green now instead of brown, larger than life, naked and glistening. 'Now you are doomed, Lord Elric!' it squealed. 'Touch but one limb with that blade –' Its legs telescoped out rapidly, flailing slimily against Elric's back and legs. Moonglum dodged as one came slicing past, missing him by inches. ' – and you are mine throughout eternity!'

Elric dragged his face clear of her enveloping stomach. It came away with a sticky, squelching sound. 'This is no ordinary blade, foul creature! This is *Stormbringer*,' he screamed, his voice breaking, 'the Stealer of Souls! Blood and souls for Lord Arioch!'

Moonglum winced as the cavern filled with blinding red light and the stench of sizzling ectoplasm. The keening of the hungry sword was ten times louder in the confines of the cave.

And the demon laughed on. 'I know your sword, Prince of Ruins, as I know you! Destroyer of your own kind! Your own darling cousin!' it taunted him. '*Stormbringer* cannot harm me, my soul is long gone. Gone in fee for my invulnerability!'

The laugh grew higher, harsher, like the cry of a mad giant sea bird.

But Elric replied, and for all his frenzy there was pity in his tone. 'Is that what he told you, Stiis? Is that what Theleb K'aarna wished you to believe? Then laugh at this!'

And with a clumsy, powerful jerk of his arm, he drew back the black blade and plunged it up between the writhing breasts.

The demon screamed. 'It burns! It burns! Help me, Lord K'aarna! Help me –'

But there was no response to her prayer.

Moonglum averted his face from the flashing, flailing,

screeching wreck. When he heard the grating, gurgling sound of *Stormbringer* starting to feed, he decided he truly was going to be sick, and bolted for daylight.

Afterwards, while Elric lay resting in the cave mouth beside a small and cheerful blaze, Moonglum turned over the stuff he had picked out of the rubbish down inside. 'She was no demon,' Elric said, drowsily.

'Was she not,' said Moonglum automatically. Problems of classification he left to Elric.

Elric picked up a pebble and turned it idly between his long white fingers. 'She was human as you, once, when he took her.'

He tossed the pebble into the darkness. It fell feebly, a couple of feet away.

Moonglum, squatting over his finds, turned and looked suspiciously at his friend, his hands cupped on his knees. 'How did you know she was a puppet of Theleb K'aarna?'

'Her eyes, Moonglum. What the Sorcerer of Pan Tang took, he marked. Quite visibly, to one who has the witch-sight.'

Moonglum threw down the fistful of coins, careless how they scattered on the ground. He half-rose, crouching as though to leap on Elric and throttle him.

'And we followed her all the way up here? You slept with her, knowing that?'

Elric was not angered, or distressed, or apologetic. His voice creaked like a gate in the wind.

'I felt sorry for her, wandering in the world, not knowing that her master is dead and food for worms.'

The old familiar mocking tone was back in his voice, and he smiled; but his companion saw how he shivered, despite the fire, and how pale his pale lips had grown. Moonglum's rage turned suddenly cold as fear, a fear he had not even felt in that hellish cave. He wondered what manner of man this was, this bleached, driven scarecrow he had linked his fate to.

'She pleased me, Moonglum.'

One evening in what I suppose was the latter part of 1992, my phone rang, and a soft, slightly urgent, Lancastrian voice asked to speak to Mr Greenland. When I assured the man he already was, he apologized for disturbing me, and in the most courteous manner imaginable invited me to address a future meeting of the Preston SF Group; and he gave his name as Bryan Talbot.

'Bryan Talbot?' I said.

'Yes,' he said.

'Luther Arkwright,' I said.

'Yes,' he conceded.

I was mildly astounded. Bryan Talbot, creator of Luther Arkwright, was ringing me, inviting me to give a talk to him and his friends, calling me Mr Greenland!

At that point I knew the transcendental Luther only from the early chapters of his adventures published in the late seventies, in the Edinburgh sf comic Near Myths. When I made the promised visit to Preston, Bryan insisted on giving me the complete trilogy, rare as those intricate and minutely-drawn volumes have now become.

Luther Arkwright, an agent able to travel between parallel universes at will, was much inspired by Michael Moorcock's

Jerry Cornelius; and as with Jerry, there was a notion that other writers should be encouraged to make fictional use of Luther and his crew. Before I had even begun to consider the possibilities, Mary Branscombe, then involved in organizing the 1996 Easter sf convention where Bryan and I were both guests of honour, told me most directly that the character I must write about was (once again) not Luther himself, but his tutor and lover Rose Wylde; or rather, Rose's alternate selves, on all the other numbered parallels, whose feelings she can share by telepathy.

I think Mary must have a glimmer of telepathy herself.

A Bunch of Wild Roses

01.53.11

LIKE A ROUND white bird, the moon sits in the bare branches of the lime tree. The lime tree stands outside the window, like the streets, like the rest of town, like the rest of the world.

The sky behind the moon is flat and grey as the paper they give me when they want pictures from me. The pictures I make are a joke. I don't know what anything looks like there, and I couldn't draw it if I did.

They ask me to paint my sisters. I say no. They say, don't your sisters want to be painted? I tell them, I don't feel like it. Then they say, why don't you paint a picture of the feeling? What colour is it? they ask me.

I give up. I tell them it is green, and when they say, green, I say, no, more blue, actually. I told Carl the truth, that it is red, red as fire, red as the guts of a volcano.

Carl said, a volcano! That would make a good picture, hey, Rosie?

The only colour inside here is white. They dress in white. They wear white dresses, and dress us in white gowns, and cover us with white sheets. A servant in white comes to draw the curtains and shut out the moon in the tree.

Some of my sisters don't know what a moon is. Others know lots of moons.

'Hello, Rosie,' says the servant in white. 'Are you going to help me with the tea today?'

*

259

00.21.31

The apartment is at Vyšehrad, above the cold grey river. The drawing room we have had papered in olive green, with some of the new automatic découpage on the walls, exact silhouettes of famous personages cut out of black paper. I am at my desk beneath the window. Flags are flying from the towers of the castle.

I am not looking at the flags. I am looking into my mirror.

The door of the drawing room is open. From the studio sounds a perpetual chipping of chisel on stone. It is the sound of Johen, putting feathers on the wings of an angel.

I have ceased to hear the chisel.

I am feeling pain in my arm, the pressure of upright bars of metal. Inside I feel boredom, and a slow deep anger like a buried mill eternally grinding. The buffeting of the wind in the hills changes to a distant growl of internal combustion vehicles, hundreds upon hundreds of them, rushing through the streets of some other city.

'Rosa?'

Johen is at the door, looking in at me.

I become aware that the chisel has stopped. I feel for a moment as if I had been asleep, and dreaming. It is more like dreaming than anything else.

Johen hesitates on the threshold, like a wary old animal tasting the air. His hair and beard are woolly grey. The cloth I tie around his head against the dust has slipped, as usual.

I say: 'Do you want tea?'

He comes in smiling. He comes close. His eyes are shrewd and brown as chestnuts. 'Here,' he says, holding something out to me.

It is a cup of tea.

*

29.06.06

This one doesn't drink tea. She never drinks, or else drinks constantly, water sluicing into her mouth as she swims. She eats nothing but fish, and eels, and soft grubs. She teases the sea snails out of the weeds and eats them, crunching them whole in the shell. She browses the cliffs of the continental shelf, chewing up jellyfish.

Her hair is long and silver-green. Her hands are small, the fingers webbed. Her body is long and lithe, her eyes are large, her skin has the faint phosphorescence of good health.

She is never alone. Her tribe is always all around her. The tribe swims numberless and strong. They are perfect kin, and know one another's minds. Thought flowers amongst them, common and luminous as bubbles.

They call to one another, marking out positions, alliances. From the muscular throats of the signallers, strange music warbles, glottal, imperative.

On, on, on.

Beneath her silver hair her gills pulse red as wounds.

01.53.11

It is winter. At the end of afternoon when the servants in white come to close the curtains they say: 'What happened to today? It was so short!'

To us, each afternoon is eternal. The interval between a pink tablet and a blue one stretches out like driving in fog. Outside the cars growl in the street.

My sisters come and go like angels in my head.

Mrs Cadmorland is shouting at the television again. Something she sees, from long ago. Such a bad thing, it keeps coming back. Mrs Cadmorland hasn't got sisters. No one here has, no one here whatever they tell you, no one but me me me me me.

Some of my sisters are happy. Some of them are not. A lot of them are fighting. I scratched Carl's face once. That was a time I had a fighting sister on me. They have big machines, some of them, for killing people, but I had only my fingernails.

I told Carl I was sorry for scratching him. I told the doctors about the killing machines, the crucifixes on the dashboard, the houses exploding. Sister touched my forehead and smiled while the doctors spoke in numbers. 25 mil, 30.

That was a long time ago. Now I help serve the meals, fetch the papers, fill the water jugs. I am stable now.

00.21.31

Johen glances at the mirror, the papers on the desk. 'Have we got a visitor, darling?' he asks. 'Which one is it today?' He does not mean to be flippant. My absences make him nervous.

I bend my head. He strokes it. There will be stone dust in my hair now. I do not care.

My hand stirs the papers. Blank forms, scraps, sketches with arrows and notes. Remarks and question marks.

Johen releases my head. He tries so hard. 'Is someone hurting her?' he asks.

I sip my tea. Rosie's feelings are like loud music, a crazy orchestra all playing at random, *fortissimo*. I feel the hot sheets, the drugs she loves and hates. Sometimes she is afraid.

'They're exploiting her,' I tell him. 'That's how they do it there. They lock you up and tell you what to do. If you don't do it, they ignore you.'

Johen does not understand. Johen trusts only what he can

touch and feel. Earth and stone and flesh. Me. Not all these not-me's.

I stand up and lean on the desk, looking down the windy salient. I can feel Rosie weaving her arm through the bars at the head of her bed again. She pushes, jamming it tight. The pain tells her she is alive.

When I was sixteen, I went to a fortune-teller. It was in St Moritz, at a matrimonial ball. I did not want to go, but all the other girls had been, so I had to.

Johen is at my back, nuzzling the short hair above my ear. 'Rosa. No one could ever ignore you.'

29.06.06

The tribe rushes across the uplands through the indigo cold.

On this parallel, clearly, life returned to the sea, or never left it. Civilization is unknown, unless it means this motion, all forging forward through the water together, feeding and protecting each other.

The sea maiden swims in the first third of the tribe, low down. She swims with the mateless females, the ones whose job it is to groom the chief elders, to minister to minor injury or disease. She sees the ocean floor pass beneath her, a furry tract of microscopic shards and shreds, discontinuous and vague in the indigo murk. The uplands are pitted, eroded. From black crevasses attenuated forests of weed reach up. Spindly fronds finger the darkness, waving ceaselessly.

Overhead a couple are mating. The male grips the back of the female's neck with his powerful jaw. If impregnated, the female will spiral up into the centre of the tribe, remaining there among dozens of others who have recently given birth, or are about to. Around the nursery swims a protective sphere of adolescents, female and male alike.

As the infants grow and mature, they start to grow bolder. They stretch their bounds. They swim out from the centre, a little way at first and clumsily, tiring soon. Soon they will progress through the body of the tribe to places ordained for them by talent, kinship or affinity. Individuals with good eyesight move up towards the light; those with good hearing move down and out to the sides. Those elders who have not become navigators or war leaders fall year by year to the rear, from which they urge the whole tribe on, calling the tune.

The sea people sing. The song runs through them all, holding them together, sustaining them in formation. Its rhythm is the tireless beat, beat, beat of their gigantic tails.

01.53.11

'Let's sit you up, Rosie. That's the way.'

A white servant is smoothing my white sheet over me, tucking me in. 'You've got visitors, Rosie!'

Sister and a doctor with some students. They home in on me, a purposeful formation, they have some business with me.

The doctor is in front. His hair is like sheep's wool caught in a fence. His face comes up pink and creased everywhere and every way. His face speaks.

'Hello, Rosie.'

White sheep beard, white sheep hair, white doctor coat open over brown corduroy jacket, blood-red sweater.

'This is Dr Shivers, Rosie,' says Sister, in her voice like a bell that rings.

I say hello. The woolly man is holding out a bar of Turkish Delight. 'I know you like Turkish Delight, Rosie.' He is gentle. 'Do you want it? Here, it's for you.'

Turkish Delight. There isn't any here.

'Isn't that nice, Rosie?' say the servants.

'Thank you, Dr Shivers!' says Sister.

The woolly man gives an absent-minded smile and puts his hand back in his pocket.

I pull the paper off the Turkish Delight.

'Would you like a bit?' I ask them all.

'No, thank you, Rosie,' says Sister. 'It's all for you!'

The woolly doctor leans on the bottom of the bed, one hand on each corner, looking up at me. He watches me eat.

'We're going to try you out of here for a bit, Rosie,' he says. 'See how you do one-to-one.'

I don't understand him. Really he is talking to the students, of course. His name is Dr Shivers. It is a cold name. That must be like always taking an icicle with you, always wherever you go.

00.21.31

The fortune-teller's tent was full of clouds of steam and incense smoke. There sat a crafty-looking old woman, shuffling a pack of cards. Her face was stained with what I supposed must be beetroot juice. When I came in she stared at me as if I was a painting on a wall, and grinned triumphantly. There was not a tooth in her head.

'Rose,' she said. 'I knew 'twas you.'

I said: 'My name is Rosa.'

She nodded. 'It can be that,' she said.

Someone had told her, obviously.

'I don't believe in fortune-tellers,' I said.

She chuckled and shifted in her chair, leaning to a little teapot she had. 'You'll take a cup of tea with me, though, *Rosa*, won't you?'

Reluctantly, I accepted.

The old woman shuffled her pack, fanned it out and offered it to me.

'And you'll take a card.'

'If I must,' I said.

It was a picture of a man about to step off a precipice. He was not looking where he was going.

'That'll fit you,' she said.

Le Fou, it said beneath. I knew that was *The Fool* in French.

Insulted, I would endure her no longer. I tried to stand up. I could not.

It was drugged, of course, the tea.

I can picture the ward where they keep Rosie. White beds, big windows, a tree outside. It never changes. Other things get confused. There was a man that came to see her and I tried for a picture of him, but all my mind would show me was Johen.

Johen leans down his dusty head to mine.

'Which one have we got today?' he asks. As if they were entertainments, kineo shows.

I hold him. I feel the energy thumping in his body, smell the sweat of his labour.

I must not be cross. He cannot understand.

02.75.02

In New Amsterdam, in a north side apartment on the twenty-seventh floor, Rose Wylde is having some people over for dinner. Her kitchen looks scarcely large enough to boil an egg, but Rose is having eight people over and doing five courses. She does it automatically, frenziedly. She loves to do it. She balances pans on every available surface and fills the room with steam.

The first course, very tiny, very potent grapefruit sorbets, were made last night and are safe in the chiller. The leek and lentil soup is simmering on the back left burner; the Palphramond celeriac custard on the back right.

In the oven are an earthenware casserole and a blue-figured pie dish of Nederland china. Rose lifts the lid of the casserole and gives the garbanzos a stir. She slides out the shelf and frowns at the meringue.

On the stereo Bessie Smith sings about her handyman, how he fixes her leak so well. Rose chops spinach, singing along. She is in a state of bliss, though she would think you were crazy if you said so. 'State of chaos, you mean.' How could she have forgotten the apricot jelly for the First Lady Pudding? And she hasn't even phoned Jan yet, to remind him he's supposed to be coming, and get him to bring some of his Ghandian tea.

'Half the time I don't know where I am!' says Rose.

01.53.11

Dr Shivers says: 'Call me John.' He takes me out of the ward, out of the building, along some paths and up some stairs to a flat.

There is a bathroom and a kitchen and a living room. No one is at home.

'Who lives here?' I ask.

He says: 'This is my home, Rosie. Where I live.'

There is a picture on the wall of sheep in a field.

He says: 'You're going to stay with me for a while. You're going to have my room,' John Shivers says, 'and I'll sleep in the spare room.'

He talks as if we were old friends. Why should I be his old friend?

'How much is the rent?' I ask.

He snorts as if I have said something funny and scratches his woolly head.

'As my guest.'

There will be something. Some reward for taking me out of the ward.

Suddenly there is a battle, and I, I am in charge. There are aeroplanes buzzing overhead, shouts, explosions. *Blue Base to Major Wylde*, says a metal voice. *Captain Pascal reports ground casualties severe. Recommends further strikes. Shred the place, he said.*

I run into the bathroom. There is a lock on the door. In the ward, our bathroom doors didn't have locks. I lock the door, then unlock it because I'm frightened, then lock it again. I sit on the toilet.

Base to Major Wylde, Base to Major Wylde. The planes are trapped behind the mirror. They sound like angry birds.

Go away, I think, but they can't hear.

John Shivers is outside the door. 'Are you all right in there, Rosie?'

I don't answer. My sisters say, *Don't answer!*

'You don't have to lock yourself in the bathroom, Rosie, you know,' he says. He is speaking to me in an ordinary voice, as if there wasn't a door between us. 'You've got the bedroom,' he points out.

I screw up my eyes. 'I'm all right!' I say loudly.

I hear him going away.

Time skips, jams. I am at a party, laughing, kissing someone, a young man. I am running through a jungle city, firing a handgun at a dark shape in a doorway. I am stretched out on a pallet, dying of fever, drowning in putrid sweat.

I unlock the bathroom door.

He hears the sound, but does not come. He calls out: 'Is there anything you want, Rosie?'

Things I want:
A big garden with fish.
A telephone.
Goldfish. Gold.
A man with a penis.
'I'm making some tea, Rosie, do you want some?'

00.21.31

While Johen directs the siting and unwrapping of his new angel, I drift away among the graves.

Line upon line they stand, precise and pretty as the shops of Malá Strana. They are engraved with emblems: hour-glasses and bones, medallions and musical instruments, like so many signs of articles for sale. Little cupboards with glass doors display a dusty vase of perished maidenhair, the black twist of an extinct carnation.

'The fossil record,' a poet once called these memorials. Individual lives, portions of time, all faithfully preserved in stone.

The fortune-teller asked me to say what number was printed on the card of The Fool.

I did not mean to speak, but my will was no longer my own.

'Zero,' I said.

'So what number, now, would two fools be?'

I had begun to blush.

'Say it, child,' urged the sybil, grinning her horrible tooth-less smile.

'Zero–Zero,' I said.

'And what do you know about Zero–Zero?' She made it sound like something wicked and forbidden.

The heat was rushing all the way down my body. I felt as if I had become hollow.

I heard my voice say rapidly: 'When I was little I used to have dreams about a magic world –'

The fortune-teller tutted at me.

'You still do.'

I was dizzy. 'You can't know that,' I said. 'I've never told –'

She took my hands in her wrinkled old ones. 'Rosa, Rosa, hush,' she said. 'This is the wonderful news. Are you ready for this? It is real, child. Zero–Zero. It is *real*.'

The fortune-teller's tea opened my mind. I sailed out into the multiverse, understanding everything there is with every cell of my body. I heard a voice calling. The voice was my own voice.

It was the Rose of Zero–Zero.

29.06.06

The sea maid catches a stray jellyfish, a small one with brown and white stripes, not big enough to share. Indulging an ancient reflex, her neighbours try lazily to snatch it from her. She defends herself easily, and tries to bolt her catch. Her neighbours laugh, pointing at the slippery mass of it bulging from her mouth. She flicks herself away, ignoring them. The jellyfish she subdues, gnawing it into a sticky pulp.

Her neighbours often find her odd. She moves sometimes to a song no one is singing, no one can hear. She makes the shapes of unknown words.

The language of the tribe has many words. *Sunlight, child, vortex.* The word for *sky* is a gesture of the hands above the head, pushing away. It is the same as the word for *death.* They have no word for *air.*

A school of tiny purple fish erupts out of the undergrowth,

scattering from the intruders. To the scanning tribe the intricate trajectories of fifty score tiny purple fish appear, like a billowing fan of time. The tribe recognizes the fish, and decides in a second to disregard them. Better prey ahead.

01.53.11

'Fully equipped, we are, here,' says John Shivers, the woolly corduroy man. He stands in the kitchen, opening cupboards. 'Corned beef, rice pudding. Knives and forks. What do you fancy, Rosie?' He holds his head on one side. His beard is like things exploding in a comic.

'Fancy some rice pudding?'

'No.'

No one asks you to fancy things. Fancies get you tablets.

It is not as hot here as in the ward. There is no Mrs Cadmorland shouting, no disinfectant smell. I don't have to fill the water jugs, or even make my bed. Green servants come and make the beds and clean.

John Shivers wants me to talk. He keeps trying. He wants me to talk about when I was a girl. 'Did you ever wish you had brothers and sisters, Rosie?'

'What would I want with brothers?'

He knows about my sisters. Of course he does. In the files. Papers, pictures, tapes. Truth, stories.

He has a picture, in his wallet, a picture of three boys on a boat. 'Look, Rosie – me and my brothers. I was eighteen.' He wriggles his bottom in the chair, opens his corduroy jacket and slaps his woolly belly. 'Put on a bit of weight since then, eh, haven't I?'

I go in the bathroom, where he doesn't come. In the bathroom mirror, my sisters come one by one.

*

00.21.31

I dreamed we stood, the Rose of Zero–Zero and I, in a clockmaker's shop, surrounded by clocks that all showed the same time. She called them *The Parallels*. Parallel worlds, she meant, that run on forever side by side, like these graves. There are countless parallels, she told me.

We are the places where they touch, said the Rose of Zero–Zero. We must touch each other, she told me, as often as possible.

A touch is often all there is: pain without an injury; an enigmatic scent; the feel of unknown clothes against the skin.

Here is a Modernist grave, square and bare as a suburban fireplace. ENSKA 1870–1931.

When one of us dies, there is a shock, like being woken suddenly by a frightening noise. You never get used to it. You feel the seizure of the heart; the rude explosion; the sudden stop of breath as death impales you.

Here is the bench where I have come to sit, with my mirror and my files.

Sacrifices, wars. Rose of Zero–Zero, collecting souls for her Valhalla. I wonder about it all sometimes.

A bird sings briefly. Over the monuments a familiar sound: the sound of chipping stone. Johen, putting the finishing touches to his angel.

03.04.88

Rosemary Wylde was always close to the sky. She was born in the high country near Spitzberg, on 24 July 1960, in her grandparents' house. Her mother, Elma, was the daughter of a judge; her father, Edmund, was a northland timber trader. It was a love match, and did not last.

In her tenth year, as a reward for coming first in a national maths examination, Rosemary's grandmother took her to an airshow. To the ecstatic child the pilots seemed to be rolling their wings especially for her. Five years later, she had talked and charmed and wheedled her way to the controls of a DN307. She became the youngest person ever to fly, quite illegally, across the Baltic Sea the long way. In the air, the problems of home and family were beneath her. So also in the elevated realms of mathematics, at which she continued to excel, when she could be persuaded to study.

Licensed at eighteen and with her inheritance prised prematurely from the durable old lady, Rosemary bought herself a bright yellow Maserati Vega, which she crashed on take-off eighteen months later, at Laagen. After that there was nowhere to go but the forces.

The Herzogovinan War brought out the best in Rosemary Wylde. Separation from her increasingly quarrelsome mother; the joy of flight justified by duty; an external enemy on whom to avenge her woes. Her calculatory skill re-emerged as a flair for strategy. Assisted by the influential if elusive Commander Arkwright, her promotion was rapid.

'Message from Blue Base, Major Wylde,' says the saluting subaltern. 'A Flight is on her way. Orlov, Mittenaud and Pascal coming home.'

The major's leather gauntlets caress the railing of the balcony. It is a tough engagement. Across the reservoir, the big guns flicker, pounding the enemy positions.

'Home for tea,' says Rosemary Wylde.

01.53.11

'Not Shivers, Rosie: *Chivers*. Like on the marmalade.'

There used to be a little black cartoon man on the marmalade label, a little black golliwog. Now he has gone, vanished from the earth like the dinosaurs.

This morning, I made the tea myself. I filled the kettle and plugged it in and turned it on, and when it boiled I warmed the pot and put two tea bags in and poured boiling water on them. I put milk in the mugs and then the tea, when it was ready.

'Cheers, Rosie,' John said.

I took the last pink tablet on Thursday. Another doctor came and looked at me, and John said we'd see how we got on without pink tablets. The blue still at night, but no more pink.

I carry a mirror around now, from room to room to room.

When John sees me, he says: 'Ooh, another wrinkle, Rosie? A grey hair?'

Some of me are laughing, some of me are crying. One of me is underwater eating fish. One of me sits in a cold garden under heavy trees. I feel the thick fur of her collar, the taut metal clips on her nylon stockings, the wooden slats of the bench beneath her.

Sometimes that one knows me.

I grope behind me with my hand. No bench. The settee, in the living room. We are having our supper. The radio is playing.

I say: 'I am disturbed.'

'Not really, Rosie,' says John Chivers from his armchair. 'You only think that because that's what everyone's always told you. You're pretty stable, really, I think.'

I look at him. He is a sweet daddy sheep. 'Do you like living here with me, Rosie?' he says. 'You do, don't you?' As long as you obey him and agree with him, he's happy.

'You're pretty stable now.'

'Until my sisters speak,' I say.

He stretches, scratching his chest. 'We've talked about your sisters, Rosie,' he says. 'Don't you remember?'

00.21.31

The graves are decorated with blots of candle wax, fresh sprays of larch. In the distance, a muffled figure stoops.

Others come here to commune with the departed; I with those who were never here. On the bench I open my attaché case and take out my mirror.

I hold the mirror to my eyes. I concentrate.

The sound of the hammer and chisel fades again.

The eyes in the mirror are mine; then not mine, and I flip. I feel a pull, as if I were travelling rapidly backwards through the back of my head. The bench has become an armchair. There is music playing, a little audio receiver on a shelf.

And there is that anger, like a banked fire, like the dull tiger in the Petrin Park Zoo. It is Rosie. She is out of the ward! She is somewhere else, in someone's living room, eating a slice of toast.

There is a man in the room with her. He is talking to her. I cannot make out a word, but I can hear his voice. I know his voice.

Jolted back to myself, I gaze stupidly around me at the names on the stones, ANTONIN MOSER, MARIA JARO-SKY, the cameos with their perfect profiles. Rosie's new companion does indeed look exactly like Johen. There was no mistake. He is Johen, on that world.

00.00.00

Rose Wylde is working to bring up a contact, somewhere in the New Puritan sector: a Rose in motion, a Rose stretched to the limit, a Rose trying to protect her patch. What is she defending with such dedication that she cannot open her mind and hear the call? What battle is she fighting, what great feat of co-ordination performing? What wriggling net is it that she is holding so tight?

Rose, Rose, Rose. The agent presses the cups of her earphones, as if trying to follow a tiny signal among noise. Rose, Rose, Rose, Rose, Rose.

The cause of each is the cause of all. Everybody must come in. Come in, everybody.

Banked overhead, the faces of Roses on parallels where the technology is: the legion, the full-timers. Pink dots on screens for the others, contacts strong and weak, pulsing pink beads on wires of light. Everybody pushing together, like a bloody delivery room.

Rose, can you hear me? Can you hear me, Rose?

'Valency peaking,' reports a programmer. A light flashes. 'Probability one,' she says; and the machines echo her, '*Probability One, One, Probability One . . .* '

The screens merge into a giant picture of a young woman on a green hillside holding up a chrome silver model aeroplane. Above the waist she is wearing lipstick, and nothing else. With her long golden hair she looks like a mermaid holding a Y-shaped mirror. She seems as if she might be very young indeed. There is an insolent look on her face.

'Rose, dear, listen to me when I'm talking to you.'

'Identity drift three parallels thirteen . . .'

Gone again.

Flux.

01.53.11

I am lying on a pallet, dying of fever. I am flying an aeroplane, firing a gun that shoots rays you can only see on a screen. I am redecorating my bathroom.

My night-light glows like a devil's eye. *I see everything*, it says. *I will not save you!* I sit on the edge of the bed, holding my shoulders. My feet are on cold stone, cold lino, cold industrial matting of steel wires and plastic beads. I rub my toes against the nap of the carpet, rub rub rub, rub hard.

Cold boots. Dawn alarm.

I stand up and walk a straight line, one foot directly in front of the other. Out of the bedroom and into the hall.

I go into the spare room.

There is just a woolly shadow on a pillow. Woolly pillow. Maybe he is nothing but wool.

I push my fist into my mouth so as not to laugh.

Raid! Raid! The sirens roll. *Bandit attack, Blue leader scramble!* Tarmac. Heavy smell of juice. Parachutes drifting down onto the parade ground, Captain Orlov's orderly cursing. Raiders hatching out of grey silk cocoons, hacking their way out with knives. I have my knife in my hand.

'Oh, Rosie, no. No, Rosie, no.' He tuts. He is up and padding about in his nightshirt. His beard explodes over his front like gun smoke. His hands are on my forearms.

'It's me, Rosie. John. John Chivers. Don't you know me, Rosie? Rosie? Rosie, what are you doing?'

I am pouring martinis out of a stainless steel cocktail shaker. I am slaking a managing director's lust with my mouth. I am riding by night with a consignment of prohibited antibiotics for the Resistance in Connecticut. I am standing on the landing with the bread knife, watching the bandit's blood pool. It trickles to the edge of the top stair and starts to drip on the next one down.

'I am disturbed,' I explain, though I don't think that explanation satisfies anybody any more; not even me.

They find me wandering the hallways, red-handed. Carl helps them put a harness on me. I would not have let them, but I thought it was my parachute. The doctors speak in numbers. 35, 40, double it. Sister touches my forehead and smiles.

00.21.31

'We heard you shout. The men came running. Jirí found you lying on the ground.'

Johen beside me, naked, warm. His warm brown eyes. She stuck the bread knife in his side.

'He says they think they picked up all the papers. I'm afraid you broke the mirror, though, falling off the bench.' I can hear it in his voice: *Good riddance.*

I stop him talking by pushing my tongue into his mouth. I take his hands and put them on my breasts.

The bread knife.

I find I am weeping again. 'There was nothing we could do,' I say, wiping my face with my fingers. 'Any of us.'

'Darling. Darling.' Johen is tenderly reproachful. It distresses him when I cry.

'It wasn't me, darling.' He kisses me. 'I'm still here.'

I want him desperately. It is the way we know, when things go bad, to push back the pain, to drive away the horror. The bread knife in his side. I run my hand down beside his belly and reach for his cock. It is still too soft.

That red mess on the stairs. I double up on him and work on him with my tongue until his cock swells and trembles against my lips. That hideous red mess on the stairs.

Hot and moist, we grapple, panting. Johen's broad hairy thighs, pinning me.

She was like one of those warrior women with their ghastly swords. Johen's belly squeezes me repeatedly to the bed.

I arch my neck. His beard scrubs the underside of my chin.

He died in agony.

I wrap my hands around the broad hill of his back, wanting to hold all of him, wanting to cram as much as possible into me, inside me, where he will be safe.

I know I can never forgive her.

29.06.06

The sea maid mourns a loss. She drifts, head down, heedless. The others cluster around her, the pod sentries, the unmated females. *Sssad?* they think. *Sssad, Rosamaris, sss, sssss?*

Her aunts and cousins touch her head with tendrilled fingers, seeking the source of this strange pain that only she can feel. Their big round eyes are white and misty blue, opaque as long-drowned jewels. Their tongues are narrow, their teeth are pointed, the gills pulse red through their weedy hair, like wounds, like hungry mouths.

The sea maid jerks her head, displaying her throat. She thrashes the water with her tail. She leaves the tribe and swims away, alone. At a distance she will follow them through the glaucous darkness, keeping her trouble from them.

They cannot understand.

The Midnight Rose team included not only Neil Gaiman but also Mary Gentle, Alex Stewart and Roz Kaveney, so it was a wonder to many of us that the enterprise didn't immediately collapse under the sheer weight of its combined intelligence. One of their shared world anthology series concerned the Weerde, a race of shapechangers who, we were to suppose, are the truth behind all our legends of vampires, werewolves, silkies and such. The human race is of little concern to the Weerde, who have been on Earth far longer than we, and are preoccupied with internal feuds and cosmic enmities of their own. Weerde live a remarkably long time, and each periodically has to revert to their basic form.

I don't remember why I chose to set my first Weerde story in the American north-east in the 1960s. Perhaps it seemed appropriate to encounter that species, whose ideas of history and identity are so alien to any of ours, in the epoch of the hippy existentialism that Stephanie voices and tries so hard to achieve: that you are only and entirely 'who you want to be'. Also very much in the background here are Carolyn Chute's chronicles of the brutal, tenacious Bean family and their 'kingdom of blood and dirt'.

Going to the Black Bear

'THIS IS A SONG I wrote about the war, it's called "A Letter from Kenny".' She played the intro looking down at the bare board floor with the beer stains, then when she started to sing she lifted her head. They didn't stop talking, though, they didn't want to hear about the war. They were just loggers and quarrymen, all they wanted was Brenda Lee or Connie Francis, or some of that country music. She sang over their heads into the smoky air of the bar room. The season was over, all the vacation cabins were locked and shuttered, the colours of fall had faded and gone from the trees. Tomorrow she'd head out for Bangor, find the Black Bear, they were cool there, they had the Kingston Trio, Phil Ochs. Bob *Dylan* had played the Black Bear. Tomorrow she'd try for Bangor, and after that she'd quit. Go back home.

She sang the chorus, sang it louder. They had to listen. There was one guy, a young guy over in the booths, sitting on his own. He was listening. She sang it to him.

> *'I'm still waiting for a letter from Kenny*
> *To tell me when he'll be coming home . . .'*

He looked kind of a nice guy, he had real nice blue eyes. They seemed to shine through the smoke, brighter than the beer lights at the bar. He didn't look like a logger. He had a jean jacket, but he had a white shirt on, like from India or somewhere, with a little embroidery on the collar. Maybe he'd been in the war, maybe that was why he was listening. Maybe that was why he was sitting on his own, not talking to any of the logmen.

He wouldn't stop looking at her. She gave him a special smile. Maybe he had a car, maybe he was going somewhere towards Bangor. He wasn't from around here, that was for sure.

She finished the song, and some of the people clapped. He didn't clap. She was disappointed. He just sat there drinking and smoking and watching her. He was amazing, so blond and tanned and everything, she thought he was a lifeguard up from Florida or maybe all the way from the West Coast. Everybody was talking about the West Coast, everybody but her had gone this summer, she was up here at China Lake, playing for truck drivers. Couldn't get much farther from San Francisco if you tried. She did the short set, all the way through 'Pretty Boy Floyd' she kept thinking, Please don't go.

He didn't go.

She came down from the stage, between the tables, into the crowd, holding her guitar up so it wouldn't get hit. She hated this part, when the gig was over, down on the floor with the people. They all knew her now, but she didn't know them. They didn't mean any harm, she just couldn't handle them. She smiled, said thank you, didn't look at any one of them too long.

'That was real good, honey,' said Myra from the bar, passing her a Michelob. Then the jukebox came on, pretty loud: the Drifters, wiping her out of the air. She was history. She drank deep, wiped her mouth. She went along past his booth, caught his eye.

'Hi,' he said.

'Well hello,' she said. She smiled, and he smiled too, sort

of. She hung around there a second, another second, he had to say something else or she had to walk on by.

He gave the slightest nod at the empty seat opposite, kept looking at her. His eyes were steady as blue stones. She found herself putting her guitar in the window seat, sitting down facing him.

So that was that.

She drank fast, she was thirsty.

He spoke then. 'You ready for another?' he said.

His cheekbones were like gulls' wings. She wanted to fly on them. He was drinking an Old Milwaukee, straight out the bottle like the logging men. She had one too.

She flexed her shoulders, rubbing her back against the partition. 'I curl right up when I'm playing,' she said. 'Like a caterpillar or something.'

Most guys would think that was cute, he just sat there like an Indian. Well, he was no Penobscot, not with that hair. 'You have a name?' she asked him.

He kept looking at her a while before he answered, something was going on in his eyes like he was trying to remember his own name. It would have been kind of spooky if he hadn't been so beautiful. She could watch him a long time, she thought.

'Tom,' he said.

'Hi, Tom,' she said. 'I'm Stephanie. I guess you know that, right?' She reached up and traced the letters of her name, backwards on one of her fliers Myra had taped to the window.

'You're good,' he said.

'Well I'm glad you liked it,' she said.

She drank some more beer. He didn't say anything. Usually guys tried to impress her, they wanted to put the make on her right away. Like the guy last night in Augusta who wanted her to be a star. 'Stephanie, you've got it,' he kept saying. 'You got the message.' Nobody that she didn't know had ever watched her as hard as this one, yet now he wasn't paying her any mind. She was pleased and insulted, both at the same time; and ashamed of herself for being insulted. She was sure he was a veteran, some of them were kind of remote, and confused in themselves. That would be a pity.

'Did you like "Letter from Kenny"?' she said. 'I saw you listening to *that* one. Were you there, in the war?'

He considered, rubbed his hand over his jaw. His nails were worn right down. He moved like he was real tired, like a much older guy. 'Wars,' he said. She thought he nodded.

They didn't like to talk about it, that was cool too.

They went out back and sat on the hill, suspended right up above the lake. 'It's so beautiful up here,' she said. She saw the stars in front of them reflected down in the water, black water in the spaces in between them. Pretty deep, she supposed. She asked him, 'What sign are you? Scorpio, right? I bet I'm right.'

There was enough light from the windows of the bar for her to see he was looking wary now, like he was afraid she was going to lay some heavy trip on him. 'I'm Aquarius,' she said. Even if they didn't know anything, they could usually relate to that. 'Well, I'm Capricorn really, but I have Aquarius rising,' she said. Then she got frightened because she didn't usually tell men that, and she wondered what she was saying. She made a D major and strummed it softly, so as not to have to say anything.

His cigarette burned down and he flicked it away. It fell through the cooling night like a dying firefly. It seemed to fall a long time, like it was going to land way down in the lake.

'I guess you're who you want to be, really,' she said, conceding. 'I mean, you're not from around here, right?'

'No,' he said at once.

'Where are you from?'

He gave her a slow look. He took a drink. 'Just now I'm wandering,' he said.

'Like me,' she said. 'I'm from Boston. I'm on the road,' she said. She could never say it without feeling like she was reading the words off something, like they were true but she wasn't supposed to say them about herself. 'Tomorrow I'm in Bangor, were you ever there? Did you ever go to a place called the Black Bear, a bar, up in Bangor, called the Black Bear?'

He shook his head.

'That's a good place,' she told him. 'That's where I'm heading.'

Looking across the dark shoulders of the trees at the white lights and the red lights creeping down Highway Three, she picked the melody of 'Mining for Gold'.

To her surprise he started to sing.

> *'We are miners, hard rock miners,*
> *To the shaft house we must go . . .'*

He sounded different when he was singing, sad and husky like he really did have the rock-dust in his lungs. She turned and looked at him again. She wondered if he was someone she should know. 'You're really good,' she said, 'are you a singer?'

'I can sing,' he said.

'But on the road, I mean, in clubs and stuff?'

The idea seemed to amuse him. 'No.'

'You should! People should sing, in their lives, not just people like me who get paid to sing . . . Sing some more,' she said. 'Do you like Bob Dylan?'

But just then with a big hiss of brakes and a low rumble from the empty bed, a log truck pulled into the parking lot. Stephanie felt exposed, she didn't want to play sitting there with the headlights scything round the place, the engine coughing and hawking in the broken night. She sat still as Tom was sitting, with her hands still on the strings until she heard the driver jump out of the cab and go into the bar. When he slammed the cab door it sounded like something finishing.

There was dew on the grass, her dress would be wet. She stood up and felt it. She stood with her arms down by her side, holding the guitar off the grass by the neck. 'I should go in,' she said. It sounded like she was apologizing to him for something. 'Got to get up early, get the good rides.'

He sat there like some old statue, arms round his knees. His white shirt was a pale glow in the light coming down from the bar.

'I love your shirt,' she said softly.

He said, 'Come with me.'

Her heart jumped in her chest. 'You going to Bangor? Or Belfast would do.'

He said, 'Sleep with me tonight.'

Her head spun like a firecracker. Man, he was cool. He was so cool her throat seized up that minute. She wanted to smile, she froze right up. She wanted to say yes, but how could you say yes when he just came out with it like that?

She never made love with men she didn't know, she always said no to the truck drivers, no matter how sweet they were, the big old men in their big old trucks.

But she knew one thing: she wanted to be free. Everybody had gone off to the West Coast this summer to be free, well she could be free right here in China Lake. If you couldn't be free like, right now, then it wasn't freedom at all, right?

She said to him, 'I have to get to Bangor tomorrow. Anyway.'

He said, 'Okay.' He looked like he'd been carved out of wood.

She stood up. She stood over him. She was ten feet tall, she felt herself growing bigger every second, she was shooting up into the sky. 'I have to go and get my stuff,' she said, 'say goodbye to Myra.'

He said, 'Okay.'

Still he hadn't even touched her. She was so big she was going to burst. She gave a little shaky laugh. 'Well, stand up,' she said.

He stood up. He was tall, not too tall. Just right. She held her face up, wanting him to kiss her.

He lifted one finger and put it gently on her lips. She closed her eyes and gave a little shiver, he was the coolest man she'd ever *seen*, she wanted him now, on the wet grass. His finger smelt of tobacco and something else she didn't know, a scent like some strange kind of animal. Maybe he was a hunter. He was still enough to be a hunter, he had a hunter's eyes that didn't blink, ever. She kissed his finger. She loved him with her eyes. 'Hold this for me?' she said, giving him her guitar. Now that was really free, trusting him to hold her guitar for her, her *guitar*! And she went running back inside, skipping up the back stairs light as a willow leaf.

His car was just some old Pontiac, nothing fancy, cracked plastic seat-covers bleached by the sun, a pair of jeans on the back seat, gum wrappers, empty packs of Chesterfields. Smells of cigarettes, old hamburgers and fries, smells of man. Stephanie felt shy suddenly, sat with her feet up against the dash, her long skirt pulled tight round her legs. She watched the road. The road went up and down, up and down. Wherever the road went the pine trees went too. They looked like ranks of stern black sentries. Beside the road they loomed over huge boulders, thirty-foot boulders that just sat there like someone had dropped them.

The big trucks went grinding by, that was a good word, a good line. With their banks of lights on top and all down the sides they looked like big pinball machines, towering over your car, grinding out of the deep forest. Stephanie tried to think of another line for a truck song, but she was too nervous. She looked sideways at Tom, so he wouldn't catch her looking. His jaw made her think of a hard blade, like a snowplow, like he was part of the car now, pushing through the trees. She looked round at her guitar in its cloth case on the back seat with his spare jeans tucked under it so it wouldn't slide off the seat on the curves.

A sign said WALDO COUNTY. Someone had scraped out the second O.

'How far is it?' she asked.

'First place we see,' he said.

She felt nervous a moment, thinking well, what did he mean by that? Was he staying close by or did he mean he was going to pull off and start in on her right there at the road side?

He drove past a big firebreak without stopping, she calmed down. Free, she reminded herself. It's cool. Beside the road is cool too, she imagined, in the country anyhow.

'What kind of tree do you like best?' she said.

'Tree?' he said.

'Yup.'

He looked around like he'd never seen the trees before, never seen them up and down the road and all around everywhere.

'Redwood,' he said. 'Oldest tree in the world.'

She thought of California, where her friends had gone. She looked around. 'I see oak, I see pine, nope. We're fresh out of redwood.' He didn't laugh.

She shifted in her seat, sitting up more.

'Can we have some music?'

He looked at her, like he thought she was strange. 'Sure,' he said. 'You sing us something.'

'No,' she said. 'You.' She put her feet down and felt the peeling edge of the plastic under her with the tip of her finger. 'I've been singing all night.'

He sang.

> *'They dressed Kenny up in a uniform –'*

'Hey!' she said again, in surprise, delight.

> *'And they sent him off over the sea . . .'*

He remembered the whole thing. Every word. Sang it really well too. It should have sounded funny, a man singing it, about another man, but it didn't.

That song wasn't written down anywhere. It wasn't even on anybody's tape she'd ever sung on. 'Ahh, you saw me before some place, right?' Stephanie said.

He shook his head no. He blew out smoke in a long plume, as if he was about to speak, but he didn't.

'You remembered the whole thing just hearing it once?' she said. 'That's incredible. I mean, that's really amazing, you know?'

They crested another steep hill. She put out her hand and patted his arm, just above the elbow, suing for his attention.

'I think you've seen me before!' she said.

He signalled then and she dropped her hand. Her hand remembered the feel of his arm through the cloth. It felt soft, sort of, like a kid's arm, nothing like a lifeguard's muscle at all. Probably she'd been romanticizing him, in the dim light of the bar. She did that, she knew: romanticized men.

He was swinging the wheel round, turning off to the right down a deep gully. She felt vertigo suddenly, as if he was going to tip them both down a big hole in the ground.

The road was a switchback, just a logging road cut out of the hillside.

'Down here?' she said. It was dark down here.

He didn't answer.

It's cool, Stephanie reminded herself.

The road curved, climbed again, fell. She saw the lights of a town off through the trees, like neon snowflakes in the distance. The Pontiac bounced, she clung to the handle over the door.

'So,' she said, 'you know any more songs? You write your own songs?'

He threw her a sidelong glance, gave the smallest shake of his head.

'Oh you should, you have a good voice, you know.' Her voice sounded small over the engine sound. 'Everybody should have their own songs, like for when you're feeling happy, you know, or when you're kinda down . . . like the blues . . .'

He wasn't responding. She looked out of the window. Stiff black trees replaced each other endlessly along the road.

There was something down there, she could just make them out among the trees as they came round a bend: hard-edged shapes, were those houses there?

Tom was slowing right down.

They were some mobile homes, away back under the trees. In a second she'd be able to see clearer. Logging camp, she guessed, only now it looked more permanent than that. The headlights showed aluminum siding, ribbed and dented. Old paint, wintergreen, brown streaks smeared across it. Pale pink curtains at a window. Over the mutter of the car engine she heard a dog bark once, saw black shapes stirring restlessly behind chicken wire, saw their eyes give back the headlights, red and orange.

The trailers looked ancient, long ribbed things with round ends, sat there in the mud like tanks, like some kind of invasion craft. They had cables hooked up to some generator somewhere, she could see blue TV light stirring through the curtains of the one nearest the road. There was a car up on blocks, some kind of engine lying on a couple of planks in the mud with a tarpaulin half over it. Kids' toys lay around, garbage of all kinds, she couldn't see what, she didn't want to. Everything she could see looked dirty, neglected, like you wouldn't want to touch any of it in case it gave you diseases.

She asked him, 'Is this it?'

Lord, she hoped it wasn't.

Tom reached for the key and turned the engine off.

Stephanie's heart thudded hard and low. He hadn't put the brakes on, they were rolling slowly and silently past the camp down the gradient of the road. He was staring out of his window, staring at the trailers as if he wanted to know who was home, and thought he could see right through the walls if he stared hard enough.

Stephanie looked away to the left, up the road, down the road. Nothing but trees. Nothing but black needles. But when she stared into the dark she felt like something she couldn't see was staring back. She looked up at the treetops, the black sky. It was there too, she knew it, staring at her.

The car crept on down the road, twigs and rocks crunching under the tires. Tom was sitting stiff as a shepherd dog, just staring into the camp. One of the camp dogs was starting to whine, starting the others off.

The car felt thin as a paper shell, suddenly, no protection at all from anything. 'Who is it, Tom?' asked Stephanie, her voice sounding high and squeaky in her ears.

He didn't turn from the window. Nor did he stop the car. She could smell the strange smell of him again, real strong.

'Cousins of mine,' he said.

She swallowed. The dogs were barking, a light went on in one of the trailers.

'We going to stop?'

His hand found the key again, and he gunned the engine back into life. 'No,' he said, determinedly, and they were gone, surging down the hill, leaving the place behind, out of sight in a second behind the trees.

The feeling something was staring lingered a way down the hill, then quickly dwindled to nothing. Stephanie felt relieved, ashamed of herself, her imagination. She wasn't free at all, she was spooky as a Radcliffe girl at a reefer party. Goodness sakes.

She wouldn't look at Tom. She looked out of the window.

A half-mile further down, they took a fork and soon came back out on the highway. She saw an orange gas sign standing up above the trees, meat trucks growling up the gradient, a pick-up loaded with churns, a tan VW van broken down, a fat guy in a Windcheater with his head stuck in the hood, a frightened-looking woman with a permanent and rhinestone glasses in the passenger seat, gazing hopelessly into every car that passed. Tom drove on by.

They pulled in at a motel. 'You folks are lucky,' said the fat old man in the eyeshade, struggling up out of the basket chair where he had been drowsing in front of the late show. 'I was just about to close up for the night.'

He beamed widely, showing bare gums, turning a dog-eared register towards them and taking the cap off a ballpoint pen. 'Mr and Mrs – ? ' She looked at Tom.

'We ain't married,' he said softly, flatly.

She saw the old man stiffen like a startled chicken. She looked at Tom warily, astonished herself. Cool was cool, but you couldn't go letting it all hang out like that in front of some old country boy, he'd probably call the fuzz.

But the old man was laughing, soundlessly, his shoulders shaking. He winked, gestured at Tom approvingly with the pen. 'What are ya, brother and sister, is that it?' He winked, mugging at Stephanie. 'You're his sister, right?' He nodded, smiling broadly, loving every minute.

She grabbed Tom's arm and squeezed it. 'Yes,' she said firmly.

The old man thought this was even funnier. He wheezed and slapped Tom on the shoulder as he gave him their key, directed them across the yard to a clapboard cabin.

'Go on with ya!'

Stephanie turned the light on, but Tom turned it off again. He bore down on her, herding her onto the bed. She dropped her backpack. In the sick, pale light through the drapes his face looked intent, heedless, blind. She felt herself swelling again, this time beneath him, her breasts rising up to fill his hands. She was full of herself, filled with hunger for him, with his hunger for her. His mouth was hot, the back of his neck hot where she clasped his mouth to hers, was he sick? Did he have a fever? He was fiery, furious, writhing in her arms. She clung to him as to a frightened horse, they plunged and reared together, sweat coursed down his sides. Veins stood out in strange patterns on his neck and forehead. He cried out in a language she did not know.

In the morning she woke feeling sore, ragged, proud. She could smell him on her, all around her in the sagging motel bed. She turned to him, but he was not in the bed beside her. She almost cried out, she felt so desolate, so deprived. The power of the feeling frightened her. Then she saw him sitting in his pants and no shirt, backwards on a chair at the window, smoking a cigarette.

Naked, daring, Stephanie got out of bed and put her arms round him from behind, kissed the back of his neck. He hadn't opened the drapes. He was staring through the gap between them, as if there was something special he was hunting, moose or deer, up the ridge behind the yard. She nestled her cheek against his, peering over his shoulder. There was nothing there she could see, just brown trees. It was broad day out there, she'd slept half the morning away.

'Well hello,' she said.

He reached up a hand, patted her bare arm. Didn't look round.

She felt sweaty, stale. 'I have to shower,' she said. 'So do you.' She pressed her fingertip against his naked shoulder. His skin was still warm, as if he had been working hard. He was hairier than she'd realized, in the urgent darkness of the night.

'Does this place run to breakfast?'

His voice was low, steady. 'I want you to come with me today,' he said.

'I have to get to Bangor today,' she said.

He looked at her then. His blue eyes were opaque, pre-occupied, her problems were nothing.

'I can go that way,' he said. 'I have folks there, someplace.'

It was fine. Still something made her hesitate. Not that she didn't trust him, only, only something.

'Well, okay, only I have to get to Bangor today, then I can maybe get a gig at the Black Bear tomorrow. You know where that is? The Black Bear?'

His face was impervious as the face of the Angel Gabriel. He looked at her like a big shot record producer she met once at someone else's show. 'I'll take you to Bangor,' he said.

'Well, fine,' she said, uncomfortably.

She wished he would come and talk to her while she was in the shower, but he didn't look like he would think of it, and you couldn't just ask. She showered and dried herself on the little scrap of hard towel, then dressed in her road shirt and jeans. The old man was pottering around in his singlet and overalls, he chuckled and greeted them courteously, made them a pot of coffee thick as creosote.

'Dja sleep okay, little lady?' he asked, treating her to another exhibition of his gums. He seemed to think she and Tom were staying there expressly for his entertainment. 'Dja get enough sleep?'

She sat in the car with the door open, her feet outside, tuning her guitar. She looked at the motel, she saw those were blueberry bushes around the cabins. Usually that would have cheered her up, today she was not so happy. She wondered very much where they were going. And she had a problem, she didn't like a man to take her for granted, but she didn't want to start a fight and spoil their last hours together. He was someone special, she was already writing a song about him, two songs, in her head.

He came and got in the car, started up. She put her legs inside, slammed the car door. She kissed his cheek. The late morning sun was the colour of corn oil through the raw branches of the trees. A rust bucket pick-up came clanking and squealing past them as they bumped out onto the road. Stephanie held the guitar upright on her lap, trying to keep the head from banging on the windshield as they bounced and swayed.

Tom glanced at her. 'Put that thing in the back seat,' he said, coldly.

'Tom? Are you mad? What's wrong, is something wrong?'

That wasn't very cool, nagging him like that. It upset her when someone spoke slightingly about her guitar.

'Nothing's wrong,' he said. Either he was mad, or he was sick. He sounded short of breath. His face was dark, dark shadow under his eyes and over his cheeks. His hair that was as blond as cornsilk looked dark too, coarser, maybe it was greasy. Maybe sex made his hair greasy.

She lifted her guitar carefully over the back of the seat, trying to reach the cloth case with her hand, her fingers, she couldn't do it. She abandoned it and sat round straight again, facing the front. She reached up and touched him on the cheek. His beard was strong, he hadn't shaved this morning.

She saw then where they were headed. Off the highway, back up the logging road. Back up towards that place where his cousins lived. In daylight it looked perfectly normal up here, pine, oaks and maples, pigeons flying overhead, road signs all dented and scratched up from buckshot, nothing spooky at all.

At that moment they passed something dead, something quite big, it looked like. Stephanie glimpsed a staring eye like a deer's, four spindly legs at bad angles, a great deal of crimson blood. She flinched.

'I'm going to have to leave you for a while,' said Tom suddenly. His eyes looked haggard, unfocused. There was sweat on his face like last night. Suddenly she was aware of the powerful heat coming off him, filling the car.

'Tom, what is it? Are you feeling okay?'

But he shrugged off her hand, muttering.

And then they were at the camp.

He stopped the car with a jerk, reached his arm across her to open the door, he was bundling her outside.

'Tom? Tom, please!'

The last thing she saw of him was his grey face looking up at her through the dusty window of the Pontiac as he slammed the passenger door, looking up at her open-mouthed, his head lop-sided like he was under water.

'Tom! Tom, wait! My guitar!'

She stood holding her hand out grabbing at the empty air, watching the Pontiac weave back onto the road and roar away uphill.

She cursed in alarm and shock. He had her guitar, she

had to wait here, couldn't move from this spot until he came back. No, she wouldn't think what if he didn't. She was despondent at her own helplessness.

A bad smell hit her nostrils. There was a cage of goats next to the cage of dogs, both ankle-deep in filth. The dogs were climbing on each other, rearing up against the wire with their whole bodies, trying to get at her. She didn't much care for dogs. She also had that sensation again, that something she couldn't see was staring at her from some-where. She looked around, combing her hair frantically back from her face with her fingers. She looked into the encamp-ment, over the blackberry bushes.

There were babies watching her, children, two four six of them. They were practically naked, streaked and spotted and blotted with dirt. They all had noses with huge nostrils. Most of their noses were running.

Stephanie came round the bushes and approached them.

The eldest looked to be a little girl about eight, skinny as a post, her hair matted in tangles and tufts. She had an unravelling sweater that hardly reached over her dirty little pot belly, and a skirt the colour of mud. Her feet were bare.

'Whatcha want?' said the little girl, screwing up her eyes.

'Nothing,' said Stephanie. 'I don't want anything.' What was she going to say? 'I just have to wait here a while for someone.' It didn't sound good, even to her own ears. She looked nervously at the trailers. The door on the nearest one was open, it looked dark inside, she couldn't see anyone in there.

'Who you waitin' for?' asked the little girl. There was something funny about all their heads, their skulls were very long, as though they had an extra bit on the back. Their eyes were all the same colour, the ones close enough to see. They were a sort of yellow colour, like a glass of beer.

'You waitin' for that man?'

'Yes,' said Stephanie. She didn't know where to put her hands. He'd left her here without her pack, without a thing. Goddamn him!

'Who was that man?' asked a little boy, his hair cut so short he was almost bald.

Stephanie took a breath, trying to breathe through her mouth, trying to shape up to all this. She still had the feeling she was being watched. 'Well, he's your cousin, I guess.'

This meant nothing to them.

'His name's Tom,' she said. They just stared.

There was a black dog with them, some kind of crazy mongrel mix. The girl pointed to it, it was bigger than she was. 'This is Dory,' she said. 'She's a dog.' She looked up at Stephanie as if for approval.

A young woman came to the open trailer door. She was wearing long wrinkled yellow woollen underwear under a grubby mauve nylon dress and dirty sneakers on her feet, laced with string. She held her hand to her face, propping up her hair, which was flopping out of a home-made permanent. It had been violently bleached and was growing out dark.

She had the same nose as the kids. And her eyes were yellow.

Goodness sake, these were genuine hillbillies, just like Woody Guthrie sang about, that were in Oklahoma. Or was it Kentucky? Even as her disgust faded, Stephanie began to feel sorry for them. And to see herself back in Boston, at the Blue Jar: 'This is a song I wrote for a hillbilly family I met up in Maine . . .'

'Nadine,' said the young woman, 'you best tell Carter.'

The eldest little girl ran off behind the trailer.

'Hello,' said Stephanie, with a sympathetic trust-me smile.

'What you want?' said the woman.

'Your cousin Tom just brought me,' she said. 'He'll be back in a little while. He had to go off somewhere, I don't know where he was going, he didn't say.'

She heard herself babbling, stopped abruptly.

'Don't know no Tom.'

'I don't know his other name,' said Stephanie apologetically. 'Blond hair. Beautiful shirt, white shirt. Drives a Pontiac, it's brown, with orange hubcaps. He said he's got cousins here.'

The woman was no older than her, yet some of the kids were probably hers. She was standing there behind them as if she'd go for an axe if Stephanie moved any closer. She was looking at Stephanie like she was the nut, as if she had two heads, as if she was some old dinosaur that had crawled out of the woods.

Probably they were all retarded. Jesus what a terrible life.

The woman didn't seem to be worried. 'You have ta come in,' she announced, as if it were a fact of life. She disappeared inside her long-immobile mobile home.

Taking a deep breath, Stephanie stepped up after her, Dory and the kids following.

Inside, the sense of invisible eyes on her did not decrease.

The first thing she saw was an unmade bed, a greasy quilt and comforter tumbled on it. There was an ashtray spilled on the quilt, an empty beer can lying at the foot of the mattress, up against the footboard. The place smelt of cigarettes and beer and animals. There were Coke bottles everywhere, paper sacks bulging with unconsidered garbage, piles of newspapers, some of them *old*. So old they were brown. Alongside the bed was a chest of drawers, two drawer fronts missing, limp clothes dangling out. You could see no one had cleaned the windows for years.

It was horrible anyone should be so poor as to have to live here, like this. The government really should find them proper homes. She wondered how long they had been living here, forever it looked like. Where had they come from originally? Maybe their parents had been transients. She wondered if they knew any songs. She couldn't see a banjo, an accordion, even a kazoo. Nothing but the TV flickering on the chest. A woman in lace and a man in buckskins were arguing playfully on the porch of an airless frontier set. '*If you think I'm marrying you, Mr Grace, you can think again!*'

'Sit down,' the hostess said.

Stephanie sat at the head of the table. The kids immediately took the rest of the seats, Dory too, squashed up on one chair with one of the babies.

'My name's Stephanie,' said Stephanie.

They all sat looking at her, three of them sitting in the same attitude: right elbows on the table, sucking the edges of their hands. The table was littered with dried-up plates, an oily black handgun, a catsup bottle, a mangled Red Indian doll of bright red polythene with one leg missing. No child claimed it. Stephanie sat tight, not wanting to touch anything. Everything smelt just awful.

The woman was opening a cupboard under the sink. 'You want some coffee?' she said.

'Yes please,' said Stephanie. 'That would be very nice.'

There were clattering footsteps. Nadine was back. She had brought Carter with her.

Carter was very tall. He stooped, avoiding the electric heater on the wall above the door. He didn't look so old either, though older than the nameless woman at the cupboard, plus he was almost bald.

He wore a black cord shirt with the sleeves rolled up, a pair of jeans that had once been blue. He had the yellow eyes, the gaping nostrils. What hair he had was a dark grey that looked like motor oil rather than age, and hung down in straggling hanks from little asymmetrical patches around his head. It did not disguise the shape of his skull. The woman's husband or her brother? Or both?

When he smiled Stephanie saw his teeth, and wished he hadn't.

'This is her,' said the woman, rising from the floor, her hands still empty.

'You must be Carter,' said Stephanie.

Carter said nothing, nodded, smiled vacantly. Stephanie wondered if there was something seriously wrong with him, but his eyes were very steady on her, unblinking, inscrutable, like Tom's eyes. Hurry up, Tom.

Behind her the TV made a squeaky burst of helter-skelter discords, slithering strings, racing brass.

'I don't suppose you get many visitors way out here,' said Stephanie.

Carter spoke. 'Not too many.' His voice was high and musical, like a child or a whimsical old woman. He went to where the woman was standing in the kitchenette and put his arm around her, pinning her arms to her sides. 'Get our visitor a drink?' he said, not taking his eyes off Stephanie.

The woman was indifferent to his grip. 'I was just goin' t'make coffee . . .' she said, lethargically.

'What a shame,' said Carter to Stephanie. 'We're all out of coffee. You'll have to have a real drink.'

He fetched out an unlabelled bottle of something clear as water and thumped it on the table.

Stephanie looked at it, looked at the icebox. 'Maybe a Coke, if you have one.'

The couple looked at each other as if they didn't know what it was. Stephanie would have said water but she didn't trust their water. 'I don't need anything, really,' she said. 'I'm fine.'

Carter leaned in front of Nadine and poured an inch of the colourless spirit into a plastic glass. It had a chipped decal of Donald Duck on the side. Stephanie smiled weakly. Be free.

The drink smelt of nothing, nothing at all. She took a sip, inhaled sharply, choked, her throat gripped by claws of fire.

'Good, heh?' Carter said.

He did not sit down, stood leaning on the sink with his arm around the woman, smiling his hideous smile.

Stephanie took another drink. This time it went down pretty easy. Her throat was completely numb already. 'I mustn't drink too much,' she explained, 'I have to keep a clear head for tonight, I have a date. I mean a gig. In Bangor, at the Black Bear, maybe you know it.'

Carter leaned forward again. He topped up her glass.

'I'm a folk singer,' she said, drinking. She smiled, bashfully, at the children around the table, at their probable parents. 'Some of us think it's terrible the way the old songs are just being forgotten, like the old Kentucky miners' songs, maybe you know –' She drank, nodding. 'And blues. Nowadays it's all Tin Pan Alley, right?'

She smiled. They didn't understand her.

'The Hit Parade. You know? Some guy in an office writing songs for money.'

She drank.

'It's chaos now!' she said.

At some point during this, she thought, she had turned around in her chair and watched TV for several minutes. She had a distinct memory of doing it, of watching two men chase each other through an obvious studio swamp and pointing it out, laughing. She remembered doing it, but she did not know when she could have done it. She was sat facing the table again now, the way she had been all along. Perhaps she had hallucinated it, the way people said you did when you took drugs. Perhaps the drink was drugged.

Her glass was empty. The children and their dog were

sitting motionless, staring at her. Her body was quite relaxed. There was a warm fug in the trailer, it wasn't unpleasant at all, nothing was watching her, there wasn't anything out there. It seemed to have got dark outside pretty early. Where was Tom? Where was her guitar? Her glass was full.

She saw Carter standing in front of her, drinking a bottle of Coke. She finished her drink.

So did Carter. Then he held the bottle horizontally between his hands and broke it in half. He snapped it just as if it was made of sugar. Stephanie cried out, no one else reacted at all.

Something outside scratched on the aluminum wall, scratch scratch.

Those newspapers, she remembered, seeing some by the door. Some of them must be older than the trailer. Some of them were brown as old leaves. Her head was whirling.

Carter grinned, letting the big chunks of glass fall spinning from his hands onto the table, clatter to the floor among the garbage. His nostrils gaped like drains. His hands were completely uninjured. He wiped them on his hips and went outside.

The woman went past Stephanie's chair, pushing her hair behind her ear. She opened a drawer in the chest and pulled out something long and white. She held it up to show Stephanie. It was a long white dress, shiny like satin, like a wedding dress. It was soiled, like everything round here. Where the hell was Tom? Why was the woman showing her her wedding dress? Were they even married, the two of them? 'Pretty,' she said, humouring her.

'Put it on,' said the woman.

'Me? No.'

'You hafta,' the woman said. Stephanie could see her thinking before she spoke. 'Carter says the women hafta wear the dress.'

In terror Stephanie slammed down her glass. She grabbed
hold of the seat of the chair. 'No! No!'

The woman picked the gun up from the table.

She handled it loosely, as if she thought it was some kind
of kitchen utensil.

'Ya hafta put it on,' she said.

Stephanie stood up. Time jerked. She was changing into
the dress, there with them all watching with their yellow
eyes. The dress was tight and smelt of cheap soap. 'You're
not going to shoot me,' she heard herself saying. The woman
said nothing, just stood there with the gun stuck onto the
end of her arm. Stephanie was trying to fasten buttons behind
her back. Her fingers were frankfurters. She was very drunk
and very scared. The woman pointed the gun for her to go
outside.

They were all out there, women and men both, in bib
overalls and shapeless mud-coloured dresses, bizarre
make-up on their faces, lipstick and eye-shadow in the wrong
places. Their heads were long and their eyes were yellow
and their noses were snouts. Carter was with them. One of
the other men had a flashlight, there was a fog, you could
hardly see the trees all around. Stephanie's eyes prickled, as
if the fog was irritating them. Perhaps she had been watching
TV in the trailer all afternoon and night had now come.

'Tom!' she shouted. 'Tom!'

Gently they ushered her through the wood. The children
followed, Dory pattering alongside. From behind the next
trailer Stephanie could hear a noise she recognized, very
lucid suddenly, as a grindstone. It was the continuous scraping sound of someone pedalling, stopping as if to check the
blade, pedalling again.

The shed was older than any trailer in the world. There
was a rotten old well beside it too, under a sumac bare as a
bone. The well-cover lay cracked in two in a drift of red

leaves. The shed was half-collapsed, inside it had ancient junk, farm stuff, chains, she saw, scythes. The place was lit by rows and rows of candles, big black ones standing in catering-size syrup cans, oil cans, soup cans, dog food cans. There was a powerful ammonia smell, like industrial cleaning fluid. Stephanie saw bones on the dirt floor. She looked away.

Carter's twin brother climbed off the grindstone and came towards her around the block that stood in the middle of the shed.

The block was waist-high, long and bare. Its wooden top was scrubbed raw. It looked quite clean apart from some dark stains. When they stretched her out on it Stephanie tried to pull away. She was shouting and screaming. They held her head. She could see small tendrils of dark fog curling through the holes in the ruined roof.

The women daubed paint on her face. They were chanting low, mumbling something all together in the back of their throats. Their hair was matted with dirt into slabs like tobacco. Stephanie was beside herself. She heard herself sobbing, whining, pleading, but they were holding her tight by the wrists and ankles. Suddenly Stephanie jerked her head free and vomited straight out sideways, clear liquor and clots of motel eggs and donuts.

They grabbed her again, someone cursing. She heard high thin voices laughing wheezily, felt them tug as if they were trying to pull her in quarters. She thought of the Coke bottle. She was breathing hard, snivelling, puke in her nose, she thought she was going to throw up again.

The chanting continued, though it sounded faint, even half-hearted, like prayers at high school, as if they were only doing it for Carter's sake, or someone's sake, because they were told to. Because they always did. When she saw the knife Carter was holding, a big chopping knife with a long pointed blade, she made a shrill sound and shouted sharply, 'Oh, God, no!' In disgust, appalled that this was all life had held for her. She felt moisture seep up the fabric of the white dress. Her bladder had let go.

'*Escouriath nemeth hi jevelion!*' shouted Carter. There was more, nonsense language, what he was shouting didn't mean anything.

A man took a handful of Stephanie's hair and pulled her head back over the end of the block. Upside down she could see the women, their painted faces like clowns pretending to be whores. She could see Nadine picking her nose. The blade was cold on her throat, then hot as it pierced the skin and blood began to seep out along it, spilling down both sides of her neck.

When the creature came in, it slammed through the doorway, sending jars cascading from a high shelf and snapping one of the posts with its shoulders. It cleared the block lengthways at a spring, candles flying in all directions, and knocked Carter to the floor. Stephanie saw it pass over from underneath, it was like a long dog with long hair and no tail. Above it, the dark clouds were writhing in at the holes in the roof. Then, abruptly, her head and hands were free. She jerked up away from the thing that had landed on the floor behind her, snarling, gnawing savagely at something. Carter was shouting, gurgling. People were moaning, yammering in high voices. Stephanie kicked out and freed her feet, slid from the block, banging her hip. The din was incredible, Dory and the newcomer were fighting. Stephanie could see them, their bodies surging and slamming down beyond the far end of the block. Dory was getting the worst of it. She was squealing, a horrible, thin sound like air rushing from the valve of a rubber tire. The creature was standing up on its back legs, Dory hanging from its mouth. It was cuffing her savagely. There was a gunshot, incredibly loud, Carter's woman shrieking, waving her gun around. The thing threw Dory aside and lunged at her.

Stephanie turned to flee. The babies were at her feet, reaching up to her with little white hands. The shed was filled with black dogs suddenly, someone had opened the pen. Some of the dogs seemed to have breasts like a human woman, more like chimpanzees than dogs. Stephanie kicked out, shrieking, and fought her way outside.

She flung a glance back over her shoulder as she fled. They were all going for it, heedless of its strength and size. Some of them were on fire.

She ran into the road, crying, sobbing incoherently, blood splashing from the cut on her neck, dripping down her white dress and around her bare feet as she fled through the fog. Blackberry bushes loomed. She swerved, ran out into the road.

'Tom!' she shouted. 'Tom!' There was no one about, only confused screaming and howling at her back, behind the trailers. Gasping, she staggered up the road.

Up around the bend there was a car parked, facing uphill. A brown car, a Pontiac.

She ran up to it, sobbing and swearing.

It was just left there like he hadn't even been anywhere. All the windows were closed. There was no one inside.

She grabbed the driver's door handle. The door opened and she fell inside, blood dripping on the seats, slamming the door behind her, banging all the locks down. His clothes were on her seat, white shirt, jacket and jeans, she was kneeling on them. She crawled into the back seat, found her guitar, held it up in front of her like a shield, there was nothing else.

She could see his shoes and socks, on the floor by the pedals.

Nothing happened. No one came after her.

She pulled his jacket around her shoulders. It smelt of him. She rubbed her face, smearing blue paint on her hand. She clapped her hand to her cut. It felt long, but not deep. If she held her chin down, maybe it would hold closed.

She panted and cried and shivered. A dog ran out into the road from the bushes and she shrieked. It looked around in all directions excitedly and dashed straight back in again. She could hear a muffled, heavy crashing, as if the shed was being pounded severely with a big soft weight.

Stephanie felt she was about to throw up again. She looked around, wound down the window fast and threw up outside. Then she wound it up again and collapsed back in the seat. Her head was pounding. Adrenalin or no, she was still extremely drunk. Poisoned. She tried to stay awake, but her eyes kept closing, she was jerking herself out of a series of dreams, Nadine trying to strangle her, a big jolly fat man with a face like Santa dangling a length of something dripping cockroaches in her face, she was a little girl again and her mother was beckoning her to follow her along the crossbar of a goal post.

Eventually, still holding her guitar, she slept.

She did not know how long she was asleep. She only knew her eyes were open again and the sun was hammering at her eyeballs. The sun was high, and Tom was standing there holding the car door open.

In the silence Stephanie could hear the TV still playing in the deserted trailer. A woman's voice was excitedly recommending Kolynos toothpaste. The sound was way over there, but it drilled into Stephanie's head. Her throat was dry from the drink and sore from screaming. She nearly screamed again with shock. Tom's face was covered in dark brown blood, it was caked around his mouth and on his hands. 'Tom! Tom . . .' she croaked.

He leaned in over the driver's seat, took the guitar away

from her and put it in the front passenger seat, on top of his clothes. He looked into her eyes like a veterinarian looking at a pet. He looked like he hadn't slept. He was wearing a plaid shirt that was too small for him, a pair of greasy jeans torn in the crotch.

He took hold of her head gently, spanning her paint-smudged face with his dirty hand. He turned her head to the left and then to the right. It hurt. Blood seeped from her cut. He touched her neck and she flinched.

She kept saying, 'Where have you been?'

He didn't reply. He was a soldier. He let go of her and sat down in his seat, shut the door. His head and shoulders blocked out the sun. He lit a cigarette and started the car.

The engine noise made Stephanie's brain throb in her skull. She could smell the strange smell of him, and the blood on him. Now he was here his presence seemed to fill the car, she couldn't think what to say, what to think. She was wearing his jacket. Her clothes were left behind in the trailer. She looked back among the trees as he drove down the hill. Nothing was moving there.

'They tried to kill me, Tom!'

Her voice sounded foolish and feeble. She was starting to cry again. She swallowed hard, trembling.

'Are *you* hurt?' she said. 'You're all –'

He shook his head, not looking round. He wasn't hurt or else he wasn't saying. He wasn't saying anything. Stephanie felt a surge of panic.

'What was that thing?'

It was like a creature in a dream. Flashes of drunken memory, like stills from a movie, scrambled, meaningless. It was all like a dream. She had heard the TV chirruping, a crow calling harshly, echoing above the noise when he started the engine. Underneath everything was a big hollow space that nothing in the world would fit.

'Bear, I guess,' said Tom, around his cigarette.

'No. No. Tom, it wasn't a bear.'

'Wolf, then, I guess.'

It was because of her he was making like he didn't care, because she was a stranger. She was ignorant, things happened in the backwoods, life and death were different there, he wasn't even going to try to explain it to her. She wanted to scream at him, 'Why did you leave me there?', but she was too afraid of him now. He wasn't cool, he was made of stone.

The big dark space moved away, closed itself off, they left it behind. Stephanie felt exhausted, she felt numb. She looked at the back of his head. He looked like someone she didn't even know.

'We going to the cops?' she asked, very quietly.

He didn't answer. Maybe he didn't hear. She couldn't say it again.

The bright day opened wide above the road.

Stephanie sat up and reached for her guitar. She pulled it to her over the back of the seat. Her backpack was in the trunk, she didn't dare ask him to stop so she could get it.

Her cut throbbed. She shut her eyes and her head span. She opened them. 'I need a doctor,' she said. Her voice shook. It was her last demand.

He pushed the gearshift. Sitting forward, she could see his hand. His nails on the stick were long, thickly rimmed with brown.

'I'll take you to Bangor,' he said.

He turned his head and smiled at her, a tight, meaningless smile of dried blood cracking around the white stick of his cigarette. She felt a wave of cold come from him over the back seat. She could feel it against her skin, the cold.

'I have folks in Bangor,' he said.

Another of the Midnight Rose shared worlds was one where a tiny but recognized minority of people are born with (trivial or vast, useful or inconvenient) supernatural abilities. Some can light fires at a distance, or influence the future. One, in a memorable story by Dave Langford, is able to levitate precise amounts of alcoholic beverages from other people's glasses into his own. To deal with such talents among British citizens, HM Government has established the Department of Paranormal Resources, at whose local offices, each with its identical cloned uncooperative receptionist called Marcia, the differently abled are required to register for temporary employment.

In 1986, when I was very much in need of temporary employment, I was approached by my local polytechnic to work as part-time personal tutor to a group of students on a course of independent study. It was a job I might have been reasonably good at, if I had had any training, if the course had been organized properly, if the poly itself hadn't been convulsing like a large, maddened animal from lacerating funding cuts. As it was, I was prevailed upon to try to ride this unpredictable alien beast, clinging on with one hand while trying to support a dozen students with the other.

One of the students who fell off was an Indian boy who, like many, simply hadn't the immense resources of stamina and self-reliance the conditions demanded. I was forever on the phone to other members of staff in other departments in other buildings, trying to sort out what on earth could be done for or with or about him. Assuring me, with the groundless, heartless, senseless optimism which was the prevailing ideology, that the boy's insoluble problems were actually wonderful opportunities, one woman suddenly added: 'I don't know if there are any mental complications.'

I was confused. It had seemed clear to me that the reason this student was struggling was the same reason so many of them were: a desperate admissions policy that accepted anyone who could pay, regardless. I asked the woman what she meant. She was unwilling to be specific. 'There is the physical deformity,' she reminded me, darkly.

Now I was utterly bewildered. I saw him every week (when he turned up), often at close quarters, sometimes for half an hour or more. What physical deformity?

'His hand,' said the woman, impatiently. 'He's got two thumbs.'

He had, too. And I had never noticed.

'You're supposed to be a writer, Colin,' said my temporary colleague, as she put the phone down.

Well: so I am.

Nothing Special

IT WAS MONDAY, but Hussein's giro hadn't arrived. 'Go and see your Mr Cartwright,' said his father. 'Go at once, today,' he said, frowning. 'Do not let them think they can overlook you.'

Hussein's mother said nothing. Hussein knew she disapproved mightily of what her younger son did now that he had left school. She did not understand what it was, she only knew this new job was not a proper one like his brother Jamshyd's. She was deeply suspicious of this 'Department'. It would be no surprise to her that its promises went unhonoured. She opened another tin of condensed milk.

'Go and see Mr Cartwright,' said Hussein's father again, not looking at his son, but at his reflection in the side of the toaster, checking the trim of his moustache. And because Hussein was a dutiful son, and always obeyed his father, he did.

At least, he tried. He went on the bus to the Regional Office where he had been interviewed, where he had been tested, after a fashion, and accepted onto the register. Mr Cartwright had asked for his personal details and signature on a number of forms, shaken his hand heartily, and given him a shiny leaflet to take away with him. 'See Marcia about your money, um, Hussein,' he had said, glancing at the forms before dropping them into a wire tray already overflowing with pieces of paper. 'And don't forget your suit!'

So Hussein went into the Regional Office, which was at

the end of Park Street between a video shop and an off-licence, and he stood in front of the woman's desk until she noticed him.

'Can I help you?' she asked, in a voice that implied it was a great condescension on her part to offer, a great insolence on his to be there at all.

'My name is Hussein Azdrubal,' Hussein told her. 'My giro has not arrived.'

'Are you registered?' she asked, looking harder at him. 'You could be anybody, you know. I mean, how am I to know?'

'My name is Hussein Azdrubal,' Hussein repeated. 'I was registered on Thursday the 27th of September. You registered me.'

With an effort, she searched a file. Grudgingly, she admitted that his name did indeed appear to be in it.

'We can't remember everyone that comes in here,' she said, airily. It was obviously unreasonable of him to expect anything more. 'You haven't been for your training yet, have you?' she added accusingly, reading his card.

'You put me on the waiting list,' Hussein reminded her.

'Well, then,' she said, in self-exculpation. 'What was it you wanted?'

Marcia had no idea why Hussein's giro had not arrived. She said it might be the post. 'You'll have to talk to Mr Addison,' she said.

Hussein bowed his head slightly towards her. 'I would like to see Mr Cartwright, please,' he told her.

She pursed her lips. 'Mr Cartwright's a busy man,' she said. 'He can't see everyone that comes in here. You'll have to see Mr Addison. Mr Addison's Mr Cartwright's assistant,' she said, pointedly, as though she thought the word might be a hard one for him to understand.

'All right,' said Hussein. He stood upright, expectantly.

The woman glared at him, exasperated now. 'Mr Addison's not here *today*. It's *Monday*, isn't it? You'll have to come back tomorrow.'

Hussein left the Regional Office and went to the railway station. He caught a train to London, and then a bus to Whitehall. Today was the day he had to get his suit, and they did not keep the suits at the Regional Office. After his interview with Mr Cartwright he had had to go to the stores at the Department itself, in Whitehall, to be measured, and today was the day they had told him to come in and collect the suit.

The stores were in the basement of the Department, in the corridor that led one way to the laboratory, the other to the canteen. After being measured, Hussein had gone into the canteen because he had missed his lunch. He had ordered a kebab. It had not been very nice. Today the smell of chips was powerful from one direction, the smell of battery fluid from the other. Hussein stood in the middle, at the door of the stores, and waited.

The storeman was a tall skinhead with HATE tattooed on one hand and KILL on the other. He was talking to a friend, who had enough hair for both of them, tied back with an elastic band. He also had a broom, though he was doing nothing with it. The two men were discussing footballers, or perhaps it was wrestlers. The storeman, grinning, said he had a room full of suits, but no authorization to give a suit to Hussein. There was no record that a suit had been ordered for him. He was sure there wasn't, even though Hussein was able to tell him that the order had been placed on Thursday the 27th of September, when the storeman himself had measured him. The storeman said he would look.

Hussein stood and waited for the storeman to stop talking to his friend and go and look for the order. While he waited, he took off his glasses and wiped them with his handkerchief. He listened to the transistor radio the storeman had behind him on a shelf. 'The gunman, who claims to be holding top secret government documents, has gone to ground in the four-star Covington Hotel,' said the radio newsreader intensely. 'He is demanding a press agent.'

Hussein smelt the chips and wondered how long he would have to wait here. He started to ask the men if they knew what time it was, but as soon as he spoke the man with the broom said, 'Get some music, Dave, for fuck's sake.' The one called Dave reached for the radio and changed the station, though the newsreader was now telling them reassuringly about what the police were doing. Instead, Dave discovered the voice of a woman who sang yearningly that she wanted him to touch her body, to the rhythmic sound of metal cans being crushed. This pleased him, and he turned it up louder, then continued to talk about wrestling, unless it was football.

Hussein waited a little longer, then realizing he would have to leave at once to catch his train, he went.

Next morning at breakfast, Hussein's father looked round from the television and saw his younger son sitting across from him. 'Hussein, has this giro cheque arrived yet?' he asked, and frowned when Hussein admitted it had not. 'Go and see that Mr Cartwright,' his father advised him.

'They said I must see Mr Addison, father,' said Hussein, who had told him so the previous evening. His mother said nothing. She sighed deeply and stared at the television, where a woman with a singing cat was explaining how all its fees went to help the rainforests. Hussein knew it had been deeply humiliating to his mother to be told one of her sons was 'Paranormal', even if it was only the younger one. She was sure the neighbours were talking about him. It was useless for Hussein to assure her the neighbours never gave him a thought, being unconcerned which of the young brown men in the locality lived next door.

It was raining. The bus was almost full. Several people who arrived after Hussein got on before him, and he had to wait for the next bus. He returned to the Regional Office. He reminded Marcia she had told him to come back today to see Mr Addison, and apologized for being rather late.

'He's not here, is he?' replied Marcia, as though she had mistaken his talent. Perhaps she thought he was the one the papers called X-Ray, or another one, Precogno. 'He's got flu.'

'May I please see Mr Cartwright, then?' asked Hussein, hopefully.

She did not answer his request, but said only, 'Where's your suit?'

'I went to the stores at the Department in Whitehall,' Hussein told her. 'The man there is looking for my order.'

Marcia looked suspicious. 'Are you sure you ordered it?'

'Yes,' said Hussein, patiently. 'I ordered it on Thursday the 27th of September. You gave me the form.'

'You'll have to have your suit to talk to Mr Addison,' she said. 'All trainees are supplied with suits. You have to go to the Department, in Whitehall,' she said, slowly and clearly. She lifted her head and looked along her nose at him. 'All right?' she enquired, sounding as if she was challenging him to say that it wasn't.

Hussein bowed slightly. 'I'll go there this afternoon.' And making an appointment to see Mr Addison the following day, he left the office and went to the railway station.

Dave the storeman was on duty again. His friend with the broom was nowhere to be seen. Dave was sitting with his chair tilted up on its back legs, reading a newspaper. He had a matchstick in the corner of his mouth.

'Yeh?' he said, when Hussein made his presence known.

Hussein smiled, hoping not to offend the storeman. 'My suit,' he said, as though it was a trifling thing. 'You were going to look for my order. My name is Hussein Azdrubal.'

The man seemed to have forgotten him completely. He went away for a long time, then came back, thumbing with one hand through a stack of crumpled dockets. From the other hand his newspaper was still dangling. 'Jet pack, wasn't it?' he said, not looking at Hussein.

'No,' said Hussein. 'A suit. I'm a trainee paranorm.'

'Yeah,' said the storeman, unwillingly, 'but you was the one wanted the jet pack, wasn't you?'

'No,' said Hussein. 'I don't know anything about a jet pack.'

The storeman squinted at him with half a smile. He was obviously used to stupid foreigners who said one thing one day and something else the next.

'Have you got the suit?' Hussein asked.

'We've got suits,' the storeman admitted, scratching his HATE hand. 'I'll have to have a look what we've got. What size?' he asked, taking the match out of his mouth and looking Hussein over vaguely.

Hussein gave his measurements.

The man didn't move, or even acknowledge he'd spoken. 'Small, medium or large?' he asked.

'Medium,' said Hussein, supposing it was safest.

The man moved his head slightly, sideways. He put the match back in his mouth.

'Come on, then,' he said, and disappeared deeper into his territory.

Hussein followed, walking curiously after the shuffling man between towering shelves of maps, socks, briefcases, wigs and inflatable dolls. They went down some concrete steps in the glare of a bulb hanging from a white celluloid shade, and into a large room that stank of old wool and mothballs. On either side, stretching away into the shadows, were racks made of dull steel tubing. Hanging from the racks were suits, rows and rows of suits, on plain wooden hangers: more suits than Hussein could count, or even imagine.

Dave the storeman grabbed a jacket at random, gripping a sleeve between his thumb and finger.

'You can 'ave grey,' he said, his voice sounding strangely flat and dead in the clothy aisles, 'or grey . . . we got, lessee, I think we got brown . . . Wassis?' He snickered. '. . . grey . . .' He slouched away along the rack, tugging suits out at random and shoving them back. 'We got brown somewhere, I know we 'ave. There's grey . . .' As he moved further away, hangers clattering right and left, his voice grew fainter and fainter.

Frightened lest the man should go away and not come back again, Hussein called out, 'Grey is fine.'

'What?' called the man.

'Grey will be very nice thank you,' called Hussein.

'Grey?' The man came back with a suit in his arms. 'What size?' he said. 'Medium,' Hussein said.

The storeman plonked the suit in Hussein's arms. Dust swirled up in the air, making Hussein blink behind his glasses.

'If you don't like it, you can take another one,' said the storeman, chewing his splintering match. 'They're all the same.'

Hussein pulled the suit on. It smelt very old. The trousers were baggy, the turn-ups dragged on the floor. The shoulders were too big and the arms too short. The storeman tugged at them without result, and shrugged. 'They're all naff, ent they,' he said. 'Demob.'

Hussein looked at him blankly, looked down at the suit. It seemed to be much too loose and, at the same time, stifling.

'What they 'ad left after the war,' explained the man.

'Blokes stayed on in the army rather than wear them suits. Sign here,' he said, and handed Hussein an inky ballpoint and a clipboard.

Hussein signed his name, thanking the man for his trouble. He bent down and hitched the turn-ups up above the tops of his shoes. When he straightened up they flopped down again.

The storeman was staring vacantly out of the basement window, which gave onto a view of grimy brickwork and an iron downpipe, painted grey. 'You have to sign for it,' he said, searching haphazardly for his clipboard.

'I have,' said Hussein. 'Already.' He picked up the board from where the man had put it down and showed him his signature.

'You'll have to see the lab about the jet pack,' said the storeman. 'Along there.' He gestured down the corridor.

Not liking to contradict the man yet again, Hussein decided it would be best to go to the lab and ask, at least. Perhaps this was some other item of equipment compulsory for trainees that Mr Cartwright had just forgotten to mention.

The lab tech was stooped, Scottish and in a bad mood. He did not like being asked about jet packs by soft-voiced refugees from church jumble sales. 'They're all in for their MOT,' he said angrily. 'I don't know how many times I've told you.' Hussein apologized. He did not mention that he had never been into the lab, never seen the technician before.

On the train home, young girls pointed at Hussein's suit and whispered to each other, holding their noses and giggling. Hussein took no notice. He read another page of his second-hand copy of Thus Spake Zarathustra. It was difficult to understand.

Hussein's father wrinkled his nose and frowned vaguely at his son's suit as though wondering whether he had seen it before, and whether he was expected to comment; but he did not, though he greeted him with exaggerated pleasure. He and Hussein's mother had just been arguing about him. 'Tell me, my son,' he said. 'Where is the money they said they would send you, this Department of yours?'

'They say it may be stuck in the post, father,' said Hussein.

Hussein's mother said nothing, but stood with her back turned, dusting the photos of Hussein's brother Jamshyd's wedding. Jamshyd was a management consultant now, or perhaps it was a consultancy manager, and he lived in Milton Keynes, the city of the future. Hussein's father glared at her rigid back. He was proud of his younger son for being selected for this scheme of the government's, whatever it was. 'Go and see your Mr Cartwright,' he advised. 'He will sort it out. It is his job.'

Next morning Hussein got up and went to fetch the post. There was a plea for funds from a snail sanctuary, an offer of a collector's edition satellite dish in real Wedgwood, and an advertisement of fantastic free prizes you could win simply by paying your poll tax. There was no giro.

Hussein washed, shaved, cleaned his teeth and looked for his new suit. The trousers had slithered off the hanger in the night and were sprawled under the wardrobe. He tried to brush the fluff off, but it seemed to have bonded with the cloth. Hoping it wouldn't look as bad to everyone else as it now did to him, he put the suit on, hoisted the turn-ups, and took the bus to the Regional Office, where he asked to see Mr Addison.

Marcia looked distastefully at Hussein's suit as if it was an offence to all right-thinking people, and reached into her desk cupboard. 'Mr Addison's not here today,' she told Hussein, bringing out an aerosol and spraying the air pointedly, her little finger crooked at an angle. 'He's on holiday. You'll have to make an appointment.'

'But I made an appointment yesterday,' said Hussein, hitching the shoulders of his jacket up again. Seeing that she didn't believe him, politely he showed her, written down in the book in front of her, 'H Azbrul'.

'Is that you?' she asked, banging the aerosol back in the cupboard and peering at the book.

'I think it must be,' said Hussein diplomatically.

Marcia shrugged. 'I wasn't here yesterday,' she said. 'It must have been my replacement. I'll have to call up now,' she said, sounding annoyed, and picked up the phone with a flourish, as if she was going to hit him with it.

Just then the door opened and with a rush of air that fluttered the notices about NALGO meetings and AIDS testing, Whizz Kid was standing beside Hussein, leaning on the desk.

'Hello, darling,' he said loudly to Marcia, and grinned. 'I hear you've been trying to get hold of me.'

Marcia's face lit up. She held the phone up in the air, several inches away from her ear, as though unaware she had picked it up. 'Whizz Kid!' she said with pleasure. 'Long time no see! Can I get you a coffee?'

Whizz Kid was over by the noticeboard, picking up all the notices he had blown down, reading them and pinning them back up again. 'Nope,' he said decisively. 'Given up coffee.' He was dusting the leaves of Marcia's sickly Swiss cheese plant, fetching water from the toilet out back and pouring it into the pot. 'Given up smoking, given up –' He popped out to the shops and was back again in an instant, flourishing a packet of chocolate-coated Hob-nobs. '– red meat,' he said. 'But I must admit, I do have a weakness for a choccy biccy.' Smiling winsomely, he offered Marcia the last one, crumpled the empty wrapper and lobbed it over the desk into her bin. 'Hi, you must be new,' he said to Hussein, holding out his hand for him to shake. 'Whizz

Kid,' he said, smiling a smile of devastating candour and naturalness.

'Hello,' said Hussein, clutching at the hand as it zoomed by. 'I'm –'

'Like the suit,' said Whizz Kid, wiggling his eyebrows. 'Very retro.' He smirked, and rubbed his nose. 'Is the great man in?' he asked, leaning over Marcia's desk and fiddling with her typewriter.

'Just a minute,' she said. She got up and went and knocked on the door of the inner office.

'Come,' called a voice, and she went inside.

Without ever stopping long enough for him to answer, Whizz Kid asked Hussein what his 'act' was, what projects he was working on at the moment, whether he knew the truth about unsaturated fats and intestinal flora, and whether he had any connections in Japan. 'That's where the future is,' he said. 'Have you ever been to Tokyo? Amazing place, very technical, people living like sardines.' His face was very close to Hussein's suddenly, making him jump. 'Do you know how many acres of rainforest it takes every week to supply the Chinese with chopsticks?' he asked. His conversation seemed to have moved on to Hong Kong, DAT, the Mandelbrot Set, call forwarding. He flossed his teeth. When he stood still for almost a second, Hussein could see Whizz Kid's suit was not demob. It was creamy, glossy, with big shoulder pads, sleek all over him like a fresh coat of paint. Curious, Hussein reached out a finger. 'Uh-uh,' said Whizz Kid, halfway across the room. 'Don't touch the suit. Unstable molecules. You like? Still running it in.' He grinned again, self-consciously.

Marcia came back in. 'Mr Cartwright will see you now, Whizz Kid,' she said, smiling sweetly, and Whizz Kid was past her, inside the office, his voice sounding recognizably from beyond the still reverberating door.

Marcia sat down. She yawned, and covered her mouth and nose. She got out her aerosol and sprayed it all around again.

Hussein sat down. He took off his jacket, but his trousers looked so fluffy he put it back on again.

Before he could button it up, Whizz Kid was back out, hanging on to the doorway of Mr Cartwright's office with both hands, swinging backwards and forwards. Beyond him, Hussein could just see Mr Cartwright himself. He was saying, ' – Covington Hotel.'

'I don't know, Dennis, it's not really me, is it?' Whizz Kid said with easy good humour. 'Rushing armed desperadoes, rescuing hostages, yes, but government documents –' He pulled a mournful face. 'What's in them anyway? Government documents – I mean, it's not exactly *sexy*, is it?'

Mr Cartwright seemed to be attempting to reply.

'Tell you what, Den,' said Whizz Kid, 'give me a call. Give me a call say Friday.' In one smooth motion he produced a sharkskin Filofax, opened it, scanned it, replaced it in his utility belt. 'Call me Friday, we'll have a bit of a natter. Tell you what, if he gets a hostage, call me anyway. A nice hostage, I mean. Photogenic. Children are good. Or a woman. Preferably.' He was at the door, grinning. 'Ciao, everybody. Ciao, Marcia. Take care.'

Then he was gone. All the way up the road Hussein could hear brakes screeching and angry horns honking.

He stood up, hoisting the shoulders of his jacket back into place. 'Mr Cartwright?' he said, cautiously.

Mr Cartwright gazed around the room, and saw Hussein there for the first time. He looked blank.

'You interviewed me on Thursday the 27th of September,' Hussein said, going towards him. 'My name is Hussein Azdrubal.'

Mr Cartwright looked disappointedly past him, at the

closed door, and then at Marcia. 'Is there anyone else, Marcia?' he asked. His voice sounded very tired and resigned.

'Only this gentleman,' Marcia said, in a voice that suggested Hussein was nothing of the kind and she was corrupting the word by even associating it with him.

'I am Hussein Azdrubal, I have an appointment with your assistant Mr Addison,' said Hussein, not wishing to push himself forward.

Mr Cartwright rubbed his forehead. 'You'd better come in,' he said. Obviously he didn't remember Hussein, from the 27th of September or any other time. He held the door open for Hussein to step into his office.

Inside, everything was much as it had been, except where papers from the wire tray had now overflowed onto the floor. Hussein wondered if his registration was still among them.

'Sit down, um,' said Mr Cartwright, sinking heavily into his own slumped chair. 'What have we found you?'

'This suit, sir,' said Hussein, pulling at the cuffs.

'Remind me, um, Hussein, isn't it, what is it you do?' Mr Cartwright asked him, looking wearily at him as if he was just another item in the mess, something he'd put down earlier and forgotten about. 'I suppose Marcia has all your details, hasn't she? Paperwork,' he said, and smiled lugubriously. 'Never mind that now,' he said, and slapped the desk decisively. 'How do you fancy working with Scotland Yard, um –? ' He looked among the papers under his hand, as if hoping Hussein's answer might be written down somewhere there already.

Scotland Yard, thought Hussein. The police. He wondered what use he could possibly be to the law of the land. 'I am happy to try, sir,' he said, obediently.

'Good boy,' said Mr Cartwright. He opened a drawer and rummaged in it without result. 'It's this Covington Hotel siege thing.' Giving up the drawer, he turned to his briefcase and rummaged through that instead. He pulled out a folded paper and showed it to Hussein.

It was a copy of the *Evening Standard*. On the front was an identikit picture of a scowling man. It looked like the Duke of Edinburgh. 'Some bloke who's got his hands on some documents or other. Oh, and a gun. Not bulletproof, are you, um –'

Hussein swallowed. 'No, sir,' he said.

Still rooting through the drawer, Mr Cartwright waved an airy hand. 'Well, don't worry. They never shoot anyone, these blokes. Haven't got the bottle. And you'll have Scotland Yard there right behind you, don't forget. Finest marksmen in the land. Pop down there, anyway, would you, um, and if you get stuck, give me a call here, you've got the number, haven't you? And we'll see who else is available.'

Hussein stood up. He'd got it, his first agency job. Assignment. He didn't like the sound of it, but he would manage. He hoped. 'Marcia will give you the forms,' Mr Cartwright said, shaking his hand vigorously again and clapping him on the shoulder as he ushered him back into the outer office. 'Marcia, would you –? ' he said, looking at his hands, then at Hussein's jacket, then diving into his pocket in search of a handkerchief.

Marcia did. There were several forms, all to be filled in in triplicate, because the photocopy budget had run out.

Hussein got the next train, then a bus to Marble Arch. He tried to read his Nietzsche on the way, but was too excited to concentrate. Instead, he looked through the papers Marcia had given him. One of them said fares by public transport would be refunded on receipt of an application countersigned by his section head. There was a leaflet advising him what to do about a pension. Another form was for claims by seconded operatives in the event of loss, damage, theft, injury or demise, which stated that it was not to be returned to the Metropolitan Police, but directly to the DPR.

Hussein folded all the papers and put them in his inside pocket. They felt very bulky there. He looked out of the window of the bus. The streets were nearly dark already. He would be late home for tea. He wondered if he would have a chance to telephone his mother.

There were several police cars and several more radio and television cars parked in front of the Covington Hotel. Around the front steps was a sort of fence made of orange tape, with some policemen inside it. The policemen's main occupation seemed to be looking stern and capable while the television people pointed their cameras at them.

A small crowd of spectators had gathered. They were women and men, young and old, black and white and in between. The only thing they seemed to have in common was that none of them looked as if they had enough money ever to set foot inside the Covington Hotel.

Excusing himself as he went through the crowd, Hussein lifted the orange tape and ducked under it. He went towards a police inspector with bushy eyebrows and a flat cap who was leaning on the roof of one of the cars, his foot on the sill of the open door.

As Hussein approached the inspector was talking on his wrist radio. 'Hot-dog surveillance bandage on thirteen at oh-seven-five, if you ask me,' he said rapidly. 'We've got chummy here sweating antifreeze, over,' he said proudly, casting a flickering glance at an upstairs window of the hotel and baring his teeth, which he tapped intently with his thumbnail, listening to whoever was on the other end of his radio. Another policeman was sitting in the car, in the passenger seat, staring expressionlessly straight through the windscreen.

Hussein waited politely. Suddenly the inspector barked, 'Don't give me any aggravation, Lychgate! Looks like a rub-

ber lightbulb job, repeat rubber lightbulb, and if Special
Branch don't like it they know what they can do with their
bathcubes. Out.' Brusquely he jabbed the miniature cut-off
switch with the tip of his little finger.

'Sir?' said Hussein. He got the papers out of his pocket.

Instead of speaking to him, the inspector leaned down
into the car. 'Bloody bathcubes,' he said disparagingly to his
subordinate.

'Sir,' agreed the subordinate, unmoving.

'Hand me that bloody horn, Wallis,' demanded the
inspector.

'Sir,' said the subordinate, and passed him a gleaming
white loudhailer.

Switching it on, the inspector pointed it up towards the
hotel window and bellowed into it, *'Throw the gun out, Atkinson! Give yourself up!'* He glared at the window, and so did
one or two of the other officers, in a manner that was curious
rather than hopeful. There was no visible result.

'Chummy's not bloody budging, Wallis,' said the inspector to his subordinate.

'Sir,' Wallis affirmed.

'We're not going anywhere, Atkinson,' threatened the
inspector through the loudhailer, then switched it off and
threw it contemptuously back into the car.

At that moment he noticed Hussein, standing two feet
away from him, trying to wriggle his jacket to lie straight
across his shoulders.

'How did you get in here, Ali Baba?' demanded the inspector. 'What do you want?' Then, focusing on Hussein's suit,
on the sheaf of forms he was holding out towards him, he
groaned. 'The bloody Freak Show, Wallis,' he said. 'That's
all we need.'

Wallis's eyes flickered sideways at Hussein. 'Sir,' he con-
curred.

The inspector took Hussein's forms without looking at them and threw them inside the car. 'What can you do, then, sonny, walk up walls?'

'No, sir, I –' began Hussein; but the inspector didn't wait for his answer.

'I'll tell you what you can do, sunshine, you can stay out of my bloody hair.' He advanced on Hussein quickly, in a threatening gesture that turned into a paternalistic squeeze of the shoulders. He spoke very softly. 'Leave it to the professionals, okay?' He looked at his hands, grimaced.

Hussein was not sure that Mr Cartwright would be very pleased if he returned to the Regional Office and said the officer in charge had sent him away. He thought perhaps he should assert himself a little, on behalf of the Department. He pointed into the car. 'My papers,' he said.

'I'll sign your papers,' said the inspector aggressively. 'Fucking Bob-A-Job, here.' He dug unproductively in his trouser pocket. 'You got any change, Wallis?'

'Sir,' said Wallis, and passed him some coins from the glove compartment of the car.

The inspector held the coins out to Hussein. 'Here,' he said, and gestured back in the direction of Oxford Street. 'Two teas,' he said. 'Two sugars in mine. Sugar, Wallis?'

'Sir,' said Wallis.

The inspector leaned his elbow on the car roof again and started talking aggressively into his wrist radio. 'Random turkey Senegal luncheon voucher in a baby's bottle, Lychgate,' he snarled, 'and I want it *yesterday*, over!'

Hussein walked away. He did not go in the direction of Oxford Street. He walked around the back of the Covington Hotel, where the tourists didn't go. There was a filthy young couple sitting in a doorway beside a mound of torn and overflowing rubbish bags and sodden cardboard boxes. Their legs were wrapped in a tattered sleeping bag. 'Spare some change, please,' chanted the girl, not even looking up as Hussein passed. She was shivering.

Hussein stopped. As he reached down to give them the policeman's money, his jacket slipped suddenly sideways and slid down his arm. The collar flipped up and knocked his glasses off.

The couple looked at the glasses as if they didn't know what they were. Hussein bent down and picked them up. He checked that they weren't broken. Then he pulled off the jacket and gave it to the girl. 'Here,' he said. 'Are you medium? I don't think I am.'

Leaving the couple staring at the jacket as if it had just materialized out of thin air, Hussein put his glasses back on and walked round to the back door of the Covington Hotel.

There was another police car there, and an armed police-man on the steps. He looked bored. His radio was squawking but he was paying no attention to it. Hussein walked right up to him.

'You can't go in,' said the policeman stolidly.

'I have been sent,' said Hussein. 'I have been given this job.'

The policeman nodded, dully. 'Your uncle's place, is it? Wrote you a letter, did he?' Seeing a thousand illegal immi-grants skivvying for rich Japanese tourists, he stared hard at Hussein, who had been born in Swindon. His face went blank. He looked at his watch and stifled a yawn.

Hussein opened the heavy door and went into the hotel. Everything was quiet. He walked along tiled passages and found a room full of shelves of toilet rolls. There were overall coats there, hanging on a rack. He put one on, and pulled on a pair of rubber gloves. Then he took a dustpan and brush from a hook, and went upstairs.

There was a security cordon at the fourth floor: more armed men, more orange tape. Carrying his dustpan, Hussein went past them totally unnoticed. Along the corridor, one door was surrounded by trays full of dirty tea-cups. Stepping carefully over them, Hussein knocked on the door. 'Mr Chummy?' he said.

The door flew open.

Inside stood a wild-eyed man wearing a brown suit and two days' stubble. He looked nothing at all like the Duke of Edinburgh. He was clutching an automatic pistol, which he pointed eagerly at Hussein. Hussein raised his hands, dust-pan in one, brush in the other.

'What are you,' said the man, 'the cleaner?' He was clearly disappointed, and seemed to have been expecting more illustrious company.

'They sent me, sir,' Hussein said.

A crafty smile flickered across the man's gaunt features. 'You'd better come in, then,' he said, holding the door wide.

Hussein went in. Like the corridor outside, the room was littered with empty teapots and full ashtrays. On the wall was a picture of a very green countryside place, with some brown water and a big cart in the middle of it. There was a big television, which was on. A bouncy song about peace and happiness was playing, while people dressed up as rainbow-coloured teddy bears hugged each other cumbersomely. On top of the television lay a large brown envelope.

The man with the gun shut the door with a bang and locked it, then walked energetically across to the window. 'I keep shouting, but they don't take any notice,' he said. He strained at the window, trying to push it open. 'Here,' he said, 'maybe you can get this open, it's stuck.' He stood back, dusting his hands, the gun in his pocket.

Hussein examined the window. 'I'm afraid it's not meant to be opened, sir,' he said. 'It's screwed shut.' He pointed to the screw heads in the frame. 'I could go and get a screwdriver, sir, and try to open it for you, if you like.'

'Oh, no,' said the man, shaking his head with gleeful malice. 'You're not going anywhere.' Then he squashed his long nose against the window, standing with his head at an exaggerated angle to squint down at the police behind the barrier below. 'I've got a hostage here!' he bellowed. 'If you don't get me Alastair Burnett, I'll shoot him!'

He reached for Hussein, as if to pull him to the window, but failed to complete the motion. Instead he looked Hussein over vaguely, his previous expression of disappointment returning. 'They could have sent someone a bit more glamorous,' he said. 'What is it, Equal Opportunities? I thought they had women cleaners, hotels. I don't suppose there are any children around anywhere, are there? Double your ratings, if you can get children. Even one child.' He seemed to be talking to himself.

Muffled through the glass, the loudhailer interrupted him. '*You haven't got a chance, Atkinson! Throw down the gun and come out now!*'

At once the man threw himself at the window and started to wrestle with it again, as if he still hadn't understood that it was screwed shut. '*Addison!*' he bawled. 'It's *Addison*, for Christ's sake! Trust the bloody British copper to get everything arse-backwards. What's it going to look like on the captions if they can't even get my bloody name right?'

In a fury, he lashed out at the litter with his foot. There was a clang, and an aluminium teapot flew through the air and splashed messily all over the picture of the cart. 'Damn,' said Addison, annoyed. 'There was still some in that one.' Dispirited, he started crawling about the room with the gun under his chin, opening teapots at random and peering into them hopefully.

Forgotten, Hussein stepped over him. He picked up the brown envelope from the top of the television and looked at it.

The envelope had printed boxes with names written in them, one after the other, and all crossed out. There was a piece of green string wound round and round two little metal clips, keeping the envelope closed.

Hussein put the envelope in his dustpan. He unlocked the door of the room, opened it quietly, and went out, closing it behind him.

On the back stairs, he put down his brush, unwound the string from the envelope, and looked inside. There was a single sheet of paper. He took it out. It was a photocopy of a page from the minutes of a meeting of the British Cabinet. Hussein read a bit of it. It was about the privatization of the DPR.

Hussein put the paper back in the envelope, wound the string around the clips until there was no more to wind, then went the rest of the way downstairs. He put the rubber gloves back where he had found them, hung the overall coat on its peg, and walked through to the front of the building in his shirtsleeves.

In the hotel lobby, the receptionist and some more policemen were sitting watching another big television. On the screen was a picture of the front of the hotel, with the policemen inside their orange tape fence looking menacing. Hussein wondered if he would be on the television screen now as he went through the front door and down the steps.

The sky was quite dark now, and it was growing chilly. Hussein walked over to the police inspector's car.

The inspector was sitting in the driver's seat, with his subordinate next to him, still staring straight ahead as though he hadn't moved. The window on the driver's side was up, but the one on the passenger's side was down. Hussein walked around to the passenger's side and handed the envelope in at the window.

'Here you are,' he said.

The policeman looked at it as if he didn't know what it was. Then he turned to the inspector. 'Sir,' he said.

The inspector turned from contemplating the street ahead and looked at what his subordinate held in his hands.

'Bloody hell, Wallis,' he said, and snatched the envelope from him.

'Sir,' said Wallis.

'He's dropped the bloody documents, Wallis!' said the inspector intently. He held the envelope and rapped its edge enthusiastically against the steering wheel.

'Sir,' said Wallis.

'He's only bloody dropped them!' said the inspector, baring his teeth in a ferocious grin. 'That's all he's bloody done!' He shot his cuff and started jabbing the tiny buttons on his wrist radio.

Wallis was looking around, through the windows of the car, as if something out there in the street had caught his eye, something moving; nothing special, just something he had seen out of the corner of his eye, and only for a moment, so he wasn't sure what it was or where it had come from.

But the Invisible Boy was walking away, back towards the city.

V

TABITHA AND COMPANY

Even when it was a singleton, before anything resembling a trilogy had come looming over the interstellar horizon, it was always my intention that Take Back Plenty *should contain as much as possible of the universe inhabited by Tabitha Jute and all the other people she encounters, of whatever shape, colour and chemical composition. This is the Plenty Principle: to make each book as full as I can pack it of places and adventures and images and dreams and stories.*

One of the stories I never managed to do more than allude to was the story of the Zodiac Twins, Saskia and Mogul, and how they weren't twins at all, originally, but the survivors of a most unusual experiment in a most extraordinary laboratory, from which they had been rescued in the nick of time by the renegade Cherub, Xtasca. Fortunately, the following year, 1991, the Birmingham Science Fiction Group invited me to be their guest at the 21st Novacon. As a part of their duties, each Novacon Guest of Honour must provide a short piece of writing for publication as a souvenir chapbook. That duty, like all the others, it was my very great pleasure to fulfil.

In the Garden

1

IT WAS SUNNY on the side of the hill. The grass was green and the sky was blue, the china blue of late spring, dotted with high tiny clouds. Bumble bees bowled ponderously from cloverhead to cloverhead, their shiny black legs hanging beneath them, gilded thick with pollen. In towelling romper suits the children crawled in the grass, patting each other's soft bodies with their little hands. The suits were pastel colours, each one different; pink, blue, green, yellow and mauve. The children were thin, with long heads and fey, delicate features.

The hillside rolled away far below, out of sight. There looked to be trees down there, positively a forest of dark pines and shaggy firs. Beyond that was the valley, the geometric patchwork shapes of farms. Small blue and yellow birds skimmed the tall grasses, seeming to catch insects on the wing, snatching them out of thin air.

The children laughed, and put their fingers in their mouths.

They could come to no harm here, for all the altitude seemed to be so high, the slopes so steep. Nothing here could sting or scratch or bite. It had been provided for them, this place, after extensive work. It was a place of sweet scents and tiny flowers, small bushes round as cushions, the sound of birds that piped from distant unseen trees and hedges. A butterfly whirled past, flapping friskily.

A little girl lay on her back in the grass, waving her hands and kicking her feet in the air. The breeze swooped down and kissed her and fluttered the flossy locks on her narrow forehead. She laughed, squeezing her eyes shut and opening her mouth. Beside her a little boy pulled daisies. His face was like hers, his eyes were the same moist, colourless colour. He fisted the daisies towards his mouth, but got lost halfway somewhere and dropped them on the front of his suit. Then he tore up grass leaves and pushed them at the little girl's cheek.

One of the others came up, crawling rapidly through the grass. She was another little girl, though you could not tell them apart, any of them, except by the colour of their suits. She crawled towards them, and kept crawling once she'd reached them, so she ended up jammed in between the two of them, with the little boy lying on her back. They were very supple, all of them. The birds sang, the sun shone, the children ate daisies.

If you could have stood amongst them, five children wriggling and bobbing around your feet, and looked south towards the edge of the meadow, where the hedgerow would have been if there had been any hedgerow – if you had stood and looked over there, shading your eyes with your hand against the golden dazzle of sunlight, you might have blinked suddenly, your eyes confused by a twist in the distance, like a flaw in the perspective of the landscape.

An instant later it had healed itself, and left nothing there to see. In the steady sunlight everything looked just as it had the moment before. The swell of the green meadow ruffled like a sea in a breath of wind. Perhaps a cloud had passed, or the shadow of a crow flicking across the sun. Perhaps it was an atmospheric kink, some local inversion of heated air.

Whatever it was, the second little girl saw it too. She

reached her hand up, as if she was trying to grasp hold of the scene before her eyes. She spoke. 'Fairy!' she said.

Her sister had seen nothing, but now she sat up and stared in the same direction, with the same intent expression on her face. 'Where?' the boys started asking. 'Where?'

'Fairy,' said the little girl again. 'Fairy!' She patted the nearer boy on the leg, spreading her hand and waving it into the sun. Then she stuck her fingers in her mouth and sucked them. She put the heel of her other hand in her eye. 'Was a fairy,' she said, indistinctly, to no one in particular. 'Saw her.'

Her sister turned from the landscape to look at her. She crawled across her feet. Then she stood up.

The boys were throwing bits of grass at each other.

2

Sometimes it was night. The light went away, and the pipes played softly. The children slept where they fell, surrounded by the stars. Stories told themselves in their eyes and ears, big, brightly-coloured stories. Then it was day, and everything started again.

Zidrich wanted to go up to the top of the hill. Suzan wanted to go with him. They held hands and toddled up through the grass.

It was a long way to the top of the hill. Zidrich was distracted by a white flower, then by a patch of white flowers, and then by a bee that was nuzzling the white flowers. Suzan saw another bee and chased it. She ran in a big circle around Zidrich and the white flowers. She hooted and waved to Goreal and the others, who were playing hide and seek. They never went very far from each other, any of them. Zidrich and Suzan had walked a long way, walked until they were tired and their feet hurt, but they hadn't really gone anywhere.

'I'm tired,' said Suzan. She lay down on the ground with her bottom in the air and closed her eyes.

Zidrich stood and looked around. There was the green field on either side of him, rolling on until it dipped out of sight around the hill. The ground ahead seemed to rise up like a wall. When he looked up, right up in the air, there was blue sky and nothing else, only the sun that swung slowly round them every day. The little blue and yellow birds flew about, exactly the same as they had the day before. Here came the butterflies too, just the same as yesterday. You could never catch one, no matter how hard you tried.

Zidrich felt cold suddenly. He did not know what it was. He had never felt cold before. The blue of the sky over his head went dim and pale, and something seemed to be coming in through his clothes.

Zidrich began to blink. He felt unhappy and frightened. He did not know what they were either. 'Suzan,' he complained. He did not want to go up the hill on his own. He turned face about on the hillside and shouted to the others.

He could see Goreal running in the meadow. 'Goreal!' he shouted. He could see Saskia tiptoeing from one bush to another. They were playing hide and seek. Zidrich shouted 'Saskia!' and waved.

He could not see Mogul. Mogul was hiding. He was hiding behind a bush. There was nowhere else to hide except behind the bushes. They never went down into the forest.

Suzan was standing up, pointing excitedly. 'I see Mogul!'

'I see Mogul!' shouted Zidrich too. He laughed.

'Ow!' shouted Mogul, crossly, and ran out from behind his bush. Goreal ran too, the wrong way.

The children were happy together. They ate coloured jellies out of plastic bowls. The jellies tasted of everything you could imagine, lemon and paper and seaweed and lamb. 'This one tastes like Vaseline,' said Suzan.

Goreal laughed. 'Suzan's is Vaseline,' he told the others. He had finished his jelly now, and started running around, doing somersaults. Below the hill the farms seemed to be moving, as if the wind was blowing the fields about. Goreal stood and watched the beige and spearmint green pentagons shifting slightly, drifting in and out of each other. Above them the forest held out its furry arms and quivered.

There was a shiny, globular, black thing flying between two trees.

'There's one!' Goreal shouted. Five pairs of identical colourless eyes stared where he pointed. They looked so alike, the children, but they never made a mistake.

You didn't see many fairies in the day. Most days you didn't see any, even when they were there. But in the night when you slept sometimes there were lots of fairies, and tall people with loud voices, all floating about in a huge round room, and you couldn't move.

'Fairies shone lights at me,' Zidrich remembered. 'I was sick.'

Goreal said: 'I wasn't sick.'

The others looked at each other. 'We weren't sick,' they all said; and they looked at Zidrich.

Zidrich looked down at the forest, but the fairy had gone. The fields below had fallen still.

3

The next morning, or perhaps a few days later, they woke up and couldn't find Zidrich. He wasn't behind a bush. He was neither up the hill nor down.

Between the field and the forest was a big ditch full of

dead needles and black moss. They often saw fairies there and sometimes an angel. It made them feel bad to be down there. It was a cold, scary place.

The children stood there now, holding hands in a line along the ditch, looking into the forest. They shouted for Zidrich.

Mogul was on the end. He held Saskia's hand tightly. 'I can't see him,' he said.

'We ought to go in,' said Saskia.

It was very dark in the forest. The trunks of the trees seemed to rise up in front of them like a wall. To left and right, the forest curved away out of sight. The gaps between the trees were so small the idea of squeezing through was suddenly very very frightening.

'We don't go in there,' said Suzan.

'Zidrich might be in there,' said Mogul.

'He isn't!' said Goreal. His voice was very high, he was piping like a bird. 'We don't go in there, so he isn't in there!'

He was on the other end of the line, holding Suzan's hand. In his other hand he had a long stick. He plunged his stick again and again into the ditch, shaking the leaves in his agitation. Then he let go of Suzan's hand and ran back up the hill.

The rest went back up too.

The children drank plastic beakers of milk. There were only four beakers today. The children sat in a lonely square. Everybody knew what everybody else was thinking.

It was Saskia who said it aloud. 'He's gone *away*,' she said.

Suzan hugged her knees. 'He can't have done!' she complained, looking at her accusingly. 'When you go *away*, it's not real. You're still here.' She looked at the others for confirmation. Goreal was nodding, very vigorously. Mogul made a half-shrug, scratching his shoulder.

'Zidrich has gone *away* and he's still there,' said Saskia.

They put all their beakers on the tortoise, which ambled slowly away down the hill. Mogul watched it disappear into the grass. Where did the tortoise go, when it went? Into the forest? Or beyond, into fairyland?

Sometimes, at night, you went away. You didn't know how you went, you were just there, in the big round room. Sometimes you were on your own; sometimes the others were there too. There was always an angel, sometimes more than one. Some of the angels were young and very beautiful. Others had skin like trees, hard and brown and cracked. The fairies did things to you with their bright machines. Then you woke up.

You never remembered much, but sometimes someone else remembered the same things. Sometimes you didn't remember being there until somebody else said something. Most mornings you didn't remember anything.

Goreal hadn't been away for a long time, and he had forgotten what it was like. He had begun to wonder whether it ever really happened. He began to wonder whether the others were pretending.

But he remembered Zidrich. He hid pieces of biscuit and put them in a special place down by the ditch for him when no one was looking. He wedged them in the clefts of a shrub. One day Saskia found them. 'Look,' she said, and showed the others.

'They're for Zidrich,' Goreal said. 'I put them there for him.'

Saskia sighed and put her hands on her hips. 'Zidrich's gone,' she said. 'He isn't coming back. Never!'

'We don't know that,' said Mogul.

'He might come back one day,' said Suzan, looking at the biscuits. They argued now. They had never argued before Zidrich disappeared. Something had disappeared with him. Goreal started to cry.

That annoyed Suzan. 'Oh Goreal, you're such a baby,' she said, tossing her head, and she walked away.

Goreal wanted someone to say something or do something, to make it all right again. He looked at Mogul. Mogul thought about things. He might help. But he didn't. Whatever it was Goreal wanted, only Zidrich could do it. And Zidrich had been taken away.

'*Away* is dangerous,' said Saskia, and she ate the biscuits. Then she went off after Suzan.

Goreal went with them. They went off to play leapfrog. 'Mogul!' they shouted. 'Mogul, come and play! Oh do come, Mogul!'

Mogul sat watching the forest. He sat there for a long time, watching. Nothing happened.

When night came and the music began, an angel hovered over the hillside for several minutes, in plain view. It was an old one, with metal and plastic bits sticking out of it. A lot of the old ones were like that. There was one that looked as if lots of different people had been used to make it.

In the morning Goreal was missing.

4

The angels were people, white, and yellow, and brown. The fairies were shiny black and quite small. They looked even smaller than they were because they hadn't any legs. You could turn round sometimes and suddenly see one flying around you, swerving to avoid you. The fairies popped in and out of existence wherever they chose, apparently, riding very fast on little saucers like flat jelly dishes. They came to collect the birds, whipping them out of the air with their tails.

'I'm sure it's the same one,' said Saskia. She called to it. 'Where's Goreal?'

'Don't,' Suzan told her. Suzan was afraid of the fairies. She was terrified of the angels. She had always hung back when Zidrich and Saskia would go running after them, now she wouldn't even look at them.

'What have you done with him?' Saskia demanded; but the fairy had gone. Saskia put her hands on her knees and glared at Suzan as though it was her fault.

'I don't think they can talk,' said Suzan, justifying herself.

'They've got mouths, haven't they?' said Saskia. They had, in fact, little bow-shaped ones, and podgy cheeks and dimpled chins.

'So has the tortoise, Saskia, why don't you ask that?'

Saskia smiled sarcastically. Saskia was looking ill. She was playing on her own most of the time, and it didn't seem to be good for her. They were all looking ill, their faces pale except for dark blue circles around their eyes. The ceaseless sunshine did not seem to be doing any good.

'The tortoise is just an animal!'

'Well, what are the fairies then?' Suzan demanded, because even if she didn't want to talk about them, not to talk about them was worse.

But Saskia had completely lost interest in the argument. She had turned and folded her arms. She was inspecting the forest. She answered without looking round: 'They're fairies, you stupid!'

Mogul said, 'I think the tortoise might be a fairy too.'

He was sitting on the ground between them. When he spoke, Saskia sat down and put her head on his shoulder. She moved slowly, like a cat with something else on its mind.

Suzan stayed standing. She said: 'Mogul, we've got to do something.' She twisted her hands in her lap. She had something in her hands, a poppy, she had forgotten she was holding it. She twisted the poppy between her hands, back and forth, back and forth.

Mogul leapt to his feet. He tossed his head and bit the side of his thumb. He lifted his nose and looked proud. He did not look at either of the girls. 'We've got to search the forest,' he said, lightly.

Suzan crushed the poppy stem with her thumbnails. 'We don't go in the forest,' she said, in a tiny small voice.

Saskia was standing beside Mogul. They looked like a pair of young dancers, poised on their toes to hurl themselves into some desperate figure. 'You'll have to stay here on your own,' Saskia said.

They ran down the hill. Suzan ran after. At the end of the meadow Mogul did not stop. He swung his arms and leapt the ditch. Saskia jumped down into it and skipped across the bottom. They turned and reached out their arms to Suzan, and scared as she was, she jumped and they pulled her soaring across.

In the shadow of the forest they were suddenly chilled. The trees seemed to crowd nearer together, to close up into a wall. They seemed to grow right up to the sky.

'Mogul, we can't,' said Suzan weakly. She looked at her two companions. 'Aren't you frightened?'

'It gets a bit better if you don't think about it,' murmured Saskia, rubbing her arms. She grinned without humour. Her breath came out as steam.

Mogul put back his head and shouted. 'Goreal! Zidrich!'

Suzan cringed, expecting the forest suddenly to roar aloud in reply. Except for the creaking and soft rustle of the branches, everything was silent in there.

Mogul picked up a long stick and swished the weeds with it. 'Follow me,' he said, but Saskia had already gone on in.

The darkness under the trees looked clothy, furry. It was

confusing. The trees weren't as close together as they looked. In fact it was hard to say where the trees were, exactly. They were everywhere, all around, but they moved when you moved, and stopped when you stopped. They were always just out of reach.

Mogul gave a little giggle, though when he spoke he kept his voice down. 'It's the same trees,' he said. 'The same ones.' He pointed behind them. 'Don't you see, the trees are keeping pace with us!'

Suzan kept looking over her shoulder, whirling around as she walked, trying to catch a tree moving. She couldn't.

Saskia walked up to a pine tree. It was silhouetted in the gloom, black on dusty black. In a moment somehow the tree wasn't there, but a few steps further on. She looked round to see if the others had noticed, but they didn't look as if they had.

'Look,' said Saskia. 'Watch this.'

And she took a run across their path, running straight at another tree, her hands stretched out in front of her.

'Well?' she demanded, when she reached the far side.

Mogul looked at Suzan. 'You ran through the tree,' Suzan said.

'No I didn't!' said Saskia. 'The tree ran away.'

Suzan squeaked and hunched in her head, looking fixedly at the forest floor beneath her feet.

Saskia, meanwhile, walked suspiciously up to the tree and gave it a kick. Suddenly it wasn't there to kick. It was behind her again.

'Oh don't Saskia, don't, don't, please, don't!' moaned Suzan.

'Come on. We have to stay together now,' said Mogul, and he reached for both their hands.

'I don't suppose it makes the slightest difference,' said Saskia, giving him hers.

They walked on through the forest, which in a while went thin suddenly, flattening out like a picture painted on a curtain. The curtain was a curtain of light like a waterfall as thin as a razor pouring sideways at you, from each side. It was so bright and gold it hurt them as they burst through it.

Beyond the curtain was darkness, and the stars.

Stars above and stars underfoot. They had come to the edge of the world, and found the place where the stars were.

They seemed to stand on the brink of a precipice with nothing but space above and before and below. The only sound was a high hum, soft and directionless. Nothing moved out there in the infinite blackness. The stars hung very still, accusingly.

In terror of falling, the children sank to the floor, but their eyes were already registering that there was a wall, a clear shiny wall, between them and the stars. They could not see it, but they could see themselves reflected in it, one face reflected three times. The wall was cold and smooth. Their breath made mist on it.

The invisible wall made a complete circle. The children paced round it, the flattened, skewed ghosts of forests and fields on their left, infinity on their right. They learned that the world was surrounded by glass, and beyond that by unbroken blackness and stars.

The glass went up as far as they could reach. They climbed on each other's shoulders. It was higher than that. They found out that it curved slightly as it rose, back over their heads. It made a sharp corner with the floor. Beneath that they could not delve.

The children sat with their backs against the glass, looking into the dusty green blur of the imaginary forest.

'Zidrich!' shouted Saskia.

'Zidrich!' shouted Mogul. 'Goreal!'

Their voices blatted off around the dome.

Suddenly the dusty light turned rich and green and golden. It spread towards them in waves, a sea of light breaking over them. In among the light, the trees of the forest rushed again to surround them.

The children flinched, seeing trees hurtling at them. They huddled down against the glass.

Suzan kept her head up. The breeze of the trees' arrival blew dust and flinders in her face. But she laughed. 'Quiet!' she said as they pulled at her. 'Listen!'

Somewhere, a horn was blowing. Fifty horns were blowing, sweet and high. *Come away, come away,* they blew. *Come away with us now.*

They blew from beyond the trees. They blew from a place hidden from glass and stars. Bats flew out of it, slivers of black ice on a cold wind. Invisible owls hooted. Suzan started shouting again.

Mogul and Saskia tried to calm her, but she was too excited. But she was happy, and smiling. She held up her hands. 'Listen!' she cried. 'They are singing.'

Mogul and Saskia tried to keep hold of her, but their hands were slipping. They tried to rouse themselves, but their eyes were closing. They could hear nothing but the high wavering horns.

'Golden fires!' said Suzan happily. She pulled on Saskia's arm and pointed away through the trees. 'Singing and dancing and wonderful feasts,' she said; and she shook Saskia by the arm. 'Can you really not see them?'

She looked with pure love into their faces. Her grey eyes brimmed with joy.

At the same instant, Mogul and Saskia dropped down into a deep sleep. Then Suzan, who had forgotten that she had ever been afraid, ran to meet her silent new friends.

*

5

Mogul and Saskia woke up. They were lying in a grassy hollow, high on a steep hillside. Bumble bees roamed the clover, their black legs thick with pollen, and the sun still shone warmly, though the day was largely done.

Mogul looked around. He said: 'Saskia, I had the strangest dream. I dreamed there were three of us, and we all lived here together, on this hill.'

Saskia was sitting with her legs stretched out in front of her, her hands clasping her ankles. She lifted her head from her knees and said: 'Five. There were five of us.'

'Yes!' said Mogul, rubbing his eyes. 'Five! You were there . . .'

'I was,' she said. 'I remember. Then we were in the forest. We went down into the forest. You and me, and –'

'– and –' said Mogul, nodding. He sat back on his elbows. His face was blank, smiling uncertainly.

'Suzan!' Saskia said. She pushed her hair out of her face. 'Mogul, I think we truly were in the forest. It wasn't a dream . . .'

'Wasn't it?' said Mogul. He lay there, thinking hard. After a moment, two small tears ran down his long cheeks. 'Goreal,' he said. 'Zidrich . . .'

'Suzan,' said Saskia. 'Where is Suzan?'

They looked at each other, like two mirrors.

'We lost her,' said one of them.

'In the forest,' said the other.

Mogul reached for Saskia, to hug her tight. But she slipped from his arms and got to her feet, in a spasm of mourning. She clenched her hands at her sides and shouted accusingly into the bland sky. '*SUZAN!*'

Mogul put his head between his knees and his elbows on the back of his head.

Neither of them said anything for a long time. They felt as if their memories had gone far away, fallen down a deep hole into darkness, and now they were hauling them slowly and heavily back into the daylight. Though they had slept, they felt sore and befuddled.

Saskia thought she heard Mogul sob.

She said nothing until he spoke. 'It's my fault,' he said.

She frowned at him. 'What are you talking about?'

He raised his head and looked carefully away from her, over the deep blue valley, with its wavering fields. 'I was pretending it was a game,' he said. 'I told myself there was no need to be afraid if it was only a game. A sort of puzzle. I thought,' he said, speaking in slow gulps, fighting back tears, struggling to express his meaning to the far sky, 'that way we could be brave; and rescue them.'

Saskia wasn't looking at him. She was rubbing her calf where she had hit it when they fell. 'They're taking us away,' she said angrily. 'One by one. They blow a horn, and everything stops.'

'Or starts,' said Mogul, emphatically. He had had an idea. It seemed to bring him no comfort, but he was determined to talk about it. 'They may be taking us away to send us off somewhere, somewhere else, to fetch things for them, or, or do things –'

She could hear he was struggling with something complicated. She wanted to encourage him. 'Like the blue and yellow birds,' she said.

'Yes.' Mogul wrapped his hands around his knees, breathing deeply, collecting himself. He nodded at the dimming landscape. 'This, all this – it may be just the beginning, like the beginning of a game. We don't know.'

All Saskia could say was: 'I wonder if the others remember us.'

She was beginning to cry now. She sniffed and wiped her

eyes with the sides of her fingers. 'Suzan asked me if I thought they were going to make Goreal into an angel,' she said.

Mogul gave a slight frown, digesting this, comparing it to his idea. He swivelled round to see his sister's face. 'Do you want that?'

'Are you joking?' she returned. She looked at him, her large pale eyes damp but steady. 'Do you?'

He deflected that. 'Did Suzan?' he asked.

Saskia didn't answer. In their invisible haunts the merry birds began to sing, heralding the evening.

Now that it was too late, Mogul understood he had never known the others at all. The fairies had done something to make him forget them. He had thought they were a dream. And before that, before this morning, if it was still the same day – he had always assumed they were all the same as each other, because, because – because they always had been.

He gazed at Saskia, feeling lost and deprived and weak with despair. And then he realized.

He was going next.

Not tonight, he thought. They have never taken two in one night. His next thought was: I must not let her know.

Saskia was standing with one hand on her hip, still breathing deeply. Her cavernous eyes devoured the sunset, which was violet, rapid, and very tidy. She looked as if she was thinking unfathomable thoughts. Mogul felt very lonely and afraid, but light-headed too, now that all that mattered had revealed itself to him. He wanted her to hug him, so he got up and hugged her.

'We'll stay here now,' he said. 'We'll be all right here. The tortoise will feed us and the birds will watch over us, and we will take care of each other, and tell each other our every thought, our every passing fancy. To every plant that grows we shall be gentle, and grateful for every tiny blade of grass. The angels will love us then and bless us, and send the fairies to bring back our brothers and our sister.'

He spoke very loudly. He was holding his head up again, as he had done before they went down the hill. An owl flew by in the gloaming, lighting up the ground with its eyes.

Saskia caressed Mogul's back, feeling his ribs stiff and clear through the cloth of his suit. 'They're not coming back,' she said, absolutely, when the owl had gone. 'There's only us now.'

They lay down in the grass, in each other's arms. Mogul murmured in her ear. 'I only said that for them,' he said. 'To keep them off.'

'In the morning we'll run away,' she said.

'Yes. Yes!' He hadn't even thought that far, hadn't seen where his thoughts were tending. It was the answer. With Saskia he could go over the hill, he knew they could do it. Over the hill and far away.

There was a soft sound, a sound of music. Mogul gripped his sister harder. 'Don't sleep!' he hissed. 'We mustn't go to sleep!'

Hurriedly they stuffed their ears with grass. It was hard to keep from hearing the faint, high piping noise that hung in the air all around. They pinched each other to keep awake.

Just when it seemed the music would never stop, it did. The landscape was completely still, frozen, ringing with silence.

Mogul pulled the grass from his ears. 'We did it,' he said.

'We did it,' said Saskia. Suddenly they were very excited. It seemed an enormous victory. They laughed in each other's faces, and kissed in the dark.

They drew apart then, both sensing the same doubt in each other; the same apprehension; the same desire. Mogul flexed his long body like a dog rolling on its back.

'Oh yes,' said Saskia, and slid right on top of him. She

parted his legs with her knee and pressed his shoulders into the ground with her hands.

Mogul opened his mouth and she kissed him. He brought up his hands and caressed the little breasts that stretched her suit. She purred.

White and slender in the darkness of the hollow, their bodies flickered one on the other like sharpening knives. Moths flew about, furry and glancing. Soon two cries rose up to cut the deepening night, two cries so closely entwined they sounded like a single voice.

Afterwards, Saskia lay stroking his chest. 'Do you suppose they're pleased,' she said, 'or angry?'

Mogul, wholly and completely relaxed, felt as if the hill under them was surging unstoppably through space. He wondered how many fairies there were out there in the blackness, gathered round the rim of the hollow, watching, listening, observing. 'They could have stopped us,' he said.

'No,' she said. 'No, they couldn't.' She kissed him and reached for him, and felt him stir again beneath her hand.

The second time took longer. No one and nothing disturbed them. They lay naked and perspiring in the clear hot night. Time seemed to have stopped now altogether. Saskia wondered how long it was until dawn; if dawn would ever come.

'I can't stand this,' she said. 'Come on.'

They stood up in the hollow. There was nothing to see all around but the stars, the hard white flowers of fire that were fixed far out in the black nothing. The grass was still as they loped naked down the hill, their feet sliding under them.

They found the ditch. Mogul jumped it again, so did Saskia. Silver and black in the night, the ramparts of the forest parted for them, as before. It was cold, and nightmarish. Something seemed to quiver suddenly beneath every bush, or keep pace with them overhead, slipping unnoticed from branch to branch. Just then they saw it. It was the owl, gliding with its great wings fully spread through the non-existent trees.

'They know we're here,' said Mogul, a tremor in his voice. He sounded relieved. It was good not to have to wonder any more.

Saskia stopped. She sat down on the forest floor.

Mogul shied. 'Here?' he said. 'Aren't we going to go – through?'

'This is far enough,' Saskia declared.

Mogul sat down. They turned to face the way they'd come and looked into the night.

Saskia wondered what they were going to say.

But Mogul had it thought out. 'Listen to us,' he said loudly. 'Are you listening?' He paused. 'We know what we are,' he said. 'We've worked it out. We all look the same, and you don't. You can come and go when you like, we can only go when you take us. You made us, didn't you? You made us and you're keeping us here for something. Because you like watching us. Because we're supposed to do something.' A note of frustration had entered his voice. 'What do you want?' he said. 'We don't know.'

'And we don't care,' shouted Saskia, hugging him to make him shut up. 'We don't care what it is, we don't want to do it. We want you to let us out.'

Then they lay back in each other's arms and waited for the hill to open.

As she zooms up and down the spaceways in her antiquated barge, the Alice Liddell, *it seems to be the fate of Captain Tabitha Jute always to collide with other people's fantasies, and be the object of unsought and unfathomable intentions. Even so, not until years later, when she trespassed into the labyrinths of Plenty, did she ever set foot in a Wonderland as dangerous as the moon called Umbriel.*

I was thinking of Sunset Boulevard *here, I imagine; and* Vermilion Sands, *the luminous, languid desert colony so perfectly designed by J. G. Ballard; and the Dormouse's treacle-well too, no doubt, where Elsie, Lacie and Tillie lived and learned to draw all manner of things. A place where dreams can be pulled out of the ground, solid, prosaic and incontestable: somewhere sensible people would avoid, surely, dreams being ambivalent companions, as Olister Crane remarks to Tabitha, 'not always welcome by daylight'. Still I think the Wells of Umbriel would present an irresistible attraction to any artist – especially ones like me, lazy by nature, far fonder of contemplating the work than actually doing any.*

The Well Wishers

ON UMBRIEL, WHERE the Dream Wells are, it is always one kind of night or another. Great nights and little ones succeed each other, darkness overlapping darkness, with only the silver-fretted heavens for relief. Sol, when Uranus does not eclipse it, is too far away to be much help. Most of its light expires on the crawl out here. So daytime is a technicality, like longitude, or irrational numbers. It can be proved to exist, but troubles few sleepers.

On Umbriel you can really concentrate on your dreams.

The ship sat alone on the field beneath the beacon. The terrain was the same all over, salty white with outcrops raw and jagged black, and there didn't seem to be much in the way of occupation; but tiny, outlying settlements like this could be horribly snotty about their zoning regulations, and the agency could be brutally literal about their policy of not rehiring careless drivers; so Tabitha Jute had opted for the field.

No one appeared to give her a welcome, or even a clue. There was no traffic, no workers, no one just hanging about, as there usually was on even the most insignificant moons. The woman who had acknowledged her approach and cleared her landing had been a recording.

'NOT A VERY FRIENDLY PLACE, CAPTAIN, IS IT?' said Alice.

Captain Jute was still new enough to this ship to be surprised by her remark. She suspected somebody had fiddled

with the programming of the persona, raising the sensitivity
levels, amplifying the affinity circuits. One day she would
have to get inside and poke around Bergen Kobold Persona
5N179476.900, given name Alice, to see what made her tick.

'No, Alice, it isn't,' she said. 'Never mind. I don't suppose
we'll be here long.'

Tabitha suited up and stepped out into a landscape like
a frozen sea. She felt the salt crust crunch silently under her
boots as she sprang slowly across to the office.

No one had come to meet her. There was one man on
the inside of a horseshoe counter big enough for twelve. He
was sitting with his chair in recline, watching AV.

Captain Jute opened her helmet. 'Hi,' she said.

The man lifted an indifferent hand.

The air was high oxygen, and warm. It smelt of pepper-
mint cycler freshener.

On the AV were a young man and a young woman in a
jeep. They were pretending to be riding along, while film
of a mountain road played behind them. They were talking
to each other, and laughing.

'Is there a message for me?'

'Nope,' said the field officer, his eyes not leaving the
screen.

The Captain unpopped her left cuff. She tapped up the
job details.

'Can you tell me where this is?'

The man gave the Captain's com set the merest glance
and pointed through the wall. 'Twenty minutes,' he said.
He didn't look where he was pointing.

'Where's the phone?'

He pointed at that in the same way.

'She won't answer,' he said.

Captain Jute made a long step to the phone. She plugged
in and started pressing the tabs.

She heard it ring, once. Then a muffled tape came on playing a forgotten pop song. There was a hustling, robotic beat; a woman's voice singing sluggishly, sullenly, along with it. If there were words, they didn't seem to have anything to do with making a phonecall.

Tabitha waited for a message, but the music was all there was. After a while she pulled her plug.

'She never answers,' said the field officer. Hands laced across his stomach, he watched his show. 'Twenty minutes,' he said again. 'You've got a car.' He stated it as a general principle.

'I'm saving up,' she said.

'Forty-five minutes,' he said.

Through the triple-glazing she could see the tracks of many vehicles, or maybe the same vehicle driving around in all directions. She could see the low plateau where the beacon was. Between there and here, roughly north-west, lay a low dull brown dome. In the distance were three or four lights, small, sharp and unwavering, like fallen stars.

On the screen the young people were still taking their imaginary ride. Only the man was talking now. The woman watched his face and smiled. The scarf on her head flapped like a flag in the artificial slipstream.

'Where do I get a car?' asked Captain Jute.

The man said: 'You wait a couple of hours, I'll take you.'

She wasn't going to get into that. 'There must be a cab.'

'I doubt it. This is apogee,' he told her, as if she might not have noticed. 'No one comes here at apogee.'

'People come here?' said Captain Jute, snapping up her cuff. 'That way?' she asked him.

He pointed again, east, a short stab in the scented air. 'Big place with all the windows.'

He keyed the door for her.

'She won't let you in,' he said.

Captain Jute reached for her sealing tab. The contact name was Morton Godfrey. A man's name, she had supposed.

'I'm just making a pick-up,' she said.

The field officer watched the people on the screen with unwavering attention, like a lover or a spy. Perhaps he had written the script and wanted to make sure they got it right.

'She never lets anyone in,' he said.

The house occupied a rise on the far side of the plateau. It was a low irregular pile of silver aluminium saucers. There were a lot of saucers, and they did have a lot of windows, thought Tabitha, coming up the slope. All the windows were alight, as if Mr Godfrey's employer was throwing a fabulous party.

A camera scutinized the approaching Captain. In her phones a robot voice said: '*State your business.*'

'Careways Agency pick-up for Morton Godfrey,' she said. She went up to the camera and showed her wrist. Artworks, the goods description field said.

'*Mr Godfrey is not available.*'

'Whose house is this?'

'*This is the house of Princess Badroulboudour,*' the robot said. '*She is not available.*'

'Was it something I said?' Captain Jute asked it.

'*I am not enabled to answer that question,*' said the robot. '*No one is available to deal with you at present.*'

In her mind's eye she could see it, a Facto 4000, multi-capacitied and very prim. She imagined it with a feather duster in its manipulators, going down a line of grey plaster statues.

'Where can I reach them?' she asked.

'*No one is available to deal with you at present,*' said the robot. '*Your visit has been recorded and logged at 05.22.32. Please return later.*'

Halfway down the hill, she looked back at the house. There was no one at any of the brilliant windows, nothing moving anywhere. Behind the house, Uranus was rising with a sour and sallow face.

She called the ship.

'Where is everybody, Alice?'

'COMMUNICATIONS TRAFFIC IS LOW,' Alice reported.

Captain Jute looked out towards the little bubble domes that were scattered across the corrugated plains of chemical ice. There was nothing moving down there either. She wondered who the hell would live here, and why.

'ONE CENTRE OF SOCIAL AMENITIES IS LISTED.'

'A bar? Is there a bar?'

'VERY PROBABLY. THERE'S A HUNDRED-BED HOTEL.'

'Someone does come here.' Religious retreats, knowing her luck. The ambience was getting to her. 'Who's this Princess Badroulboudour, do we know?' she asked the ship, as she called the hotel.

There was a swift pause while Alice searched. 'I CAN'T FIND ANYTHING UNDER THAT NAME. SHALL I PUT OUT A QUERY?'

'No, Alice, doesn't matter.'

The hotel answered. Tabitha could hear slow music, a couple of people talking in the background.

'Are you open?' she asked.

'*Ask me nicely.*'

The voice was studied, coarse, good-humoured, female. She relaxed a fraction.

'I'm just in. I'm looking for fresh air and a recharge.'

'*You find something fresh on Umbriel, sweetheart, you let us all know about it.*'

*

The hotel was called Reveries. It was inside the brown dome she had seen from the landing field. There was no one in the cloakroom. She put her chip in the slot, and her suit in a locker.

The corridors of Reveries were silent, with thick purple carpets in case somebody accidentally made a noise. There were signs to somewhere called the Well. Captain Jute followed them.

The signs led her to a small circular chamber, with two other corridors leading off it. There were some steps going down. At the top of the steps was a tall blue glass vase holding a single flower.

The flower was large. It was ostentatious, and not very realistic. There were six broad petals of cobalt blue that curved luxuriously back from a soft grey centre. In the centre was a face.

The face was humanoid, life-size. It had two green eyes, a broad nose, and a pair of glistening lavender lips. The eyes looked entirely vacant, but as Tabitha appeared the lips parted suddenly, as if in a little soundless sigh.

Tabitha felt the eyes of the flower follow her down the steps, and into the Well.

The Well was clean white rockfoam and vinyl, with red-wood trim. There were eighteen tables and a grand piano. The piano had a dustsheet over it, and the tables were empty.

On the juke-box at the end of the bar a saxophone was playing, while some men sang mournfully in unison in a language she didn't know. Opposite the bar was a picture window, showing a broad slice of desolation. The glass was tinted seaweed green. It didn't help.

There were six people in the room. One of them was standing behind the bar, the other five were sitting on stools in front of her. They were all older than Tabitha. They all looked at her as she came down the steps.

Tabitha hated being inspected. It made her feel she needed to hitch up her jeans and tuck her T-shirt in.

The barwoman had a head of tarnished curls and a face life had written lines on. She smiled dozily. 'How do you like the air?'

'It would be better with a beer,' said Tabitha.

'What's your choice?'

'The cheapest,' said Captain Jute. She went and sat at an empty table.

The other customers withdrew their attention. A drowsy, rumbling conversation resumed. Tabitha wasn't interested.

The Well was like any other hotel bar on any other world. The locals were leaning on the bar as if they were glued there. They were assaulting their livers with alcohol in a relaxed but businesslike way. On the little holopad of the juke-box a blond white man in a baggy suit was nursing a black saxophone that emitted floating white eggs of sound. Everything was perfectly bland and ordinary, in fact, except for the ornaments.

They didn't make good ornaments, in Captain Jute's opinion, but that was what they had to be. They were all the same size, about thirty centimetres tall, the same as the flower at the entrance; and they were all set up just above eye level, in case you wanted something to look at.

From where Tabitha sat she could see three.

One was a big transparent egg. It was full of a clear liquid, and there was some kind of creature hunched up inside it, which the egg was barely big enough to contain. The creature looked as if it might have been the offspring of a human and a fish.

The creature was partly animated, like the face in the flower. It kept making tiny squirming motions against the inside of its egg. Every time it did, strings of bubbles floated up from the corners of its mouth.

The second ornament was another creature. It was a model of a Thrant, poised as if to spring. It too seemed to be moving a little, flexing its long muscles, without ever moving its feet. It seemed to have its eye on Captain Jute.

Captain Jute hoped it wasn't actually capable of springing. She hoped that wasn't the sort of thing they found funny on Umbriel, at apogee.

The third ornament was a life-size head. It too looked human. It was bloodless white, and completely bald. There were long metal spikes sticking out of its skull. It kept smiling knowingly, and lolling out its deep red tongue.

'Hi there,' said a man. He had got down off his stool at the bar and come over to her table. 'Can I get you another?'

She looked at her beer. Apparently she had drunk it.

'Why not,' she said.

The man was dark-skinned, with a little gold ring in each ear and a shock of shiny black hair. He was wearing a crimson blazer over a collarless shirt in blue pinstripe. He had a little beard on the point of his chin, and there was a gold ring around that too. He was dressed up a lot for someone living in a place where no one came.

Perhaps he had been expecting her.

'You're not Morton Godfrey,' asked Captain Jute, 'by any chance?'

They all heard that. They laughed at her, sideways.

She ignored them and concentrated on her new acquaintance. He was grinning.

'No,' he said. 'I'm not Morton Godfrey.' He looked steadily at her, bathing her in his regard. 'I'm Olister Crane,' he said. He had that tone in his voice that allowed a chance she might have heard of him.

She hadn't.

He indicated the seat opposite her. 'Mind if I sit down?'

'I wasn't saving it for anyone,' she said.

He asked her: 'So, is that your Kobold out there at the field?'

Captain Jute said it was.

'Did Mr Godfrey send for you?'

She nodded. He hadn't, but that was none of Olister Crane's business, whoever he was. She drained her tube and began the new one.

Crane was not going to give up trying.

'Your name is Mo,' he said. 'Your name is Lucky.'

She would not play. 'My name is Tabitha Jute,' she said.

He complimented her with his eyelashes.

'You know who Mr Godfrey works for, Captain Jute.'

'A princess, apparently,' she said.

Crane found her reply amusing.

'A princess,' he repeated, affirmatively.

The saxophone record had stopped some minutes earlier. Now one of the customers at the bar leaned over to the panel and punched up something else.

There was a sound like steel brushes being dragged along a metal floor, and after a while, a woman crooning. She didn't sound any happier than the men with the saxophone had. On the holopad some kind of string puppet jerked and spun.

'This is where she is now,' said Crane. 'Princess Badroulboudour. Gracing our little colony.'

He looked at Captain Jute sidelong to see how she took this disclosure. He seemed to want her to be impressed.

There was nothing more boring, thought Tabitha, drinking, than people wanting you to be impressed. Crane reminded her of her father. This was just the sort of place she could imagine he might have ended up, drinking for consolation on a dead-end moon.

'Have you seen her yet, Tabitha?' asked a white woman at the bar. Already they had adopted her, accepted her into their club. 'Last year she bought some of my jewellery.'

'Tell her about your jewellery, Cerise,' said another man. He sounded somnolent with drink.

'You like jewellery, Tabitha?' The woman wore an iron and turquoise comb in her long blonde hair. She appraised the new member across the room. 'You should wear rubies. I've got some pieces you're going to adore.'

Captain Jute sat tight. She drank steadily.

'And you can read my poems,' Olister Crane was saying softly to her, 'and Noland's novel, and Gideam's opera.' He produced a huge white handkerchief and touched it to his eyes, as if they were wet, from humour, or emotion. He was still smiling. 'And maybe by then the Princess will let you see Mr Godfrey.'

He lay his large hand on the table between them, an ambiguous gesture of friendship or warning.

Tabitha examined the label on her beer.

Long after everyone had stopped waiting for her to speak and gone back to talking among themselves, she asked Crane: 'Where is she from, this princess?'

This stirred them all again, all her new pals sitting along the bar. They indicated the juke-box. They wanted her to look at what was on it.

While the music played, the figure in the holo had changed from being a string puppet. Now it was a living human woman in an industrial grey skinsuit, only instead of hands and feet, her arms and legs ended in sprays of electrical wiring. The wires were unbraiding, multiplying while the figure tugged and struggled.

'This is her,' said Cerise. 'Princess B.'

Tabitha watched for a moment. The trapped figure, half woman, half machine, reminded her of a woman called

Devereux. Devereux lived in a private habitat off Deimos. She wasn't someone Tabitha especially wanted to be reminded of. 'Do you like this stuff?' she asked Olister Crane, who was buying her another drink.

'Tabitha,' said Crane chidingly. 'You really don't know the Princess? She was the one who invented traipse!'

'Not my kind of thing. Put some blues on,' suggested Captain Jute.

It was useless. They found her something that was more or less R&B, then talked over it.

They had a mission, to educate and inform. Either that or they were punishing her lack of interest with a lecture on their local celebrity.

'You remember that thing people used to say,' said a fat woman called Georginelle, 'about having to reinvent yourself thirty-two times a second. That was Princess Badroulboudour. She was the one who said that.'

'Princess Badroulboudour – redesigned – the face of music – forever,' claimed Gideam, the composer of operas. He was elderly, and even more overweight than Georginelle. The gravity was kind here, to people that size. Still Gideam's breathing was laboured, his voice thick with mucus. 'She *became* the face of music.'

The face of music was equipped with breathtakingly large eyes, and a mouth that seemed to express a personal offence at the universe, or the human condition, or something. The patrons of the Well played Tabitha some more examples of her work: restless things in different speeds, but with the same abrasive kind of rhythm. The Princess appeared in a dozen different styles: in rags; in furs; once in a weird telescopic dress whose sections slid up and down her body while she danced. Untutored, the Captain might have been unsure that they were all the same woman, though there was a uniform frenzy to the appearances, as if whatever it was she disapproved of so was on the point of devouring her whole.

Captain Jute did get the sense that the Princess's reign had been pretty temporary, like all these things. She still had no idea what traipse was, or why it mattered. She had the feeling that if she told them how pointless it all sounded to her, somebody would say: 'Exactly.'

Crane was still monopolizing her. 'So what have you got there,' he asked, 'in your Kobold?'

'I'm making a pick-up,' she said.

'The Captain is making a pick-up,' said Crane to the rest of them, keeping his eyes on Tabitha.

'She's the lucky one,' grated the barwoman.

'What are you picking up, Captain?' called the somnolent man.

'I'm picking up some artworks,' said Captain Jute.

Now she had given them something. They were thrilled.

'She's working again!' Georginelle was positively exultant. She tipped back her head and clenched her fists.

The news was no surprise to Cerise. 'She couldn't just retire,' she said, as if that should always have been obvious to everyone. 'You can't *stop*. If it's in you, you *can't* stop.'

She wanted confirmation for her testimony. They gave it to her. You couldn't stop working, they all agreed. Though none of them at the moment seemed to be in much of a hurry to start again.

Everyone wanted to know what Tabitha knew. Tabitha told them again: she knew nothing. She showed them her wristcom. 'There, you see? Artworks. That's all it says.'

'What does she want with a barge?' said Crane to the room in general. 'She could just release them.'

'Security, Crane,' said Gideam. 'There are no safeguards here. Anyone who really – wants to can – steal all your ideas.'

'She doesn't want to let people know where she is,' said

Cerise. She said it loudly, claiming the credit for being the one to admit an unpleasing truth.

'Everyone knows where she is,' stated the somnolent man, truculently. By *everyone* he seemed to mean the entire population, permanent and temporary, of Sol System.

'Princess Badroulboudour,' Cerise continued in her fatalistic tone, 'could put this place back on the map, if she wanted to.'

'She doesn't owe Umbriel anything,' Georginelle said protectively. 'And she certainly doesn't owe us anything.'

This had the air of a ritualistic argument. There was no way either of them was ever going to convince the other. Maybe that was traipse too.

Captain Jute said to Crane: 'You're all artists.'

Crane nodded slowly and rhythmically. 'We are the Well Wishers,' he said.

He slid his hand across the table, and made a bridge across Tabitha's wrist. He did it delicately, slowly, looking humorously into her eyes. Perhaps the idea was that she would be mesmerized. Or perhaps he was daring her to stop him.

She moved the hand. She lifted her beer to her mouth.

'You sit here and wish,' she said.

Everything she said amused Olister Crane. 'Yeah, then, Captain, we do. But this isn't that Well. That's just the name of the bar. That's just like a joke. The Wells of Umbriel. You know?' He sat back, searching her face. He shook his head. 'You don't know anything, do you?' His voice was sympathetic, and high.

'Glory be,' the barkeeper said. She was looking across the heads of her patrons, out of the green window. 'If it isn't her coming.'

Crane got to his feet. Georginelle and Gideam and Noland turned on their barstools. Everyone gazed out of the window.

Across the rutted white waste a big grey car was approaching.

'It's her.'

They all stared. Their enthusiasm for the ex-entertainer seemed to have evaporated suddenly. They seemed oddly apprehensive, as if wondering whether she might have been listening to them talking about her.

'Do you think she's coming here?' said Georginelle, in a kind of hushed giggle.

Tabitha left the bar.

In the purple corridors, she found herself running. She did not know why. Perhaps she just wanted to get on with the job. Or perhaps the songs had got to her. Perhaps the Captain feared that Princess Badroulboudour might be an unstable presence, a manifestation likely to disappear as quickly and unpredictably as it had appeared.

The grey car was an antique Rolls, a hundred years old if it was a day. It was a halftrack now. It slipped silently towards her across the alien ice.

It came inside the dome and stopped, not entering the car park. Maybe proximity to other vehicles might be contaminating.

The driver's door unsealed. A human chauffeur got out. He wore a grey uniform two shades darker than the paintwork of the car. His face was completely concealed by the peak of his cap and a moulded grey plastic airmask.

He let a woman out of the back.

She wore the same model airmask, and three swathes of thick pink-speckled fur: one in a high collar around her neck; one around her hands as a muff; and one luxuriously around her ankles. On her head was a helmet of black velvet. Her costume was mulberry red, with a high-waisted jacket and a full-length skirt narrow as a stalk.

Princess Badroulboudour held her head high and her shoulders back. She gazed across the car park like a predator, suspecting enemies.

Captain Jute stepped out across the concrete. She unpopped her cuff, ready to display her credentials.

'Princess?' she said. 'I'm with Careways, I'm looking for a Morton Godfrey.'

With her black-gloved hand Princess Badroulboudour impatiently pulled off her airmask.

'Who is this?' she said to the chauffeur, with a dazed hauteur that made the Captain's hair prickle. 'What does she want?'

The Captain recognized now the original of the holos: the head like a mannered sculpture with its taut, hollow cheeks and affronted mouth. The eyes really were as large as they looked, and made even larger with mascara.

'Careways,' she said again. 'You've got some artworks to go to New Malibu.'

She tried to show her wristset. The woman would not focus on it. She glared.

The chauffeur stood behind his employer, too close to be properly respectful. His breast was grey and smooth and broad as a wall. His jacket bore two rows of silver buttons. The singer reached a hand back over her shoulder, as if to make sure he was there to protect her from this intruder.

'I don't suppose you're Morton Godfrey,' said Tabitha to the chauffeur.

His voice was muffled by his mask, but she knew he was smiling. 'At your service,' he said.

His employer turned on him, as though the phrase itself was an annoyance. 'Who is she?' she demanded.

Captain Jute addressed herself to Godfrey. 'How much have you got?'

'Money?' asked Godfrey.

'How much of a load,' said Tabitha.

The entertainer with the ludicrous pseudonym was staring at her as though to nail her to the ground where she stood. 'Nothing is ready,' she said.

The man in the chauffeur's uniform lifted his head a touch. His eyes were the merest glints in the shadow of his cap.

Princess Badroulboudour swept past Captain Jute. 'Nothing is ready, nothing.' Her voice was bored, remote.

The chauffeur followed the Princess into the hotel.

The Captain came after. 'When will I be able to collect?'

'How do they expect anything ever to be ready,' the Princess complained, 'when they won't leave you alone?' Everyone was to blame for her deficiency: Godfrey, the agency, Tabitha too.

Princess Badroulboudour and Morton Godfrey flew along the purple corridors, swift as children in the easy g. Captain Jute strode after. They were leaving her behind.

'Mr Godfrey,' she called.

'Not here,' said the chauffeur. 'Come to the house.'

'I've been to the house,' said the Captain as they disappeared round the corner.

When she caught up with them, the Princess had come to rest. There was another of the unpleasant ornaments, and she was standing in front of it, examining it.

The ornament was a sly-looking, dark-skinned boy with his hair shaved to a frizz. He looked about twelve. His head was too big for his body.

Princess Badroulboudour held her right elbow cupped in her left hand, her long fingers splayed against her cheek, a parody of the art connoisseur.

'It's not crap like this, you know,' she said.

The boy curled his lip at them.

'Pathetic,' said the Princess. She hit the thing on the side of the head with her muff. It did not react.

Tabitha wondered if Crane and his friends were hiding somewhere, watching this.

Princess Badroulboudour turned a scornful glance on the Captain. 'This is the sort of stuff you're expecting, I suppose.'

'I'm just the driver,' said Tabitha.

The Princess's fingers lunged for her arm. 'Come here, driver.'

Tabitha checked an impulse to kick her. She had lost a job once before, for refusing to be treated like dirt. She let herself be pulled into a position between the singer and the statue.

'Now then. Tell me what you see.'

'An ugly boy,' said Captain Jute.

'It's crap,' said the Princess immediately, as if that was the only acceptable answer, the answer Tabitha should have given. 'But is it interesting?'

The depth of insinuation suddenly in the skinny woman's voice made Tabitha turn and stare.

The Princess was smiling now, sardonically. The discarded airmask nestling underneath her chin was the same advanced design as her chauffeur's, but finished in speckled pink to match her furs.

'I wouldn't have it in my house,' Tabitha told her.

The Princess laughed throatily, seeming to read more in the reply than the Captain had intended to put there. Her chauffeur was laughing too. 'Where *is* your house?' the singer asked.

Several possible replies occurred to Tabitha, all of them offensive. She hadn't got a house any more than she'd got a car. All she'd got was her superannuated barge, Bergen Kobold 009059, registered name the *Alice Liddell*.

She said nothing.

'Listen, listen, you,' said the Princess, who seemed to be bound by no restraint. 'What you're going to be carrying is the first collection of moondreams ever to be exhibited in a decent gallery. Do you think you can handle it?'

Tabitha held her face rigid. She spoke to Godfrey, who stood behind them. 'You've got the insurance details,' she said. 'If you want it to go with Careways, I'll take it. If not, there's the usual cancellation fee.'

'Well, perhaps you'd like to think about it,' said the Princess to her, with sudden devastating charm. It was as if the Captain hadn't spoken.

'If the consignment isn't ready, there is a stopover charge,' said the Captain to the chauffeur.

The Princess closed her great black-rimmed eyes. The raspberry-speckled fur seemed to bristle across her shoulders. 'Sort it out,' she said in an undertone, to her attendant.

Godfrey placed himself between her and the offending space pilot. His attitude to his employer was soothing, conciliatory; but he did not touch her. He pulled out a phone and flipped it open. Tabitha could hear he was speaking to the barwoman. It was a moment or two before she realized he was booking her a room.

In the bar they called the Well, the locals were at the green window, waiting for the Princess to leave. More of them had gathered in the short time Captain Jute had been away. Everyone seemed to be up to date with everything. Unasked, the barkeeper pulled another tube from the fridge and held it out to Tabitha. 'On the bill,' she said.

Around the curve of the dome the grey car appeared, heading away across the ice.

'There she goes,' said Cerise, in case anyone wasn't looking.

'Now you can take it easy, Tabitha,' said Georginelle, in a congratulatory tone.

'*What* is it she's working on?' asked the novelist, Noland. He sounded like a bored parent consulting a teacher about a devious child.

'Did she tell you anything?' Cerise was avid.

'Of course she didn't tell her anything,' said Olister Crane. He was moving in on her again with his dandy beard and blazer.

'She asked if I thought I could handle her moondream collection,' said Tabitha, as much to get their reaction as to gratify their rampant curiosity.

They were startled. 'Her *dreams*?' Cerise squeaked. Georginelle muttered something incoherent.

The men smirked at each other. 'Her Highness's moondream collection,' drawled Crane.

'And where are you supposed to take them?' asked Noland. Mirth was evident in his voice, the imminence of ridicule.

'New Malibu,' said Captain Jute.

They all laughed then.

Captain Jute shifted in her chair. 'They're for an exhibition,' she said irritably.

'Poor *stupid* cow,' declared Noland explosively while Georginelle made tutting, clucking noises of pity.

'They're not going anywhere,' Crane assured Captain Jute.

Captain Jute put her head back. 'You don't know that,' she said. 'She might do it. Godfrey might get her to do it.'

Crane rounded his lips and shook his finger in front of his nose. 'No no no no no no,' he said quietly and rapidly. 'The dreams don't travel.'

He spoke with great gravity, acquainting her with a basic truth.

'New Malibu!' said a woman Captain Jute didn't know. They were still finding the idea pretty funny.

'Maybe hers are different,' said the Captain. She wanted this job.

Cerise came over to the table. 'Tabitha, look,' she said. She indicated one of the ornaments, the bald head with the spikes growing out of it. 'That's me. That's a dream I had.'

Tabitha looked. The head winked at her. She could see now it bore a strong resemblance to Cerise.

She was completely confused now. She had no idea if this was art, or a joke, or what it was.

'I wouldn't have thought you'd get much sleep with those sticking out of your head.'

To her gratification, they loved that. They obviously thought it showed the right attitude.

'That's me, look,' said Gideam, amid the hilarity. He pointed at the little fishman in the egg. 'I'm jolly proud of that one, it's the best I've ever had. That's what – inspired me – to write – *Hatchings*.'

'Those things are moondreams?' Captain Jute asked Olister Crane.

He nodded emphatically.

'What are they?'

'Our true selves,' he said, in all seriousness.

'Which one is you?'

'Come with me and I'll show you.' He stood and held out both hands.

Captain Jute got up from her chair, but she did not let him take her hands. She followed him to the stairs.

He gestured at the flower with the face. He went up the stairs to where it stood. It pursed its lips and blinked vacuously at him.

'They look solid enough,' said Tabitha.

'They are,' said Crane, touching one blue petal reverently, 'as long as we're in the vicinity. That's why we keep them

382

here in the bar.' Like everything else, he thought that was a good joke.

Tabitha hoped Princess Badroulboudour wasn't expecting to travel to New Malibu along with her collection.

'How do you make them?'

'First, you go to a Well,' said Crane, starting back down the stairs to her. 'I'll show you.'

She wasn't really interested. She was worn out from the journey and all the walking.

'I'm knackered,' she said. 'I'm going back to my ship.'

'I'll drive you,' said Crane, quick as a snake.

'We got you a room here, sweetheart,' the barwoman called out. 'It's all ready for you. Why don't you go up and get your head down for a while?'

She wondered if the woman meant to warn her against Crane. He stood there all kitted out in his crimson blazer, ready to show her his dreams.

She didn't need the warning.

The Captain rubbed her head and yawned. The ship was her cave, but it was cluttered and cramped. A hotel room would be comfortable.

She was ready for some comfort.

The room was huge. It had three enormous sofas, besides a bed big enough for four people. The extravagance of everything was almost depressing. She wouldn't possibly be here long enough to make a satisfactory dent in it.

'They really must get tourists, Alice,' she said.

'THE DISCOVERY OF THE SO-CALLED DREAM WELLS QUICKLY ATTRACTED NUMBERS OF INVESTIGATORS, ENTREPRENEURS AND CURIOSITY SEEKERS TO UMBRIEL,' said Alice, who had been doing some research of her own. 'SINCE IT BECAME APPARENT THAT THE EFFECT IS A NATURAL PHENOM-

ENON THAT CAN'T BE MEASURED, PREDICTED OR
CONTROLLED, THE INITIAL CURIOSITY HAS
ABATED SOMEWHAT.'

'Somewhat,' said Tabitha, sliding open a cupboard. It was
full of thick soft towels in pastel colours. 'I've just been
seeing some of the effect, if I understand it right.'

She slid open another cupboard. It was a fridge. It was
stocked with shrink-wrapped snacks, shiny chocolates, tubes
of the beer she had been drinking.

'Alice, will you please tell Careways the consignment isn't
ready and stopover arrangements have been made,' she said,
reaching for a tube.

'WILL DO, CAPTAIN,' replied the ship. 'SHALL I TELL
THEM YOU AWAIT THEIR INSTRUCTIONS?'

'Yes,' said Captain Jute. 'Tell them that.'

She launched herself lightly onto the bed and put the AV
on. There were so many channels she tired of pressing the
button. She put it on a fifty-second cycle and fell asleep
to dream of car crashes, Z-ball tournaments, overflowing
carbonated drinks and glossy linkmen in blue suits. The
linkmen had metal spikes growing out of their heads.

The door chimed softly, waking her. It was a squat service
drone. They had sent up her suit, cleaned and recharged.

Captain Jute slept again, woke, ate, bathed at great length
in real water, got drunk, watched some porn, called reception, called the ship. Careways had acknowledged, but left
no message. There was no word from Godfrey. At some
point, the fridge had been silently restocked.

Captain Jute did everything again, and again, in different
sequences. She ate and slept and woke and stared out of the
window at the rolling dance of Oberon and Titania, the night
that raced away across the mountains of Uranus overhead.

Soon enough, boredom drove her back to the bar. She
didn't imagine it could still be the same day by any system

of measurement, but Crane was there. He was alone. He looked up and smiled, easily, as if he had been waiting for her.

'Okay,' Tabitha said. 'Show me these Wells, then.'

They drove through a haze of salt glare. The stars were dazzling. Among them Sol was a fierce dot, as if someone outside space was trying to break in with a welding torch.

Crane looked at Tabitha sidelong. Though his ice rover was on automatic pilot, he was keeping his hands to himself.

'What, you always travel alone?' he said.

'Always,' she said.

'You don't like people.'

'I'm fine on my own,' she said.

He laughed a short silent laugh. 'You're fine on your own,' he said.

The dead land crept by.

'You'd do okay here,' he said. 'This place is made for people who are fine on their own.' He scratched at an imaginary spot on the windscreen. 'The less you need, the better you'll like it.'

'I'm not staying,' said Tabitha.

Crane chuckled softly. 'No, no,' he assured her.

The car was bright yellow. She looked at its fuzzy reflection in the ice.

'What about Mr Godfrey?' she said.

'Is he bothering you?'

She was not pleased by a proprietorial assumption that seemed to underlie his reply.

'Did she bring him here?'

'The Princess brought him.' The poet's voice was cool now, neutral. 'He's her number one fan. A good-looking man,' he averred. 'A big man.' He smiled a wide-eyed smile.

She said nothing.

385

'Best not touch.'

'I wasn't going to touch him,' said Captain Jute, unnerved.

'No no no no no no,' he said again.

She inhaled hard.

Another barren kilometre slid by.

'What about you?' she asked him, eventually. 'How long have you been here?'

'Years,' he said. 'Years and years.'

'You must like it.'

'I'm a poet,' he said. 'I have a poet's ego. I like the idea of a corner of the universe that shows my reflection.' It was obviously a line he had perfected.

'A blue flower?' she said.

'My theory is, that one was kind of a joke,' he said drily. Lights flickered across the dashboard as the car turned in the direction of an oblong dome. 'I like it. Don't you? I do. I think it's good.'

'And it just happens?' she asked. 'Naturally?'

'Well, you have to work for it,' he said. 'You have to concentrate.'

'How many have you done?'

He shook his head, not answering.

The dome looked like a simple utilitarian construction: bluish-grey fabricate with modular units budding out of it.

'Is this it?'

'This is it,' he said. 'This is the main one.'

It looked more like a public building on Luna than a place where people went to dream solid dreams.

'You spend a lot of time out here, do you?'

'A lot of time,' he acknowledged. 'It's like making babies,' he said, innocently. 'You have to try a lot of times before you get lucky.'

'Sometimes you just don't get lucky,' she told him firmly.

'That's right,' said Olister Crane. He wiped the corners

of his mouth with his forefinger and thumb as he drove on toward the Well.

'Not everyone can make a dream,' he said.

'You write poems too,' she said.

He looked at her sideways again. 'I'm going to write a poem about you.'

'Leave me out,' she said.

'That's a good title,' he said.

'I don't want you to write about me,' said Captain Jute.

Crane scratched his beard. 'Those are often the most interesting subjects,' he said, in a playful tone.

'You'd better not do it,' she said. 'And you'd better not have any dreams about me, either.'

'I think you're too late, there,' said Crane. 'Everyone's dreaming about you.'

Her jaw tightened.

'Oh, don't worry, Captain,' he said. 'Nobody's going to steal your soul.'

Where they went in, at the end of one of the tube modules, the air was warm and dank as a swimming bath. It even smelled slightly of chlorine. Biofluorescents threw sickly green light around.

A dried-up old man in a grubby white orderly's jacket sat at a desk. Crane spoke to him. They chatted for a moment, about who was in. Tabitha heard no names she recognized.

The superintendent was punching something out slowly on a keyboard. 'Who's your lady friend, Mr Crane?' he asked. Perhaps he thought she didn't look capable of saying her own name.

'This is Captain Jute,' said Crane. 'Captain Jute flies things.'

Please let's not talk about Princess Bad now, thought Captain Jute to herself.

'Captain Jute is working for the Princess,' said Crane.

But the old man merely cocked an eyebrow and laughed.

They went down a corridor. Someone had tried to make the place look impressive by painting huge diamonds on the walls. The diamonds were sombre red, with gold outlines. In the middle of the floor someone else had left a battered green folding chair and a couple of bundles that looked as if they might have been laundry.

Captain Jute followed Crane round the obstacles. The chair seemed to be a chair; the laundry, laundry.

She wondered when the weirdness was going to start.

There were doors along the corridor. Some of them were open. Inside were empty rooms.

'People still do come?' she asked.

'In the season,' Crane said.

She wondered how long ago the last season had ended.

He seemed to answer her thought. 'There's no commercial potential,' he said. 'One thing the Wells don't make is money.'

They passed a glass-walled area that seemed to hold the remains of some abandoned experiment. There was the frame of a whole body medical scanner, with all the machinery removed. On the floor were a lead-lined blanket and several empty gas cylinders.

Ahead, a woman walked slowly across the corridor, wrapped in a towel. She went through a door, which closed behind her. She did not even glance at them. Perhaps she was walking in her sleep.

'In the beginning everyone came to Umbriel,' Crane was saying. 'Everyone with something burning in their brain. Artists, scientists, people on campaigns. Pilgrims, crazy for mysteries. People with theories. People with too much time and money. People dying, with no time at all.'

He was speaking more softly now, as they neared the end of the corridor.

'People come and make a living out of the crazy people,' said Crane. 'Interpreters. Dream therapists, like Georginelle there.'

They entered the dome.

'Some people think everybody should see their own true self,' said Crane.

In the main dome the lights were low. Around the walls stood lines of hooded, shadowy booths like prayer shrines. There was more random furniture, stray pieces of equipment. Industrial friction carpet ran around a large curved pool.

'There is always some disappointment,' Crane said, 'inevitably. The truth is a stranger. Mostly. Not always welcome by daylight.'

Around the pool at intervals were stands of long-handled tools: hooks, rakes and nets. The stands had stainless steel racks on top. Most of the racks were empty.

'So the people moved on,' said Crane, going to the edge of the pool. 'The seekers decided it was something else they were looking for.'

'I imagine,' said Captain Jute.

He ignored her.

He was looking across the pool at a small tent of milky plastic. Its occupant was just visible through the fabric, a horizontal smudge.

Crane went down on one knee.

'The people who stayed,' he said. 'The Well Wishers. Who knows what they're looking for.'

He dipped his hand in the water.

It was not really water, obviously. It was dark as ale. It dripped greasily from his fingers.

The next steel rack along had something on it: something round. It was, once again, about the size of a human head.

Her hands clenched tight, Captain Jute went up and had a look.

The thing was a sort of fat bird with no legs, lying on its side. Its plumage was dowdy, its eye an unfinished socket. Inside it was dirty yellow, the consistency of dried-up sponge. It seemed to be disintegrating.

'We can go now,' Captain Jute said. Her voice was high, tight in her throat.

Crane stood up with his back to the Well. He wiped his hands together. His face seemed illuminated with a sudden elation, or malice.

'What's the matter, Captain? It's only a dream . . .'

Across the water came a shout of complaint, muddled by echoes into incomprehensibility. Tabitha could see a man's head sticking out of the tent. She wondered what they had woken him from.

The superintendent was sitting with his chair tipped back, his feet up on his desk. His eyes were closed.

Smiling, Crane rapped on the desk with his knuckles.

'You should be sleeping in there,' he said, 'not out here!'

The old man gave them a gap-toothed grin. 'Not me, Mr Crane,' he croaked cheerfully. 'I ain't got the talent.'

There was still no word from the agency. Tabitha lay on her enormous bed. 'You should have seen those things, Alice,' she said.

'PERHAPS I SOON SHALL,' answered the small voice from the wall, where the wristcom was in a power socket, recharging.

'Not if Crane and them are right.' She rolled over and back. 'Shit, this is such a waste of time.'

The AV was playing a rerun of a primitive sitcom, about two Martian salt dealers and their unruly camel. Half-finished snack dishes lay on the bed, clothes and empty beer tubes around it. She had spent the rest of the day failing to get hold of anyone that might have a truck for hire.

'We're not earning anything, lying here. We ought to check in and see if we can't get a bit of local work.'

'THAT WOULD PUT YOU IN TECHNICAL VIOLATION OF YOUR CAREWAYS CONTRACT, CAPTAIN. SECTION 24, PARAGRAPH 4.14: BEFORE THE TERMINATION OF THIS AGREEMENT THE OPERATOR MAY NOT ENTER INTO A SECOND OR SUBSIDIARY –'

'Don't read me that crap, Alice. They don't know what it's like out here.'

'PERHAPS YOU SHOULD THINK OF THIS AS A HOLIDAY, CAPTAIN,' suggested the ship. 'A PERIOD OF RECREATION.'

'Don't let Crane hear you,' said Captain Jute. She rolled herself up in the coverlet, yawning. 'He has some ideas about recreation. If something doesn't happen soon, I'm going to give in, I know I –'

The phone warbled.

She threw out an arm and hit the button. 'Yes?'

'*Morton Godfrey's here to see you, sugar.*'

'Christ. At last. I'll come down.'

'*Uh-uh. He's on his way up.*' The barwoman started to cough. '*Couldn't stop him.*'

'Christ. Christ.'

The Captain catapulted herself off the bed and started trying to kick some of the debris out of sight under it. Misjudging the gravity, she merely succeeded in scattering it around further. There was something bright pink spilt down the front of her shirt. She scrubbed at it furiously with a complimentary tissue, without result, then grabbed her jacket with one hand and the remote with the other, attempting to put the jacket on and the AV off at the same time.

She got one arm in the jacket, and managed to kill the soundtrack. Then the door chimed.

'I'm coming!' she yelled, searching madly with her hand behind her for her second sleeve.

'CAPTAIN,' said the persona, from the dangling com set, 'PERHAPS –'

'Vox off,' ordered the Captain, pointing the remote at the door.

Like a visitor from some more elegant age, there stood Morton Godfrey. His boots were spotless knee-length Repellex. The sourceless light of the hotel corridor turned his uniform into a suit of tailored steel.

He took off his cap and put it under his arm.

'Captain Jute.'

She loped towards him, still pulling on her jacket. 'You didn't have to come up,' she said.

'Sorry for the intrusion,' he said, walking in.

He towered over her. Without cap and mask, he looked as perfect as a royal accessory must surely have to be. A clinical fragrance radiated from him.

'The Princess is ready.'

'Now? It's the middle of the night.'

The chauffeur stood with his hands on hips, looking at the silently quarrelling figures on the oversized AV. 'It's always the middle of the night here,' he said.

'I was in bed,' she said.

He looked her between the eyes. 'So I imagine,' he said. He circled each of his wrists briefly with the thumb and forefinger of the opposite hand. She felt her face go suddenly warm.

'I've been trying to get transport all day,' she said.

'We've got transport,' said Morton Godfrey, looking up

at the AV again. There was something deliberate about the way he took his eyes off her. He nodded, stoically, at the screen. 'Second series,' he said. 'They were never as good after Caligula Probert left.'

Even the chauffeur was an art critic.

He glanced intently at Tabitha again, then cast an eye over the disarray of the bed, the jumble of socks and discarded meals.

'I'll come back,' he said. 'I'll come back at six. Can you be ready by then?'

'I've been ready,' she said with asperity, 'for some time.'

'Well, you're not ready now,' he reminded her, solemnly.

'Okay,' she said. 'Let's go.'

'No,' he said. 'Get your sleep. I'll come and get you.' He half winked, and held up a forefinger in confirmation. 'At six.'

She shut the door on him. She went back and lay down on the bed, hard.

It was herself she was angry with, she realized after a moment. She had been supremely unprofessional. He could complain to the agency, get her replaced.

She rolled over.

'Vox on,' she said.

The light on the wristcom blinked.

'WAS THAT MORTON GODFREY, CAPTAIN?'

'Yes. Why?'

'STRESS PATTERNS IN HIS VOICE ARE SIMILAR TO THOSE IN THE VOICE OF OLISTER CRANE,' the persona reported.

Tabitha succeeded at last in turning the AV off. 'Are they?' she said.

'SUGGESTING HE DESIRES YOU TOO,' said the persona.

The Captain felt her face heat up again. The things this one came out with.

'I don't think so, Alice,' she said. 'You can delete that, please.'

'YES, CAPTAIN,' whispered the little voice from the wall.

'The people love her,' said Morton Godfrey. 'They do. Only the networks are all against her.'

This place was full of men who wanted to tell her stories.

They sat at the bar, drinking coffee. The barwoman was in and out, working. No one else was around. Captain Jute once again had the sense they might be watching her, keeping out, leaving the pair of them alone.

Godfrey sat swivelled around sideways on his stool to face her. He held his coffee cup in both hands, and ran his thumbs around the bowl of it, caressing it. Captain Jute imagined those big hands caressing the neurotic designer cheekbones, the vestigial breasts.

'They don't understand her,' he said. 'She threatens them.'

He looked at her to see if she understood. When she didn't react he nodded, as if the point needed approval by somebody before he could go on.

'They're jealous of her talent.'

Delay had enveloped them again. Either that or Bad was being deliberately uncooperative, which seemed entirely possible. Captain Jute had been up and dressed at six. At half seven Godfrey had phoned to say the 'schedule had been changed' and he would be there at eight. It had been nearer nine when he showed up in a little metallic blue Guignuki slider, a two-seater. Now it was nearly eleven, and they were still in the bar. She did not object to his company. She was quite convinced Alice didn't know what she was talking about. Morton Godfrey was a satellite, single-minded as Umbriel or Luna. One thing only lit up his life: the reflected glamour of his primary.

'Are we going to take a look at this stuff, then?' she asked him.

'Yeah,' he said. 'In a minute.' He put his cup down beside his cap, which lay upside down on the bar like an empty dish. He seemed to suppress a sigh. Perhaps his mistress and he had had a row.

The barwoman was unloading the glasswasher. Godfrey signalled to her.

'Doreen,' he said. 'Put "Do You" on.'

Doreen was feeling uncooperative too, apparently. She apologized with her eyebrows, her hands full of glassware.

Godfrey got to his feet. He eased himself around Tabitha to the juke-box panel and pressed the numbers.

On the holopad at the end of the bar appeared a sleek figure dressed in a black shirt and oversized powder blue man's suit.

'You've seen this,' Godfrey said.

'Maybe,' said Tabitha, wearily. 'I don't know.'

The dancing doll on the holopad swivelled her hips. The ornaments on the wall of the bar showed through her as though she were made of cellophane.

'Thirty-four takes,' said Godfrey. 'You wouldn't believe it.'

He drank his coffee.

'She was as fresh after the thirty-fourth as she was at the first. She always gave it everything she'd got.'

His loyalty was touching.

Close-ups showed Princess Bad looking haughty and hermaphroditic. Her eyes had been narrower then, or they had been made to look it. She was dancing a delicate, mincing dance, while her voice on the soundtrack sang something about snow. She looked exactly like a Japanese transvestite.

'Look at that depth! Look at the resolution! They can't get work like this anywhere now.'

It was impossible to tell whether he was speaking about Princess Badroulboudour or the cinematography. Tabitha wondered whether the Princess would have had something to say about that. Perhaps she wouldn't have approved.

The music rattled to a stop. The image melted into nothing.

'This show is really important to her,' confided Godfrey, into the icebound silence.

Doreen wiped her hands. 'Captain Jute says the Princess is working again,' she said. Perhaps she had noticed the Captain's growing impatience and decided to help her out.

'Yeah. Well.' The chauffeur seemed troubled by Doreen's intervention, reluctant to expand his audience to include her. He looked towards the empty holopad, as though hoping the little ghost would reappear and guide him.

'She never really stopped,' he said.

'She's been doing some dreams,' Doreen prompted.

'Yeah.' The chauffeur rotated his coffee cup precisely in its saucer. 'This place has been really good for her,' he said. 'The new stuff is her best yet.'

'We'd surely like to see it,' said Doreen with edged good humour. She took up her crate of glasses and disappeared out the back.

Morton Godfrey's eyes flicked after her. He muttered something; and when Tabitha did not reply said softly but distinctly: 'The Princess never shows work till it's finished. They know that.'

He picked up his coffee and drank it off. He put the cup down sharply. Clearly he resented the implied insult to his mistress's artistic integrity.

Captain Jute glanced at the moondreams in the bar: the spiked head, the model Thrant still flexing its muscles.

'I've been told,' she said carefully, 'that these things won't survive being taken away from their owners.'

Godfrey looked directly at her then, for the first time since putting the disc on. In his guarded glower she was surprised by a strange vulnerability; a plea for her complicity. He was asking her to be good, like him, and not expose the bankruptcy of his mistress's expectations.

'We got to go,' he said. 'She'll be waiting.' But he didn't move. He sat there looking at her unhappily.

Tabitha decided to try taking control, to see if that was what he needed. 'Give her a call,' she said. 'Tell her we're on our way.'

His eyes still on Captain Jute, Morton Godfrey pulled his phone halfway out of his pocket. Then he pushed it back in.

His hand came up and went over Tabitha's shoulder and round behind her head. She felt his broad palm cradle the back of her skull.

'I'll call her from the car,' he said thickly. Then he opened his mouth and pressed it determinedly to hers.

Captain Jute had time to be shocked, and aroused, and amused, all at once. She put her hands between them, pushing at the wide wall of the chauffeur's chest, feeling the twin rows of silver buttons bite into the flesh of her palms.

Eyes screwed tight shut, she twisted her head away from his, coming up for air over his shoulder. Her heart hammering, she opened her eyes then and saw at the top of the steps, where Olister Crane's dream flower leaned from its blue vase, the Princess Badroulboudour, standing watching the pair of them.

That was when she jerked backwards in fright and fell off her stool.

*

Captain Jute shut the forward starboard airlock and threw her helmet clumsily into the co-pilot's web.

'Prepare for departure, Alice.'

'THE HOLD IS STILL EMPTY, CAPTAIN,' the little ship pointed out. 'THE CARGO CONSIGNMENT HASN'T YET BEEN LOADED.'

'I know the fucking consignment hasn't yet been loaded!'

She was furious: with herself; with Careways; with Morton Godfrey; with Princess bloody Badroulboudour. She had come all the way out here for nothing, and wasted a week being leched over, drinking too much and watching crap AV. Now she wouldn't get paid, and no doubt Bad still had the clout to get her blacklisted with every shipping agency in the outer system.

In the low g of Umbriel her fall had been humiliating rather than painful. It had taken her an undignified minute to get her breath back into her lungs and her feet under her. By that time they had both gone.

Doreen, crouching to help her, told her she had come back just in time to see the Princess leaving, going up the steps without a word. 'Godfrey stands there staring like a man that's seen the sign,' said Doreen.

Tabitha rubbed her hip. 'What sign?' she asked.

'The sign,' said Doreen. She ran her middle finger and thumb along an invisible line in the air. '"JERUSALEM",' she quoted. '"CLOSED FOR REDEVELOPMENT". Then he snatches up his cap, pulls it on his head and leaps off after her. Good Lord, give me a man that'll follow me that way. You okay, hon? You want some more coffee?'

'Fucking idiot,' Tabitha had said, and more in the same vein.

Doreen turned her head, lowered her chin and looked up at her from the corners of her eyes, prepared for something bad. 'Did he hurt you?'

'He fucking kissed me,' she said.

Doreen whipped out a cloth and started wiping the bar vigorously. 'Well, at least it wasn't a total loss.'

'You think it's funny?'

Doreen threw up her hands in surrender. 'Hey, hey, sweetheart, that man's all over everyone. No offence,' she purred, 'but what do you expect?' She shook her curls. 'If she don't know it by now, she had it coming.'

'How did she look?'

'Mad as hell.'

Suddenly the barkeeper had cracked up laughing, and just as suddenly the Captain had joined her.

She sat at the bar and drank a refill. 'Oh, Christ,' she grumbled, 'why can't I just get a single straightforward job for a change?'

'Hey, lover, you find something straightforward in this system, you let us all know about it,' said Doreen. 'Here, how about a shot of whisky in that? The real thing, Doreen's personal reserve . . .'

While the barwoman rummaged under the bar, Tabitha had reflected that when the local witticisms start to repeat, you might as well be going.

Now she sat in the cockpit of her Kobold preparing for take-off and wondering how long it would be before she dared go back to the Careways Agency.

'At this rate I'll be calling Sanczau for another favour,' she said. She hated the idea. It seemed like admitting she couldn't handle the ship their Grand Old Man had given her.

'YOU DID PROMISE BALTHAZAR PLUM YOU WOULD STAY IN TOUCH,' the ship reminded her diplomatically.

'Don't talk to me now about Balthazar Plum,' said Captain Jute. 'He's no different from Morton Godfrey.'

'I'M NOT SURE I UNDERSTAND THAT LAST REMARK, CAPTAIN,' said Alice, who had not been told anything.

'Just be glad you're made of steel, Alice.'

'IN FACT, STEEL PLAYS A VERY SMALL PART IN MY COMPOSITION,' replied the persona. 'MY PRIMARY CONSTITUENT IS A BINOMIAL POLYSACCHARIDE COMPRISING –'

'Status reports, please Alice.'

'EXTRAORBITAL FLIGHT APPLICATION FILED AND ACKNOWLEDGED, PLASMA BALANCE 46% RISING. IMPULSE OSCILLATIONS 120–22. PRIMARY ORIENTATION AXIS LOCK ENGAGED. VEHICLE APPROACHING.'

'What?'

The external monitors flashed up a grey Rolls halftrack racing towards her across the ice.

The Captain swore again. 'Come to tell me he can't let me go, has he?'

But in a moment she could see the Rolls now had a robot in the driving seat: a chunky custom-plated Facto 4000.

'Power down, Alice,' said Tabitha, jockeying with the magnification, trying to see into the back seat of the car. 'Christ, it's not her, is it? What does she want? If she thinks I was encouraging him, I shall laugh, I know I shall.'

But the robot was alone.

Parking the Rolls neatly alongside the Kobold, it unsealed the door and let itself gently down onto the ice. It rolled the four metres to the forward port entry ladder, then reconfigured its mobilators to climb up into the airlock.

Admitted to the ship, the robot cocked its flat head up at the Captain, who stood there in the inner doorway, leaning on her arms.

'*Careways Agency operative, I have a message for you from Princess Badroulboudour,*' said the robot. '*She is ready for you to begin loading.*'

'I've already had that message, thank you,' said Tabitha, reaching for the CLOSE control.

'*This message supersedes that delivered at 08.80.14 by Morton Godfrey,*' said the robot. '*This message originates at 15.06.36.*'

'You're kidding,' said the Captain. 'And does it come with an apology for unauthorized personal interference by a member of her royal staff?'

The robot hummed congestedly for a moment. '*That question contains more than 10% of undefined and unfamiliar terms,*' it told her. '*I am not enabled to answer that question. I am enabled only to convey you to the house and assist in the execution of your instructions, as issued by Careways Agency and detailed in Careways Agency contract 95TAF9U4.002.*'

Captain Jute whistled and shook her head as she reached for her helmet. 'Can I drive?' she asked.

'*The vehicle is currently enabled to accept only my commands,*' it said, seriously.

'It is, eh?' said Captain Jute, as she tabbed Alice down to Maintain. 'What happened to Mr Godfrey?'

'*I am not enabled to answer that question,*' said the Facto 4000.

At Princess Badroulboudour's palace all the lights were still on. The only person inside was Princess Badroulboudour; but she was all over the place. The interior décor consisted of the chromatic variations of her own identity.

A life-size holo of a younger Princess Badroulboudour in a white dress dominated the foyer. She had been made up to look like the old movie star, Marilyn Monroe, though with black hair. She was turning away from the door and looking round at you over her shoulder; and when the wind from the grating blew her skirt up, you could see she wasn't wearing any knickers.

'There are two kinds of people who come to this house,' said the owner herself, arriving on the far side of the foyer in a gold-caged lift. She indicated the replica that was wiggling and beaming and pushing its dress down with such artful ineffectuality. 'The ones who immediately they see that, have to come round the front and look; and the ones who wouldn't dream of doing anything so vulgar.' She sounded tired, but very much at ease. 'Which kind are you?'

'I'm pretty vulgar,' said Tabitha, not moving from where she stood. She had to say it loudly, to be heard over the music.

The foyer was a rounded space tiled in large rectangular sheets of something grey and opalescent. Small Princess B-style images flickered here and there like sudden puffs of orange and viridian fire, never exactly where you were looking, while the life-size holo gleamed and fluttered. Every tile, Tabitha supposed, was a possible screen. The music was not like the things they had played her in the hotel bar, but like slowed-down explosions, full of fuzz and overload. The whole effect made her feel rather sick. Presumably that was the intention.

The entertainer came across the foyer, magnificent in sleeveless lilac shimmersilk, balloon pants and fishnet cape. She wore heels and lots of bulky Arabic jewellery. She seemed pretty hyper, but pleased with herself, all trace of anger and aloofness vanished.

'Vulgarity is all we have left!' she cried. She seemed to have decided Captain Jute was now her trusted colleague, her ally against the worlds.

'I'm so so sorry to make you wait such an awful time,' the entertainer said, leading Tabitha into the lift. 'It must have been bloody dreary for you.'

She shut the gate with a jingling clash.

Captain Jute was trapped in a cage with Princess Badroulboudour. The planet-devouring eyes were fastened upon her.

The Captain made the position clear. 'I'll be gone as soon as you can hand over the consignment,' she said.

The woman looked through the bars of the cage, interested only in what she herself had to say. 'I've been trying and trying and trying to make the selection,' she said, as the lift rose one floor. 'I just couldn't decide. And you know why I couldn't. Because all along the only thing to do was send *everything*.'

They walked out of the lift into a curving corridor with glossy pink walls that met overhead. The music was just as loud up here, and the air was perfumed with a rich, dizzying musk. The whole place seemed to be a parody of the female body, as if its architecture had been extrapolated from the inner curves of its owner.

'Everything,' said Princess Badroulboudour. 'It's the logic of it. Exhibition.'

In a dimpled niche, a miniature holo of the Princess smiled, then turned sulky as they passed.

'Exhibition. That's the key, you see, the theme.'

The exhibitor smiled keenly at Tabitha. She seemed to have completely forgotten the incident in the bar. Perhaps Doreen had been right, and it hadn't been that much of a shock.

The Princess ushered the Captain into a room.

The room was large, and white, with huge paintings on the walls: enormous dull things, triangles of tan and grey on dirty white. In the far corner of the room was a compact automatic cuisine. There was a glass counter where a spherical white lamp hovered. The lamp was on, like all the lights in Princess Badroulboudour's palace.

On the counter were the messy preparations for a meal: crushed rectangular packets of white insulite film; an open jar of honey with a spoon in. On the floor, as if it had rolled off the counter, lay what looked like a big black watermelon with a piece torn out of it.

Princess Bad strode up to it as if she was going to give it a kick. She stopped beside it and swivelled with a grand, demonstrative gesture.

Tabitha went over and looked at the thing.

Inside the broken black shell was wet, glossy brown pulp. From the midst of it, as if modelled out of it, protruded the Princess's own face. Her chin was raised, her eyes closed, her mouth open in some kind of private joke or ecstasy. There was one hand, too, the fingers sticking out. They moved, thrusting, as if the dream woman were trying to surface, to push her way out of the smothering pulp.

'Now,' the Princess was saying, 'imagine.' She was taking something from the counter. 'You come in, just the way you've come in now, and here –'

She was putting whatever she had picked up into Tabitha's hands.

The Captain caught hold of it automatically. She looked up at the artist, bewildered; then down at what she was holding.

It was a long wire, for cutting cheese. It had a smooth wooden handle at each end, painted a cheerful buttery yellow. Princess Badroulboudour had put one handle in each of her hands.

Tabitha looked at the cheese wire. She looked at the wet black thing with the face in. What was the woman thinking of? Whatever it was, it was appalling.

Captain Jute dropped the wire hurriedly back on the counter. 'I don't think so,' she said.

'Well, no,' said the Princess in her hard, flat voice. 'But you get the general idea. The settings, the appliances, it's all documented, in the background stuff they're getting. But they have to see something like that, you see, at the same time they're seeing something like this –'

While she was speaking, the artist vaulted lightly across the room, shoved open a pair of high white doors and disappeared through them.

Dazed, and more sickened than ever, Captain Jute went after her.

She found her in a room of green jungle plants. There was the noise of booming water in the music now, and birds squawking lazily.

Tabitha was almost afraid to look at what the woman wanted her to see here. But this one was a harmless miniature, a pretty self-portrait covered from head to toe in brilliant feathers. She looked comical and jolly, more like a clown than a parrot.

'These are all your dreams?' said Captain Jute. The word felt daft as she said it, inadequate.

'Don't tell me about your insurance again,' said the Princess loftily, leaping ahead on some connection only she had made. 'You can't insure them, I know. You can't *preserve* them. That's exactly what's interesting.'

She took another head from among the greenery. It was yellowish white, like bone. Its eyes were closed, its mouth open. For its two rows of teeth, it had two metal sawblades.

'It's all about exclusivity!'

The artist's hysterical eyes shone. She turned the head in her hand. From the neck dangled a short fibrous root, like the root of an extracted tooth. There was blood on it.

Princess Bad laughed, putting the back of her wrist to her mouth. She looked as if any moment she might overbalance backwards into the foliage. 'Exhibition and exclusivity,' she said thickly. 'Look, look, bugger this, I want some wine.'

Tabitha was afraid that would mean they were going back

405

into the room with the watermelon thing on the floor; but instead the Princess led her on along a gallery of pine and yellow metal that ran inside the outer walls of the saucer palace, past long windows that looked out onto the ice below. There was still nothing moving out there. There never would be.

As they walked the artist went on with her theme as if she had never proposed dropping it. 'Exhibition and exclusivity. The Princess B no one can see. Not even –' She broke off; then spoke again, in a deliberate tone. 'Where do you go when you close your eyes? That's where it started. What happens when you walk away from yourself?'

Tabitha had had more than enough of this. She spoke up.

'I thought we were all supposed to reinvent ourselves thirty-two times a second, or whatever it is.'

'That's what I *mean*,' said the Princess, ushering her into another lift, this one a more conventional steel box. 'Princess Badroulboudour is the prisoner of that line. People *welded* me to it. The very people it was intended to liberate. They don't want to be liberated from themselves,' she said slowly and scornfully, as the lift took them down into the hillside, 'not for a thirty-secondth of a second. They're in love with their stupid selves. And with Princess bloody Badroulboudour!'

She looked at the toothy head, which she was still carrying. As if to underline her comment, it opened its sightless eyes and smiled up at her lovingly.

'Who I encouraged them to produce,' said the Princess. 'I know, I know.'

Captain Jute looked at her reflection in the sliding doors.

The lift deposited them in a darkened room, too dark to see anything. The air smelled stale. To the music that had followed them all through the palace was now added a buzzing, snoring sort of noise. The water motif was still there, but bubbling now, sedately, more like a big pot than a big river.

'They made me into the woman who said that line,' said the Princess, walking away in the darkness. 'I am never allowed to reinvent myself, not allowed to embrace the prospect of singularity.'

It was Princess Bad who was in love with herself if anyone was, thought Captain Jute. She couldn't even interrupt herself to turn the light on.

'Wine,' she heard her hostess say, indistinctly; then: 'Lights up.'

As illumination dawned all around, soft and pale amber, the Captain saw they were now in the bedroom. Hence the snoring, she presumed. The saw-toothed head lay on the bed, which was large and circular, with a censer of perforated brass hanging over it.

Below the bed a flight of wide, shallow steps led down to a small sunken pool. It seemed to be some kind of jacuzzi, seething with dark water.

Everywhere in the room there were clothes: clothes hanging on tiered racks, clothes discarded on the floor, clothes folded neatly or bundled together or spilling out of shelves. Here and there, images of different sizes peered out of corners. One, a skull-headed figure with several arms, lay beside the jacuzzi, gesticulating jerkily at the ceiling.

They were all her. In Princess Bad's case, her true self was her external appearance. Apparently.

'All these are going,' their maker said. She was across the room, on the far side of the bed, pouring thick red wine into two large glasses. 'I wasted ages trying to work out a selection,' she explained again. 'Now I think the point is to show them everything. Here.'

'No, thanks,' said Captain Jute.

The woman seemed not to hear her. She continued to hold out the glass of wine across the bed.

'Show them what a real artist can do here,' said Princess Badroulboudour smugly.

It wasn't a jacuzzi, of course. It was one of the wells. Princess Bad had her own private Dream Well. She had built her palace around it.

The water was murky, opaque in the low light. As it boiled, the Captain could see the shape of another image already forming beneath the surface.

'Are you sure these things are safe?'

The Princess laughed loudly.

She took Captain Jute back up to ground level. She spoke about the special amenities of the building, about its 'homeostatic systems'. She sounded more like an estate agent than an interplanetary recording star. Whatever residual awe Tabitha had felt now vanished completely.

'Let's see how the loading's going,' said Princess Badroulboudour.

The garage was spacious. The robot was there. It was pulling racks of green plastic crates out of a goods lift and towing them up into the back of a tall spike-wheeled truck. The crates were full of dreams. Tabitha saw them blink their eyes and gesture with their tiny hands, as if to say goodbye.

The blue Guignuki slider was parked over by the wall. There was no sign of Godfrey.

Over the radio, the field officer quizzed them as they came in range. It was still the same bloke on duty. Probably he didn't have an AV of his own at home.

Tabitha leaned forward to the radio. 'She let me in,' she told him.

When they reached the office, the robot stopped the truck. The officer did not appear.

'Do you want to take a look?' the Captain asked him. She got half out of her seat to see if she could see him in there.

He was in the warm. He was reluctant to suit up and go out into the vacuum. '*Just give me the figures*,' he said.

She started to read him all the values, the way the regulations said you had to: weight, cubic capacity, varietal coding. 'Fifty-eight human heads,' she said. 'No insurable value.' He didn't laugh. She could just make him out now through the layers of glass: a grey blur poking at a keyboard.

The robot drove the truck onto the field. It put it beside the *Alice Liddell* in exactly the same position it had put the Rolls.

Captain Jute gave Alice the signal to open the hold. A puff of debris blew out as the pressures equalized: particles of who knew how many different worlds, a negligible addition to the mass of this one. Among the dust she spotted a lost screwdriver, an empty krilkracker bag.

Inside the hold the cargo extensors were starting to unhook themselves. 'Just the drones for this one, Alice,' said Tabitha, sealing her suit.

'ACTIVATING,' replied the ship, pleasantly.

There was a pause, and then four squat shapes like spaceport shoe polishers waddled out onto the ice.

Beside the Captain in the truck cab, Princess Bad's 4000 extended its head, running it out along a little boom. Its selection of eyepieces swivelled rapidly until it found the right one.

'*I am enabled to transfer the consignment*,' it said in Captain Jute's earphones, as she swung herself outside.

'You can help,' she told it.

The robot clambered down, looking all the time at the drones. Its manner seemed distrustful. It approached the nearest one and flashed some lights at it.

The drone turned its upper casing around and flashed some back.

The 4000 craned its head up towards the Captain, who was opening the back of the truck. '*The capacities of this model are inferior to my own*,' it informed her.

'But there are four of them,' she said, 'and only one of you. You'd better watch your step.'

While the persona plotted a course for the Asteroid Belt, Captain Jute stood up on the catwalk that ran around the hold and supervised her metal team. Together they unloaded fifty-eight masks, models and portrait busts of Princess Badroulboudour from the back of the truck, and loaded them onto the *Alice Liddell*.

It took a while. The moondreams were apt to bob about like bubbles. One left its crate entirely. The Captain slid down the ladder and intercepted it before it floated into somewhere crucial and did some damage.

The fugitive dream was a half-length figure, thirty centimetres long. It was nude, its right arm modestly covering its breasts. Its skin was the texture and colour of graphite.

The Captain held the figure under its armpits in front of her, dangling it like a baby. The moondream did not move. Inert, it hung between her hands as if stunned by the bleak light of Uranus. Belatedly the Captain wondered if she should have done something to protect them from the vacuum.

'I told you I couldn't be liable,' she reminded it.

She thought she saw the grey lips twitch.

The Princess's robot rolled up and looked at her in a manner she could only call accusing. Behind it the drones were beginning to unroll the cargo retaining nets. 'Wait, wait,' she told them. 'Last one.' She tucked the cold grey torso safely back in its crate.

The ship went up into the cold black gulf under the yellow

circumference of Uranus, and the cold black gulf received her. 'That's better,' said Captain Jute, as the last of her weight drained away and left her floating peacefully at the controls, in her web. Space suited her, she always thought to herself at about this point: the depth and the breadth and the solitude of space. Other people always wanted something from you; usually something that you hadn't got. With a good ship, you could leave their complications and entanglements behind along with their gravity. While the charting computers made the last refinements to the vectors, she thought of Morton Godfrey, the need in his eyes, the desperation in his kiss. How entangled must he have become in the endlessly bifurcating personality of Princess Badroulboudour?

'I WONDER IF YOU SHOULD CHECK THE CARGO, CAPTAIN,' said Alice then.

'Oh God,' sighed Captain Jute, feeding the hold cameras to the console monitors. 'What's happening?'

'I BELIEVE THERE MAY BE SOME SPOILAGE,' said the ship persona calmly.

Tabitha released the latches of her web and swam back through the cockpit to the door of the hold.

They were ten thousand klicks from Umbriel. Already the moondreams were suffering corrosion. Released from the supporting armature of their creator's presence, their features were melting.

The Captain reached through the retaining net and pulled the large black spheroid to her. Inside it was dry and flaking like rotting sponge, like the legless bird she had seen at the Well. The face it bore was barely recognizable.

Before she could even start to wonder what to do, and whether she felt good or bad about it, the hold com chimed.

'*Callig Brabo Golp Ganshaf zero-zero-nider-zero-fiver-nider. Thif if the polee'h. Blease returd ibbediately, repeat: ibbediately, to Ubbriel field.*'

Yes, well: it had to be the cops, in fact. No one else could simply override her receive control. And the hoarse, non-human accent spoke for itself. Still the Captain automatically catapulted herself back into the cockpit to check the screen.

There it was, in horrible full colour: the shaven blue dog face of an Eladeldi traffic cop.

'*Captid Zhoot,*' she commanded. '*Returd at wuds to Ubbriel.*'

The inspector was an Eladeldi too, of course. She carried some kind of anti-allergen inhaler with which she made great play, shaking it up and squirting it moodily into each nostril as she stepped in through the airlock with two squad officers behind her. 'Zhoot, Tabitha, Captib,' she said formally. 'I ab authorived to tsurch your bessel.'

Tabitha wished she had an anti-allergen inhaler of her own. It was not Umbriel she was allergic to, or even Eladeldi. It was cops. The very sight of a cop made her nervous, irascible, badly behaved. She had already shut the persona down in reflex non-cooperation.

'Why?' she said, not getting up and stepping away from the controls, but rather tightening her grip on the edge of the main console. 'What's happened?'

But the cop only intoned again: 'I ab authorived to tsurch your bessel. Blease unfashed your web ad step away frob the codtrols.'

Through the viewport Captain Jute could see the patrol ship, a Caledonian Cumulus looming over the field like a miniature fortress. Its blackened engines stuck out like gun emplacements, threatening the dirty ice.

Paws in the pockets of her uniform duster, the inspector stood in the middle of the cockpit. With a sombre jerk of her muzzle, she directed one of her subordinates into the main body of the ship. He scurried past the door of the hold, which the Captain had closed and sealed for re-entry, and on down the passage that led to the squalid and rudimentary personal quarters, astern.

'Good luck finding anything back there,' Captain Jute called after him. 'I never can.'

She scowled mutinously at the inspector, who was now scowling suspiciously at her.

The inspector took in the rubbish in the cockpit, the empty food containers and unwashed T-shirts. She produced her inhaler again and took a couple of juicy squirts. 'Steb away frob the codtrols, Captid Zhoot, blease,' she said thickly. 'I'b askig you dicely.'

'And I'm asking you nicely what the fuck's going on,' said Tabitha. But she opened her web and stepped down, reluctantly, away from the console.

At once the second squad officer took her seat, slid an unlabelled disc into the drive and started to type.

'You be careful with her,' Tabitha told the interloper. 'You hit one wrong tab and you'll hear about it.'

The inspector stared hard at the Captain for a moment. Then came the sound of boots on the decking, and the patrolman came back along the passage with a small plastic bag of dried vegetable matter. Sternly he held it up for his chief to examine.

'Oregano,' said Captain Jute.

The inspector gave the bag a tired glance, took it and stuffed it in the pocket of her coat, then waved the man back to his search.

'God knows where he found that,' said the Captain.

'Obed the hold,' said the inspector to the woman at the console.

'It's a mess in there, I warn you,' said Captain Jute. 'The cargo's a bit the worse for wear. I did tell her it wasn't recommended. Told Bad, I mean. Princess Badroulboudour. You know Princess Badroulboudour.'

The inspector made a low snuffling noise in the back of her throat.

The door of the hold came open.

The mess had got worse. Some of the images had burst apart like Venusian puffballs. A sticky yellow residue was speckled all over the walls and floor like ancient kitchen fat. For a moment Captain Jute thought they might decide to pull her licence for hygiene offences.

The inspector shuffled to the lines of green crates. Between the bars she poked the flaccid remains of the parrot-princess with the end of her stylus. There was a smell like the sweet smell of corruption.

'Where were you betweed the hours of eleved ad fifteed hudred yefterday, Captid Zhoot?'

'Here,' said Tabitha. 'I was right here. Well, eleven: I suppose I was on the way here. From the Well.'

'Which Well would thad be?'

'The bar. At the hotel.'

'Yesss . . .' exhaled the inspector. She produced a zip-lock evidence bag and lugubriously packaged up the sticky glob of dead dream residue from the end of her stylus.

'Who saw you there? At the hotel?'

'Well, Doreen, obviously. Morton Godfrey. I had breakfast with him.'

The inspector stared at her. Her mouth was open, her blue tongue curled. It was hard to tell what it meant, if anything.

'Then Princess Bad arrived and they left. The two of them. Together.'

'Togedder,' said the inspector.

'Yes,' said Tabitha. 'Well. She went, and he followed. Ibbediately,' she said.

The inspector paid no attention to her rudeness. She started fishing with her stylus again in the crates of ruined dreams. 'Where did you go betweed the bar ad here?' she asked.

'Where?' echoed Tabitha. 'Nowhere. I came straight here.'

'What did you do thed?'

Tabitha's head felt hot. Everyone was guilty, to the Eladeldi mind. It was just a question of identifying the particular infraction.

'I started getting ready for take-off.'

The inspector left off fishing to pull out her notebook and call up a screen of information.

'Field records,' she said at length, 'show take-off at twedty-two hudred twedty-fibe. Loadig cobplete at twedty-wud sebety-sebed. Loadig cobbedsed twedty-thirty.'

The inspector looked at the Captain with eyes that were black and clear; thoroughly accustomed to the human discourse of evasion and deceit; endlessly, if minimally, hopeful for a glimpse of truth.

'I was going early,' said Tabitha. 'I thought Princess Bad was about to cancel. Then the robot arrived and said it was still on. That must have been about fifteen hundred. A bit after, maybe. Why don't you ask it? It's a 4000, you two should get on well.'

The inspector had begun prodding the contents of another crate.

'You think I nicked this lot or something?'

The inspector sniffed hard and slow. She began pulling something out of the sticky, dusty ochre mess.

It was a long piece of wire. The Eladeldi pulled it out from under the net, raising it with the end of her stylus, like a wary diner encountering spaghetti for the first time.

At each end of the wire there was a yellow cylindrical wooden handle. As the wire came out of the crate, the handles caught in the slots. The inspector took a piece of cloth and gently freed them.

'Whad is this, blease?'

Tabitha rubbed her forehead. 'It's like a thing for cutting cheese, I think,' she said. 'I don't know. I didn't know it was in there. It's not mine.'

'Bud you know id.'

'Yes,' said Tabitha, feeling peculiar. 'It belongs to the Princess. She showed it to me. At the palace. The house, I mean.'

She reached out to take the implement from the inspector. The inspector gave a sudden bark, shockingly loud in the confines of the hold, and snatched it away.

'It was with one of the exhibits,' said the Captain. 'At the house. The robot must have packed it by mistake. Or maybe it's meant to go with it, I don't know.'

Distantly, carefully, the inspector was coiling the cheese wire inside another, larger evidence bag.

The patrolman who had been searching aft appeared, saluting. With a few words in their own soft, coughing tongue, the inspector gave Captain Jute into his charge. Then she went back into the cockpit.

'Are you going to arrest me for stealing a bit of wire?' yelled the Captain.

No one answered. The patrolman pushed her face against the freezing metal wall of the hold, made her spread her arms and legs.

While she struggled as hard as she could with a big blue paw pinning the back of her neck, he frisked her unceremoniously, finding nothing. Then he led her forward, into the starboard airlock.

As the inner door started to close, Captain Jute took a last look at the two silky blue figures up in the cockpit. The inspector was comparing the automatic log with something in her notebook. Her subordinate looked unhappy, as if the results were not what the inspector wanted. Her ears were drooping.

'Don't tell them anything, Alice,' called the Captain, as her suit pressurized and the pumps began evacuating the lock. 'Let them find out for themselves.'

She knew the sequestered persona could not hear her.

In the office, the field officer was still sitting with his hands laced across his stomach, watching the AV screen. There was another cop with him, a human. When the door opened the cop straightened and turned, and saluted the Captain's escort. Captain Jute returned the salute, just for fun. Everybody stared at her sourly.

'At ease, boys,' she said.

The Captain's escort pushed her hard into a chair. He signalled to the human one, who came over, scanned her fingerprints and put handcuffs on her.

The Eladeldi left the ship. Tabitha sat tight. Fear and anger and disbelief swept over her in alternating waves. They obviously had no intention of telling her what she was meant to have done. The cop and the field official were both preoccupied with the screen.

'Can I watch?' she said.

In a little while the cop hitched up his trousers and came over to her. For a moment she thought he was going to hit her. Instead, he put a hand under her armpit, hauled her to her feet, and pulled her over to the screen.

When she saw what was on it, her next clever remark died on her lips.

It was a still picture of a man, a human. He was lying out in the open, on raw ice.

The view cycled to another shot of the same man. He was naked. His face was purple, his eyeballs bursting from his head. That black growth protruding from his mouth must formerly have been his tongue. The pictures had the flat, coarse, unreal quality that told the Captain she was not looking at the special effects from some murder movie.

In any case, she recognized the man.

'Morton Godfrey,' she said.

The two men studied her.

'Friend of yours?' said the cop.

'No,' she said. 'He worked for Princess Bad.'

The chauffeur's whole neck and jaw were twisted and swollen. He looked like a mad purple moondream.

'I had a drink with him, yesterday morning,' the Captain heard herself say. 'I think I'm going to be sick.'

The field officer kicked a wastebasket at her, just in time.

In a little while she lifted her head.

'What happened to him?' she asked, in a squeaky whisper.

The two men looked at each other, as if wondering how much pleasure there was to be derived from not telling her.

'Satellite picked him up at 02.90,' said the cop. 'Somebody strangled him and dumped the body.'

'He was a big man,' said Tabitha, wonderingly.

'That the way you like them?' asked the field officer.

'Fuck off,' she said. 'Why's everybody so interested in me, for God's sake?'

'You were the last person seen talking to him,' said the cop.

'I didn't strangle him!' she said.

On the screen, the distorted face of the dead chauffeur zoomed into pitiless close-up. The field officer was playing with the controls.

'Somebody did,' he said.

The screen was full of bulging red and purple flesh.

'All they have to do now is find the cord,' said the field officer.

'Wire,' the cop told him. 'Go back one. There. Look at that. See the depth of that, compared to the width. See? That's like a cut.'

Behind her the door whisked open again. The inspector came in, followed by her team. The patrolman sprang to attention.

Captain Jute looked at her. She was numb. There was a noise in her head like a hundred engines on slow burn. 'Are you going to charge me?'

The inspector barely looked at her. Her ears were stiff, the fur on the back of her neck bristling with displeasure. 'You will be held for questiodig,' she said roughly.

She reached in the pocket of her long coat and took out the cheese wire in its bag.

When they all saw that, the air in the room grew solid with investigative fervour.

The inspector held the bag out to her human subordinate. 'Figgerprids,' she ordered.

Tabitha was dreaming.

She dreamed she was swimming in a green sea, within sight of vague islands of purple-grey rock. She could taste and smell the salt of the sea. She felt uncertain about swimming in it. The sea was lively. The swell might pull her under.

In the dream, there were fountains in the sea. She could see them shooting up into the air. She felt that if she could get to one of the fountains, she would be safe from sinking.

Beneath the fountains, dark blue shapes swam indistinctly in the green sea. They were whales. The fountains were their waterspouts. In the dream, it became important that she dive beneath one of the fountains, to rescue a smaller creature which was not entirely distinct from herself.

There was a moment when she found herself taking hold

of a bulky young mauve-coloured animal by its flippers and trying to pull it towards her. It was a baby whale, she thought, though it seemed more like a seal.

Then she woke, disoriented, not knowing where she was.

She got off the bunk and stood upright. The sprayfoam floor of the cell rasped the soles of her bare feet. Uranus shone in through the high, narrow slot of the window. It was just past full, and very bright.

While she stood there, thinking about nothing, the door whined open. A cop came in, one of the human ones.

'Come on, get your things,' he said. His voice was dull and unsympathetic.

'What's happening?' she said. 'Where are you taking me?'

'Hawaii,' said the cop. He took her by the arm and led her out through the passageways of the Cumulus, that smelled of dogs, disinfectant and despair.

A small desk stood at the top of the exit ramp. Olister Crane was there, writing something on a pad with an ink pen. For a moment she wondered if it was his threatened poem.

'What am I, on bail now?'

He wore his red blazer, the gold ring around his beard. He capped the pen and slid it neatly into his breast pocket. His nails were long, but clean and well shaped.

'They know you didn't do it, Captain,' he said.

In his yellow rover they rode away from the Cumulus, across the silent sea. The shock of it all reverberated in the Captain's head. She felt exhausted, filthy.

She pulled at her hair. 'I need a shower,' she said.

'Need a drink too, am I right?'

In the purple corridors of Reveries, they walked past the model of the ugly boy that had incensed Princess Badroulboudour. It smirked and ogled them.

'Whose is that one?' asked Captain Jute.

'He's one of mine,' Crane told her, complacently. 'Handsome devil, ain't I?'

It was the local equivalent of four a.m. The bar was open. Tabitha wondered when it ever closed.

Georginelle was there, drinking alone. She was horrified to hear about Tabitha's treatment. 'Of course, there's no chance you'll get an apology,' she said, righteously.

Tabitha said little. Of the cheese wire, she said nothing at all.

She looked around the walls. The unpleasant ornaments looked tawdry and unrealistic, as if even the temporary absence of their creators was enough to shave a degree of substance from them.

Crane was sitting close to Captain Jute. She put her hand on his forearm.

'Take me to the house,' she said.

He raised his eyebrows. 'My house?' he said.

She could see he knew perfectly well which house she meant, but for some reason required her to say it.

On the way, they saw three flat blue spearheads go over, heading east: fliers out of the patrol ship, going to pay Princess Bad a visit.

The Captain imagined her sitting in her windowless basement room, waiting for them on the big bed. She saw her surrounded once again by all the moondreams that had disintegrated in the hold of the *Alice*: the parrot and the melon, the sawtooth and the skull – all the little versions of herself the superseded star had produced in her years of solitary musing. Captain Jute imagined her gazing into the glutinous water, striving to invoke one final, consummate portrait, in which all the faces of all the roles she had played would combine around a single centre, like the facets of a jewel.

Even before they came in sight of the palace of silver

saucers, the white blaze of its lights began to pale the stars.

'They're not going to let you in,' said Crane softly.

'Everyone keeps telling me that.' Captain Jute was sealing up her suit. 'Drop me at the next bend,' she said. 'You drive up to the front door, create a diversion.'

'Create a diversion,' repeated Crane, chuckling lazily and shaking his head. 'What do you think this is, a movie?'

Soundless on the airless moon, the rover wheeled away from her, off up the hillside. He would come up with something, Tabitha was sure. Perhaps he would give the cops an impromptu poetry recital.

She went up the rest of the way quickly on all fours, trying to merge with the profile of the terrain. She could feel the unspeakable cold of the surface, beginning to suck at her through the suit. She saw no one.

The robot met her at the door to the garage.

Its voice buzzed in her phones. '*No one is available to deal with you at present.*'

'It's me,' she said. 'Captain Jute. You remember me.'

The arrival of the police had unsettled it. In the circuits of the domestic 4000 there were no contingencies for the Apocalypse.

'I've come to pick up the last of the artworks,' she told it.

'*Your statement requires confirmation,*' said the robot.

'Ask the Princess,' she said. She knew they would have blocked the connection by now, isolating the system from its owner with one of their handy little discs.

'*Princess Badroulboudour is occupied,*' said the 4000. '*Your request has been recorded and logged –*'

'I can't wait,' she told it. 'The Princess would be very very unhappy if it got left behind.'

Red lights flashed on all its displays. '*Your statement must be referred to Princess Badroulboudour,*' it said. '*Please return later.*'

Captain Jute attempted to convey every impression of urgency. She swung her arms around. She hugged herself and hopped from foot to foot. 'I'm leaving in fifteen minutes,' she said. 'I don't want to make the Princess unhappy.'

The red lights flashed amber. She supposed it was re-attempting the refused communication. She hoped none of the cops had been detailed to watch the other side of their com block.

'Well, it's too bad,' she said. 'You'll have to tell the Princess I came but you turned me away. You'll have to tell her I'm sorry I can't do what she asked.'

The amber lights all went out. One light only remained. It was red.

For a significant fraction of a second, the robot struggled. Then the light went green.

'*I shall accompany you to the Princess,*' said the 4000, as it opened the door.

'No, no, wait here,' said the Captain. 'I shall need you to drive me back to the field. You must prepare the truck!'

The 4000 spun its head. It extended another pair of eyes. It considered the truck that towered over it on its crampon tyres. By the time it reversed its mobilators, Captain Jute was on her way to the lift.

In the corridor she passed a holo of an obese Princess Badroulboudour dancing in freefall. She did not slow down to examine it. She knew everything now that its frenzied presentation could possibly convey.

In the Princess's bedroom all the lights were on. There were cops everywhere. With their trace detectors they were sweeping the wardrobes, the trinket shelves, the canopy above the bed.

They would not let her out of the lift. They blocked her exit, signalling to their superiors.

The patrolman who had searched the *Alice* was there. He stood on the far side of the bed, a tracer rig around his neck. Recognizing her, he alerted the inspector.

The inspector did not even glance at the intruder. She was busy. Her shoulders were hunched, her ears up. She stood with her legs bent, her front paws on her knees, her long coat hanging open.

All the inspector's attention was on Princess Badroulboudour.

The Princess stood before her in a white cowl-shirt and black leggings. She wore the dead chauffeur's uniform jacket draped over her shoulders. It was a nice touch, Captain Jute thought.

The Princess was as thin as a cigarette. She had no make-up on. Her face looked porous and creased, her large eyes red with emotion. She looked as if she had been up all night exercising, rehearsing the part of a woman wronged.

The Princess's Dream Well was still in ferment. People in sterile suits of white paper were shining a spotlight into it. There was a woman in scuba gear perched on the edge, directing them.

'Bad,' said Tabitha over the shoulders of the cops. 'All your dreams died.'

The Princess shrieked. The audio tracers recoiled, whipping off their headphones.

'*There she is!* Returning to the scene of the crime,' said the Princess with melodramatic relish. 'Hold her tight,' she ordered them. 'Don't let her make a run for it.'

Tabitha relaxed, folding her arms. 'I'm not going anywhere,' she said.

There was a flabby splosh as the frogwoman went in.

The inspector shook herself irritably. This was hard

enough without distractions. She gestured her people to bring Captain Jute into the room.

'Why have you cub here?' she asked. 'Is there subthig you wad to dell me?'

She panted sourly.

'No,' said Captain Jute with an insolent smile. 'You're getting it right now.'

Meanwhile Princess Badroulboudour was launching into her aria.

Captain Jute often thought afterwards that it might have been her greatest performance. There she stood, dressed like a refugee, grandstanding in an overheated, overlit room for a captive audience of cops. There was nothing original about the song she sang, or the simple, senseless ideas that over the years had come to comprise her character; but her projection was thunderous and her conviction total. For a minute or so she filled the scented air with the rage of grief, while her case and the last frail shell of her sanity collapsed in shreds around her like decomposing moondreams.

'She's the one, inspector! The dirty-handed slut I saw with Morton in that second-rate hotel. I warned him about her, but he was always a soft touch. No defences. Look at her! Women like her think they can take what they want. Fly in, fuck it, fly out again. Not a thought for the lives they ruin as they come and go.'

Her voice broke. Her narrow bosom quivered. The tendons on her neck stood out like twine and pulled her mouth into a downturned crescent of disdain.

'She killed him. She *killed* him. God knows what she wanted him to do that he was too loyal and honest and sweet to do . . .' Her voice softened into tenderness. 'She wanted him, and she couldn't have him, because he was mine, so she killed him.'

She shook. Her voice began to rise again, *con tremolo.*

'Because she was jealous of me. They all are, all of them. All the women who aren't lucky or talented or courageous enough to be me.'

Princess Badroulboudour took hold of her arresting officer by the shoulder.

'Take her away, inspector,' she commanded. 'Take her away and lock her in that big black ship of yours, and carry her off into dark, cold space. And when you get to the darkest, coldest, emptiest part of space, open the door and throw her out. And let her think as the emptiness sucks her lungs out through her mouth about the man she killed and the woman whose life she destroyed.'

She threw her arms out and her shoulders back, turning her head left and right, appealing to the investigators as if to a chorus line that would now link arms and echo her sentiments in deafening harmony.

But the investigators were taking no notice. They were going about their business like souvenir hunters, picking over the bedroom of this decayed celebrity.

Below the flight of steps that ran down from the bed the greasy waters of the pool were quiet now, delivered of their final burden.

The Princess's last dream lay dripping on a white plastic sheet, where the frogwoman had dumped it. Captain Jute could see it, between the backs of the forensic team. It looked only half-made. Even so, it was completely recognizable.

Unlike most of the other moondreams she had seen, it had two heads. It had a large head and a smaller one. What connected the two heads could be thought of as a single snaky neck, so that the dream resembled one two-headed creature looking at itself. The larger head was bent over the smaller one, like a madonna over an infant.

The face on the upper head fluttered and writhed like an ill-tuned holo. Its eyes kept spreading wide and puckering up like unruly mouths. Perhaps, Tabitha thought, the image was enraged by its premature extraction from the mineral womb.

The lower, smaller head was turned up. It was blocky, unmoving, and bare of detail. Its brow stuck out like the peak of a cap, shading what there was of its face. All Captain Jute could see was a single gash, a curved line like a smile, the blissful smile of a fan in the front row at a concert.

Around the neck that joined the two heads a shiny, sticky string was twisted. Each end of the string was held tightly in one of the hands – spidery, inhuman little hands, with far too many fingers – that protruded from just beneath the chin of the effervescent upper head.

Over and over again, while the Captain and the cops watched, the little hands pulled the wet string tight.

Take Back Plenty
Colin Greenland

Winner of the Arthur C. Clarke and British Science Fiction Association Awards for the best science fiction novel.

Tabitha Jute was in trouble on Mars.

It was Carnival time and everyone was partying except her. Up against the law, penniless and about to lose her livelihood and best friend, the space barge *Alice Liddell* – Tabitha needed some luck. Fast.

Then along came the intriguing gloveman Marco Metz. He needed a lift to Plenty to rejoin his bizarre cabaret troupe – and he would pay. Tabitha knew Plenty was a dodgy place since its creators had been exterminated by the Capellans, the masters of the Terran system. But she didn't have any choice.

What should have been a simple five-hour journey and some quick cash turned into a chaotic chase from the orbital tangle into the depths of hyperspace, with the cops on her tail.

And that was only the start of her problems . . .

'A great, big, magnificent, galaxy-shaking plot that will make you forget to eat and sleep.'
Michael Moorcock

'A masterpiece. If you ever wondered why you began reading science fiction this book answers that question. *Take Back Plenty* is fun.'
Interzone

ISBN 0 586 21339 2

Foundation

Isaac Asimov

The first volume in Isaac Asimov's world-famous saga, winner of the Hugo Award for Best All-Time Novel Series.

'One of the most staggering achievements in modern SF'
The Times

Long after Earth was forgotten, a peaceful and unified galaxy took shape, an Empire governed from the majestic city-planet of Trantor. The system worked, and grew, for countless generations. Everyone believed it would work forever. Everyone except Hari Seldon.

As the great scientific thinker of his age, Seldon could not be ignored. Reluctantly, the Commission of Public Safety agreed to finance the Seldon Plan. The coming disaster was predicted by Seldon's advances in psychohistory, the mathematics of very large human numbers, and it could not be averted. The Empire was doomed. Soon Trantor would lie in ruins. Chaos would overtake humanity. But the Seldon Plan was a long-term strategy to minimize the worst of what was to come.

Two Foundations were set up at opposite ends of the galaxy. Of the Second nothing can be told. It guards the secrets of psychohistory. *FOUNDATION* is the story of the First Foundation, on the remote planet of Terminus, from which those secrets were withheld.

ISBN 0 586 01080 7

Only Forward
Michael Marshall Smith

A truly stunning debut from a young author. Extremely original, satyrical and poignant, a marriage of numerous genres brilliantly executed to produce something entirely new.

Stark is a troubleshooter. He lives in The City - a massive conglomeration of self-governing Neighbourhoods, each with their own peculiarity. Stark lives in Colour, where computers co-ordinate the tone of the street lights to match the clothes that people wear. Close by is Sound where noise is strictly forbidden, and Ffnaph where people spend their whole lives leaping on trampolines and trying to touch the sky. Then there is Red, where anything goes, and all too often does.

At the heart of them all is the Centre - a back-stabbing community of 'Actioneers' intent only on achieving - divided into areas like 'The Results are what Counts sub-section' which boasts 43 grades of monorail attendant. Fell Alkland, Actioneer extraordinaire has been kidapped. It is up to Stark to find him. But in doing so he is forced to confront the terrible secrets of his past. A life he has blocked out for too long.

'Michael Marshall Smith's *Only Forward* is a dark labyrinth of a book: shocking, moving and surreal. Violent, outrageous and witty - sometimes simultaneously - it offers us a journey from which we return both shaken and exhilarated. An extraordinary debut.'
Clive Barker

ISBN 0 586 21774 6

Red Mars
Kim Stanley Robinson

WINNER OF THE NEBULA AWARD

MARS. THE RED PLANET.
Closest to Earth in our solar system,
surely life must exist on it?

We dreamt about the builders of the canals we could see by telescope, about ruined cities, lost Martian civilisations, the possibilities of alien contact. Then the Viking and Mariner probes went up, and sent back - nothing. Mars was a barren planet: lifeless, sterile, uninhabited.

In 2019 the first man set foot on the surface of Mars: John Boone, American hero. In 2027 one hundred of the Earth's finest engineers and scientists made the first mass-landing. Their mission? To create a New World.

To terraform a planet with no atmosphere, an intensely cold climate and no magnetosphere into an Eden full of people, plants and animals. It is the greatest challange mankind has ever faced: the ultimate use of intelligence and ability: our finest dream.

'A staggering book . . . The best novel on the colonization of Mars that has ever been written' *Arthur C. Clarke*

'First of a mighty trilogy, *Red Mars* is the ultimate in future history' *Daily Mail*

'*Red Mars* may simply be the best novel ever written about Mars' *Interzone*

ISBN 0 586 21389 9

Green Mars
Kim Stanley Robinson

WINNER OF THE HUGO AWARD

The second book in the highly acclaimed Mars trilogy,
following the award winning *Red Mars*

MARS. THE GREEN PLANET

Man's dream of a new world is underway, but corrupted. The
First Hundred have scattered or died, the rebels are underground, planning their utopia, waiting. The transnational corpo-
rations aided by the UN are rebuilding the ruined cities and
mining valuable resources. They too have a dream. Mars can be
plundered, cultivated and terraformed to suit Man's needs -
frozen lakes are forming, lichen is growing, the atmosphere is
slowly becoming breathable. But most importantly, Mars can
now be owned. On Earth, countries are being bought and sold by
the transnationals. Why not here too?

Man's dream is underway, but so is his greatest test. Societies are
crumbling and re-forming, adapting and reacting to new conditions. The survivors of the First Hundred know that technology
alone is not enough. Trust and co-operation are needed to create
a new world - but these qualities are as thin on the ground as the
Martian air they breathe.

'One of the finest works of American SF'
Times Literary Supplement

'The red sand displays the recent footprints of Ben Bova and
Greg Bear . . . But the forerunner is Kim Stnaley Robinson'
Time Out

'Absorbing . . . impressive . . . fascinating . . . utterly plausible'
Financial Times

ISBN 0 586 21390 2

The Thief of Always
Clive Barker

*A disturbing fable exploring childhood fears
and delights from the maestro of dark fantasy.*

Mr Hood's Holiday House has stood for a thousand years,
welcoming countless children into its embrace. It is a
place of miracles, a blissful round of treats and seasons,
where every childish whim may be satisfied.

There is a price to be paid, of course, but young Harvey
Swick, bored with his life and beguiled by Mr Hood's
wonders, does not stop to consider the consequences. It is
only when the House shows its darker face – when Harvey
discovers the pitiful creatures that dwell in its shadow –
that he comes to doubt Mr Hood's philanthropy.

The House and its mysterious architect are not about to
release their captive without a battle, however. Mr Hood
has ambitions for his new guest, for Harvey's soul burns
brighter than any soul he has encountered in a thousand
years . . .

'A dashingly produced fantasy with powerful drawings
by the author'   *Daily Telegraph*

'Barker puts the dark side back into childhood fantasy . . .
A welcome modern-day return to classic form, this fable
lives up to the publishers' billing as a tale for all ages'
                                        Publishers Weekly

ISBN 0 00 647311 3

Arthur C. Clarke
2061
Odyssey Three

2001: A SPACE ODYSSEY
was the classic story that told of man's destiny in space

2010: ODYSSEY TWO
pushed back the frontiers of
human imagination still further

2061: ODYSSEY THREE
tells of humanity's evolution towards the stars . . .

In 2061, when two Suns share the skies of Earth, Halley's Comet returns to the inner Solar System. Soon the fates of two spacefaring expeditions are entwined by human necessity and the immutable laws of astrophysics. Centenarian Heywood Floyd must once again confront Dave Bowman, a newly independent HAL and the limitless power of an alien race that has decided humanity must play a part in the evolution of the galaxy – whether it wants to or not.

'One of the true geniuses of our time'   RAY BRADBURY

'Hugely readable . . . No one who enjoys the stimulus of ideas that are elegantly presented should miss it.'

New Scientist

ISBN 0 586 20319 2

DAUGHTER OF THE EMPIRE
Raymond E. Feist & Janny Wurts

The mysterious world of Kelewan is encircled by magic, mystery and murder. Here at the heart of the Tsurani empire, Mara, Ruling Lady of the Acoma, leads her people through terror and peril on a truly epic scale. She must contend with powerful rival houses, strike deals with sinister rebel warriors, and forge a treaty with the enigmatic Cho-ja – a race of alien insectoids. But in order to restore the honour of her house, Mara must marry the son of a deadly enemy – and carry the struggle of her people into the heart of his stronghold . . .

ISBN 0 586 07481 3

SERVANT OF THE EMPIRE
Raymond E. Feist & Janny Wurts

Mara of Acoma is a force to be reckoned with when playing the bloody politics of the Game of the Council and has made great gains for her followers within the Empire.

Against advice she buys a group of Midkemian prisoners-of-war, only to discover that one of them is a noble: Kevin, third son of the Baron of Zun. When she interviews him, it becomes apparent that he may be of great use in the Game of the Council . . .

ISBN 0 586 20381 8

MISTRESS OF THE EMPIRE
Raymond E. Feist & Janny Wurts

Now Mara faces not only the brotherhood of assassins, and the cunning spies of the rival ruling houses, but the awesome Assembly of Magicians, who see her as the ultimate threat to their ancient power.

ISBN 0 586 20379 6

'Sweeping drama unveiling a tale of love, hate and sacrifice against the panorama of an alien yet familiar society'
Publishers Weekly

The Last Raven
Craig Thomas

In the aftermath of the Cold War, the world is a less dangerous place . . . except for Patrick Hyde.

When he witnesses the shooting down of a Soviet airliner near the Afghan border, he has only one option – to reach London and Kenneth Aubrey. His enemies, American and Russian, have no alternative but to silence him . . .

To stay alive means killing and running – from Afghanistan to Delhi to California, Hyde pursues the truth as his enemies pursue him.

Can Aubrey save Patrick Hyde – can he even save himself?

The era of *glasnost* and *perestroika* is the most dangerous time for the last raven . . .

In *The Last Raven*, Craig Thomas reaches new heights of tension, suspense and action, to prove himself once again the master of the modern adventure story.

0 00 617918 5

Strange Dreams

Edited by
Stephen Donaldson

A new collection of fantasy short stories personally selected by bestselling author Stephen Donaldson, these are the 'strange dreams' that stir the heart and mind, written by authors past and present – from Rudyard Kipling, Jorge Luis Borges and Franz Kafka to Theodore Sturgeon, John Varley, Sheri S. Tepper and M. John Harrison.

Here are witches, ghosts, a demon child, a boy who never grows old, a prehistoric monster that never died, a dragon in the snow, a wolfman, an unusual private eye and a very modern woman swallowed by the past.

Including works by: Greg Bear, Jorge Luis Borges, Orson Scott Card, Harlan Ellison, M. John Harrison, Franz Kafka, Garry Kilworth, Rudyard Kipling, Lucius Shepard, Theodore Sturgeon, Sheri S. Tepper, Jack Vance, John Varley, Walter Jon Williams.

'One of the best things about this book is the astonishing range of styles, settings, subjects and characters it presents. Donaldson has assembled a satisfying and delightfully varied group of tales.' *Publishers Weekly*

ISBN 0 00 648005 5

STEPHEN DONALDSON

MORDANT'S NEED

1: The Mirror of Her Dreams
2: A Man Rides Through

King Joyse and the kingdom of Mordant are in dire need; threatened by the evil Arch-Imager Vagel and the hordes of Cadwal from without, betrayed by unknown enemies within. Terisa Morgan is Mordant's unlikely champion, plucked from a life of wealthy dreariness in New York by the accidental magic of the apprentice Imager Geraden. The kingdom is directed by the power of images, of visions and of mirrors, and Terisa and Geraden must master this power if Mordant is to survive. But the traps laid for them are many and treacherous. . .

'An impressive performance. Donaldson has created a galaxy of idiosyncratic, neatly described characters. Its greatest success lies in the complexity of its language, a fit vehicle for the intricate plot. Donaldson's style – shimmering and full of ambiguities and puns – resembles the curved mirrors of Mordant.' *New York Times Book Review*

'Donaldson does not seem to know how to fail . . . intricate, madcap, involving.' *Washington Post*